Your Mos… umble Servants

P. Henry

G. Washington

Benj. Franklin

Saml. Adams

Wm. Alexander

H Knox

Anty. Wayne

Jno P Jones

Th: Jefferson

C Pulaski Gen of Caval.d

Chas Lee

Thad. Kosciuszko

Dan Morgan

John Adams

John Hancock

STAN ELLSWORTH

Renegades & Rebels

EPIC AND TRUE STORIES OF OUR REVOLUTIONARY HEROES

A not-so-scholarly guide to the Firebrands and Philosophers of American Independence

Softcover ISBN: 978-1-944141-34-9
Hardcover ISBN: 978-1-944141-38-7

Printed in the United States of America

Book design by Morgan Crockett
Printed by Book Printers of Utah, Inc.

Front cover: *Lexington Common Minuteman, 19th of April 1775* by Troiani. Bridgeman Images, used with permission.
Text images courtesy of New York Public Library Digital Collections.
Image page 182 from Alamy Ltd, used by permission.
Image page 342 by David Millman, used by permission.

Special thanks to Perpetua Printing LLC, whose financial assistance and guidance helped make the publication of this book possible.

perpetuaprinting.com

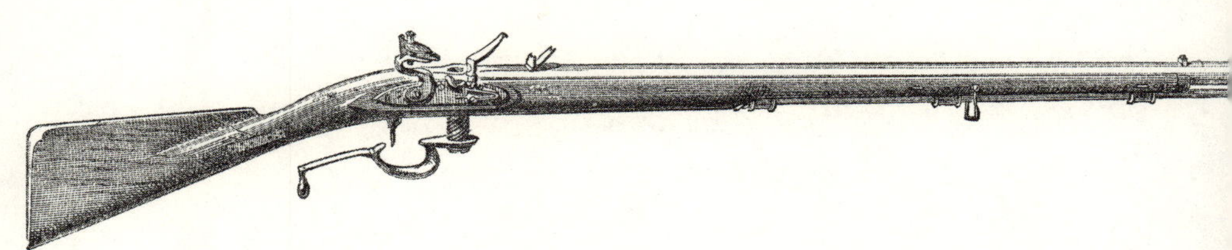

For Every Soul that has Stood
to Arms and Fought for Liberty.

For Every Heart that has Known
the Awful Weight and Burden
that is the Cost of Freedom.

And for Every Spirit who Dares
to Stand for Right and Truth
—No Matter the Price.

ACKNOWLEDGEMENTS
(THANKSGIVING)

To all who have Made a Difference in My Life;
the teachers who labored and tried,
the principals and vice principals who cursed and cried,
and Gave Me Experience.

For all the books, movies and documentaries,
all the articles, essays and commentaries
that Gave Me Knowledge.

For friends and enemies, Trials and Triumphs
that have made me what I am Today.

For family, folk and my loving Wife,
for Freedom and the Gift of Life;
my Ancestors, their Sacrifices gave me my Today—
I hope I make you Proud!
Your Stories are my Heritage,
I Will Remember!

My Children and Grandchildren, my Legacy,
I hope I did right by all y'all!
Never forget Where you come from or Who you are!

To Stephanie, Joe, and Kathy, Gregg, Scott, Linda, and Stan,
and to my Brothers from American Ride.

And to Mom, Dad, and most especially Stacey,
who stood by me through all the tough stuff;
every page, every chapter, and every rewrite.

Thanks.

Above all, Honor and Glory to God the Father and His Son, Jesus Christ;
through His Grace and Merit All Things are Possible!

TABLE OF CONTENTS

Farmer/Minute-man

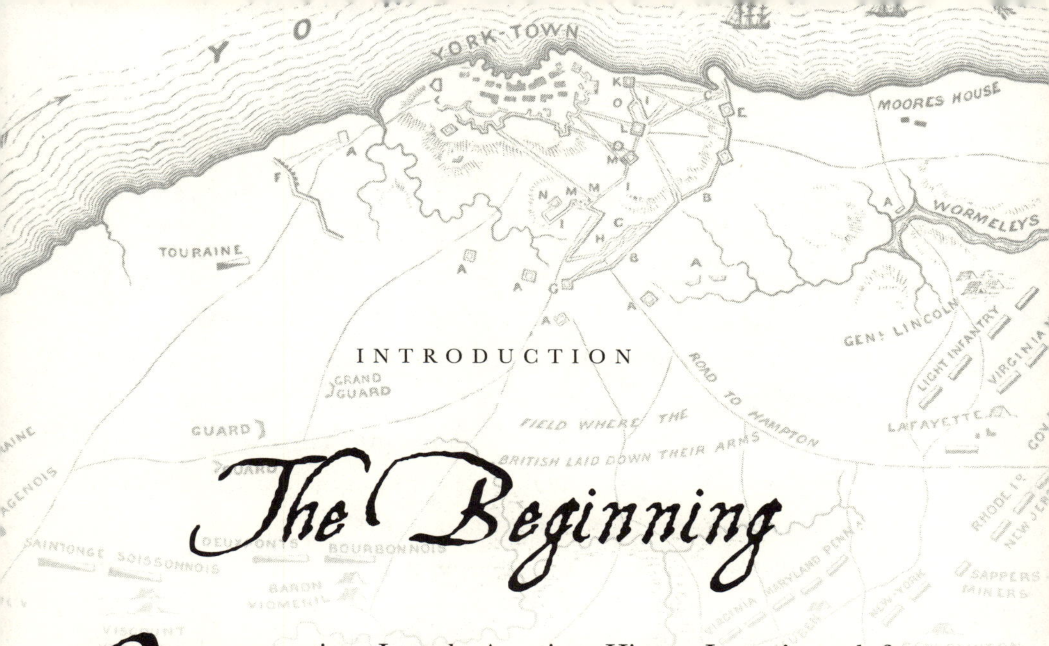

INTRODUCTION

The Beginning

Once upon a time, I taught American History. I wasn't much for school as a student, and frankly, I had my doubts I would last as a teacher. I wasn't a poor student; in fact, I got good grades. I was, to say the least, athletically inclined and "highly spirited." Like most Southern boys, I am intensely independent and adventurous. In my high school experience that was seen as a big minus, so I was on the radar of every vice principal I knew. Action was my business and trouble was my middle name. Hell, I just thought it was fun. Even so, I always found a way to keep up with my studies. Truthfully, I always loved reading and learning, but the way subjects were taught would put me in a coma! There's an old saying, "The lecture is where the notes of the teacher become the notes of the student *without passing through the mind of either one!*" And how my teachers could lecture. Still, I loved all the subjects and I had a deep passion for History. I just couldn't stand the way it was taught!

Fast forward 20 plus years.

I'd seen a lot. Good times, bad times; been almost all around the world. I'd been through a couple of careers and I'd learned a thing or two. Now I was going to *teach* high school—American History no less. My earlier opinions about high school principals, history teachers, and the standard history curriculum were going to be put to the test. Maybe things had changed in the time I had been otherwise occupied. Sadly, I've learned that things in this life change very slowly, if at all.

In my teaching experience, I found that most of the problem was the *how*, not necessarily the who or the what. I saw many administrators who got into education to make a difference, but who just became cogs in the educational machine. I saw teachers who entered the field on fire, but who now merely tended the embers until retirement. What was taught and how it was *allowed* to be taught sapped strength, hope, and spirit out of many energetic and eager minds on both sides of the blackboard.

The history curriculum was the most troubling to me. Only thin paragraphs on the American Revolution, the Founding Fathers, and the establishment of our American nation, but chapter after chapter of politically correct defamation and disinformation! Being a lifelong and unrepentant rebel—and a man who never backs down from a fight—I figured I would just teach history as it had really happened and let the chips fall where they may. And while I always loved the students, I was never big on policy and procedure. In fact, I've never been much for protocol at all: directives and such I see more as guidelines. I think you can see where this is going. After five years, I figured I'd (once again) had enough of the high school experience; it was time to part ways. I needed to find a new way to teach and reach a broader "classroom."

See You in the Movies!

While I was teaching, I had a student whose father was a movie producer and director. He invited me to be in one of his projects. I declined, saying I had no interest at all in the entertainment industry. Then he told me what the pay would be, and I said, "Sir, you have my attention."

From that opportunity came the television series *American Ride,* an idea that took eight years to sell…sort of an overnight success. In *American Ride*, I found a way to combine two of the things I enjoy the most: American History and Harley Davidsons. It's the saga of a biker who happens to know a lot about history. He talks about the truth of America's story from the saddle of his iron horse. He's no "talking head" in a sweater vest and bow tie; this guy is a road warrior complete with skull rag and leathers, boots, and biker "kutte" (pronounced "cut" as in "cut off," but it's from a German word that means a knight's battle vest or monk's frock, go figure!). Let me tell you, wrapped in all that denim and leather and chrome and steel, history became cool!

SO HOW ABOUT THE BOOK?

Yeah, how about that? Originally, I thought to title this book, *Buy This Book. It Will Help You Cheat on History Tests!* But then I remembered, this is *serious* stuff, and that might be just a little bit "over the top."

After filming eleven seasons of *American Ride* and traveling across America, Europe, and the Pacific, it became evident to me that there were many people who had been misled and misinformed by the efforts of the "let's change history" crew. From George Washington's cherry tree to Ben Franklin's kite, the stories of America's Revolutionary heroes had been hijacked by "alternative" historians and retooled, casting the Founding Fathers and America's heroes as self-serving villains or as sinister and shadowy, cloak-and-dagger members of a secretive and mystic society bent on wealth and world domination.

To me, this farcical fiction had gone too far. The time had come to let the true story of freedom ring loud and long and clear! These were men who were willing to lay down everything, *everything*, to secure the blessings of liberty, not only for their time, but for us. It was time to redeem and restore the reputations of the folks who fought, sacrificed, and laid all on the altar of liberty so that our nation could be Free.

This book represents my attempt to set their record straight; to inspire Americans of all ages with the true and epic history of our Revolutionary Heroes.

I do hope you will enjoy the read; It is written to Americans and for Americans. But no matter where you live, if you believe in liberty, in freedom, in the greatness of the human spirit, and that good will triumph over evil, then this book is for you.

—Stan Ellsworth

Some Notes on Revolutionary Fervor... American Style!

Our Revolution was homegrown and "home brewed." No foreign somebody or other came to the colonies to stir up rebellion—unless you count royally appointed corrupt colonial governors or the oppressive British Military presence—but no foreign leaders shaped the ideas of the American Revolution. At the heart of it all were two ideas: the rule of law (instead of a king), and self-governance, both personal and public (again, instead of a king).

These were new ideas!

For centuries, the king or his cronies ruled and directed public and personal thinking and morality. And the king's punishment was both personal and public. Just watch the end of *Braveheart*—that stuff actually happened! Makes you wonder why the American way of thinking took so long to happen, doesn't it?

America's revolutionary leaders weren't out for blood, they were out for change. The biggest issue was "taxation without representation." We were against it. When the British King and/or Parliament would pass some new underhanded law, our Revolutionary leaders would write a strongly-worded letter (ALL CAPS, more than one exclamation point) i.e. the minutes from the Boston Town Meeting and the Olive Branch Petition, just to name two. All in logical succession, all about the rule of law, all kind of silk stocking, ruffled shirt, passive aggressive political stuff.

Then the British pushed it a bit too far and they soon found out we wore buckskin and homespun, had guns, and weren't afraid to use them.

From Lexington and Concord all the way to Yorktown, it was "Don't Tread on Me!" for the American Revolutionary.

Some Notes on liberty, Freedom, and the Continuing Revolution

Before we go any further, we need to remember that the leaders of the American Revolution were not a bunch of wig-wearing old farts. Most people remember these men as a bunch of ancient white fuddy duddys and think of them as made of marble. But in reality, they were young and vital, vigorous and energetic! Most were in their twenties and thirties, some were younger, and only a very few were over 40. They believed in their cause, which was individual liberty, American independence, and freedom. And for their beliefs, they were willing to lay down their very young lives and all prospects of a prosperous future. These fellas were driven and motivated!

They saw liberty as the right of every man (now every individual) to act for himself, to build his own life, and to stand accountable for his actions in the public square. Liberty was seen as the right to exercise a positive morality; to be the best you could be, of your own choice. Like the poet said:

> *Cattle die and Kin folk die,*
> *And so we die Ourselves,*
> *The thing I know that Never dies*
> *Is the Fame of a Man's Great deeds!*

To our Revolutionary leaders, independence meant the right of the New American Nation to act as an individual; to exercise that same liberty in the "family of nations" as we would in our community.

And freedom. As seen by our Revolutionary leaders, freedom was the community created by every citizen upholding their responsibility to establish and create a good and moral society where all people could enjoy the blessing of the "unalienable rights" given by our Creator.

The Revolution was—and should still be—seen as perpetual, continuing forever. Each new generation standing up for the values that we hold dear and handing to the next generation the rights, privileges, and responsibilities of citizenship untarnished, preserved, and renewed. As Americans, we promise to always be revolutionary by living up to the dream of our founders contained in the Declaration of Independence, the Constitution, and the Bill of Rights by being active in the processes of government and by using our liberty to leave a legacy of greatness.

As we look to the lives of our Revolutionary Heroes, we find that they shared a unique value set that we will refer to as the "American Character." These values can be found in many societies, but they find their greatest expression in the rugged and independent American Spirit. It is the code of the Bad Ass!

> **1) Courage/Boldness, Bravery:** *to have the grit to stand, alone if necessary, for what is right. To do what must be done for the victory of liberty and freedom.*

> **2) Truth/Honesty:** *to say and do what is right, no matter the cost.*

> **3) Honor/Integrity:** *the gift we give ourselves by living up to our spoken word, keeping faith with those who have gone before, and being the example for those who follow.*

> **4) Fidelity/Loyalty, Steadfastness, Commitment:** *to faith, to cause, and to kin. To be recognized as one who will always stand for liberty and freedom.*

> **5) Discipline/Restraint, Determination:** *the ability to regulate and manage passion and response. To be proactive in a good cause and have the ability to focus no matter the distractions.*

> **6) Hospitality/Courtesy:** *to always respect yourself and others. To speak and act with dignity. Always share the bounties and blessings of life with those who are truly in need and act with charity for all.*

> **7) Industriousness/Economic Vigor:** *work ethic, ambition, and drive. To put "skin in the game" and "promote the general welfare" by labor and ingenuity.*

> **8) Self Reliance/Self Sustenance:** *to meet your own needs; financially, materially, and economically. To be a provider and not a burden.*

> **9) Perseverance/Dedication, Endurance:** *Never Give Up. To have the fortitude to continue even when the odds are against you. To see the fight through, even when things look dark and ominous—to be the one to change the outcome!*

So, kick a leg over! Let's take a ride and learn the true stories of America's Revolutionary heroes!

*An early and more accurate image
of General Washington—when he had all his teeth!
Washington was both myth and legend,
even in his own time.*

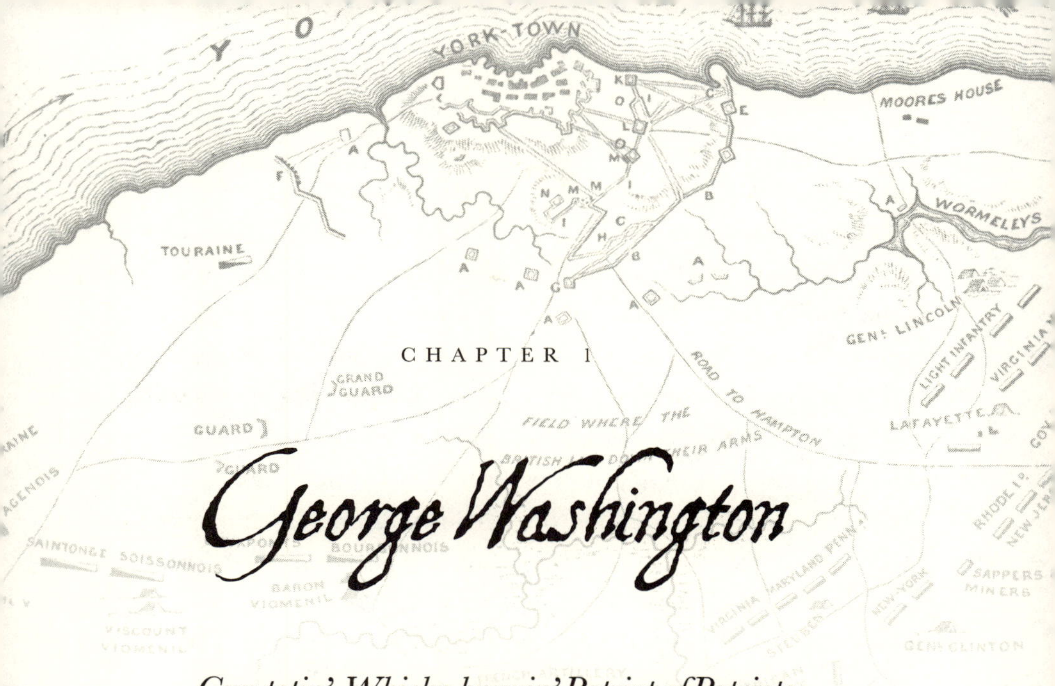

CHAPTER 1

George Washington

Gun totin', Whisky brewin' Patriot of Patriots

Among our Revolutionary Fathers, the man who was born to be the "leader of the pack" had the most complex personality of them all. George Washington was the mind behind our victory in the Revolution. He was "the man" at the Constitutional Convention. And he was a man of such epic character that the Presidency was designed with him in mind. Even to the men of his own day, Washington was larger than life. He had an almost super-human strength of body, mind, and spirit. He was the "American Character" personified. His qualities of courage, integrity, self-discipline, and devotion to duty made him the natural "go-to guy" to lead the Revolution.

We remember General Washington as the stern and resolute warrior, the unwavering father of the Continental Army. Or President Washington as the serious and somber "man in black," a leader almost unapproachable by common folk. Publicly, Washington was all those things. The true George Washington, the man, is something far more captivating. He *was* a man's man. In fact, he exuded masculinity: ruggedly handsome (he had scars on his face from smallpox), tall and broad (he was 6' 2" and over 200 lbs at a time when most men were barely 5' 8"), and he *never* wore a wig. Saddling his horse for "the hunt" (normally foxes), or for a race, or for weeks out in the backwoods in his buckskins with his hounds, his guns, and the "Good Book" was where he was most at home. He was a southern boy's southern boy after all. Washington was always willing to roll up his shirt sleeves and do the work himself. He loved a good laugh and was close in his relationships with friends, family, and even Native American tribes. He became widely known as the manufacturer of the finest whiskey, the strongest corn liquor, and keeper of the best Madeira wine in America. Most folks agreed that his wife, Martha, was a) a real beauty, b) a real "fireball", c) a real lady, and d) the brewer of the best beer in the mid-Atlantic states!

Washington was, above all, lucky. The man was impossible to kill! Diphtheria, malaria, tuberculosis, and smallpox were among the several deadly diseases that Washington survived. If we count all the battles he survived *unscathed*, as well, luck may be too poor a word. In fact, many of his contemporaries thought he was protected and preserved by Providence—that's Providence with a capital P.

The Path of the Patriot

George Washington was born "gentrified." As a younger son of a modest gentleman farmer, Washington seemed destined by birth, education, and connection to a career as a "gentleman farmer." Then the wheels of "fate" began to turn. Washington's father, Augustine, died of a sudden disease (what lots of people died from back then) and his older brother, Lawrence, took a hand in young George's raising. Lawrence brought his younger brother into the power circle of Lord Fairfax (one of the wealthiest British nobles in the colonies). Washington became the most courteous and "connected" young man in Virginia. Lawrence and the Fairfax family made certain of it. Washington was given every advantage that his new society friends could offer. He became a great fan of the theater, he was a fantastic dancer, and he learned all the nuanced and subtle ways folks in society behaved and acted toward one another and toward those of "other" classes. He was educated in the manly arts of shooting and riding—at both of which he was unequalled. Washington loved "the hunt"; goose and fox were his favorites and he is credited with helping to create the American Foxhound. As for riding and racing, George Washington was never bested in a horse race. Steeplechase, cross country, or flat out quarter mile, he never lost (the man was competitive!). He was, by all accounts, the best horseman in the American colonies.

He was well-travelled by the time he was 19 years old. Washington was appointed *the* surveyor of Culpepper County—that was all the land from the Appalachian Mountains and along the Ohio River, all the way out to who knows where. It represented Virginia's claim to the "overmountain" region of the interior. That's a lot of land! Soon he owned more land than anyone in Virginia. Okay, it was up in the "over yonder," but land was power. He also accompanied his brother, Lawrence, on a voyage to the West Indies. The trip was supposed to cure Lawrence of his tuberculosis, but the death of his older brother in 1752 changed Washington's life forever. He was now "the eldest" son—and *heir* to everything his father had built. He would be *the* Mr. Washington of Mount Vernon, a large plantation on the Potomac, and assume his brother's responsibilities in society, as well as becoming one of Virginia's four commanders responsible for militia training. Washington was sworn in as a major of militia in February 1753, at the age of 21. He volunteered for active duty ten months later and the rest, as they say, is history!

Washington entered military service just when England and France were about to "duke it out" for empire in America. The colony of Virginia was especially outraged when the French built a series of forts from Quebec southward to the Ohio River; what Virginians saw as part of Culpeper County. Reacting to the threat, Lieutenant Governor Robert Dinwiddie sent young George Washington to lay down the law and tell the French to get lost. When a diplomatic approach failed, Dinwiddie called up a force of 300 backwoods militiamen, placed them under Washington's command, and sent them to defend English (read Virginia's) claims to the "Forks of the Ohio," where the Allegheny and Monongahela Rivers come together to form the Ohio (now Pittsburgh). Washington promptly led his 300—allied with some Native American warriors—to open a can of colonial "whoop-ass" on the French; ultimately causing a world war. Washington won two battles before being surrounded and captured in a field east of present day Uniontown, PA, by a much larger group of French and Indian soldiers.

There was a lot of criticism when he returned home, especially from the English. But throughout his life, criticism and hard times only seemed to strengthen Washington's resolve and dedication. And this time was no exception. Washington wasn't anywhere near done with the French. In 1755, he volunteered as an "unofficial" aide to Major General Edward Braddock who commanded a large force of regular troops sent to capture Fort Duquesne, the newly built French stronghold at the Forks of the Ohio. Regular troops and regular tactics meant a regular "butt whippin'." Wearing bright red jackets and standing in close ranks, Braddock's boys met a terrible defeat by the banks of the Monongahela. Every officer (except Washington, of course) was shot down, either wounded or Killed in Action. Our heroic young major rose to the challenge, however, and "led from the front" as he always did. Washington took charge; he had several horses shot out from under him and had at least 4 bullets rip through his clothing (remember that Providence thing?). Washington saved what was left of the day. His display of courage, initiative, and tactical skills in battle caused his personal reputation to soar. A grateful and perhaps inspired Lt. Governor Dinwiddie gave Washington charge of Virginia's frontier defenses for the rest of the war. He not only commanded the colony's regiments and special ranger companies, but all of the Virginia militia, as well. This is where he met many of the officers and soldiers who would serve with him in the coming revolution. By war's end, Washington was a brigade commander, the highest ranking American in the colonies.

The French and Indian War was a warm-up for the leaders of the American Revolution. From his own experience in the war, Washington learned the necessity of discipline—"the soul of an army" in his mind. He learned important lessons about tactics and formations, both British and Native American. He came to realize what every great military leader understands: that the best commander pays close attention to detail, learns how to make do with less, and puts the welfare of his men first. But most important to his future, Washington saw, firsthand throughout the fighting, that American colonists were treated as 2nd class citizens. British officers largely "looked down their noses" at the colonial soldiers as being rustic ("redneck" or "yokel") and provincial (backward and backwoods). Washington was frustrated that he couldn't get a British Army commission, even though he had been honored for his achievements during the war. And he saw up close and personal that British foreign policy was skewed. It favored the British and discounted the British Americans. These observations drove Washington to have a mind "unfavorable" to the British agenda. Fact is, he didn't cotton to it at all.

Following the war, Washington went back to being a "gentleman farmer." He got more land through business savvy and his marriage to Martha Dandridge Custis, the wealthiest, most attractive, and most eligible young widow in Virginia. He also "took his place" in the community. As *the* Mr. Washington—hero of the war and all—he became a member of Burgesses, Virginia's "home" assembly, and acquired political skills and understanding that would serve him well in the future. He had always been a deeply religious man and became one of the vestrymen (non-clergy leaders) of his parish. He also became part of the southern branch of the Sons of Liberty, a member of the Virginia Committee of Correspondence (there were no cell phones, so these committees kept the revolutionary groups in the different colonies "in touch" with each other), and a leader against English "infringement" of American rights. By 1774, Washington had gone "whole hog" in supporting the revolutionary cause. He accepted command of the Virginia "provincial" militia (militiamen who were loyal to the Patriot way of thinking) and he represented Virginia in the Second Continental Congress, which he attended in his "dress blues" (his finest military uniform). For Washington, the uniform represented his feeling and decision that "taking arms" was the only choice or chance the American colonists had of equality and liberty, without a word being spoken. His lifelong motto was: "Deeds, not words."

The Revolution's Indispensable Man

As soon as Washington came to Philadelphia, the Continental Congress took full advantage of his military experience. Following the news of fighting at Lexington and Concord, he was appointed to every committee that had anything to do with military matters. And on June 15, 1775, Washington was nominated by John Adams and unanimously elected as "General and Commander in Chief of the Continental Army and all forces thereunto attached." Washington accepted the assignment only out of his deep sense of duty and wouldn't take a penny for the work. For eight years, the longest American war excepting Vietnam and the War on Terror, he led the Continental Army in the cause of Liberty and Independence—it was enough to turn your hair gray.

And so we faced off; Yankees vs Redcoats, upstarts vs empire, innovation vs tradition. Out of necessity, Washington fought a very different war than the British. You might say he was a brawler, "no rules, just fight," and the British were "in the ring" so to speak, "marquis of Queensbury rules, you know." Where the English would focus on control of money and movement, occupying cities and coastlines where the Royal Navy (the terror of the seas) could easily support and resupply the army, Washington's troops fought a more guerrilla war, like the Native warriors, more as hunters in the wild. The British would want to fight "fixed" battles where everybody lines up and we decide this affair by massed musket fire. While their grand strategy was to force a general action, a one-time, winner-takes-all battle, Washington put his emphasis on preserving his army. He believed that the Revolution could succeed only if he kept his army intact.

He would bide his time, avoiding major defeats and decisively attacking when the chance for surprise came along. But when engaging the enemy, Washington was always first on the field or first to the fight (as at the Battles of Trenton, Princeton, and in a manner of speaking, at Monmouth) and the last to leave (as at the battle of Brooklyn Heights—he took the very last boat back across the East River, leaving only minutes before British scouts arrived).

General George Washington took command of the now appropriately named Continental Army in early July 1775. He had come with orders to form the "many companies of militia from the several colonies" into a functioning army, direct the siege of Boston, and "effect the expulsion of the British presence from that city."

Upon his arrival in Cambridge, Washington immediately wanted to plan an attack on Boston, but his officers were against it. They argued that the British were too well supplied and too well covered by the British fleet. It was decided to wait until the waters around Boston were frozen. Washington would take action, though. He sent an additional six regiments north to aid in the ongoing attack on Quebec and he ordered Henry Knox to go to recently captured Fort Ticonderoga in upstate New York and bring back the post's artillery. The attack on Quebec was frustrated by weather and distance and failed to achieve the desired results, but Henry Knox returned to Cambridge in January 1776 with 59 cannons and became Washington's favorite artilleryman.

When the waters around Boston finally froze over, Washington's officers still refused to attack the city. In frustration, Washington looked for another way to remove the British. So, on the evening of March 4, 1776, he directed his men to take the cannons from Fort Ticonderoga up to the high ground of Dorchester Heights, south of the city. Washington also ordered his troops in Cambridge to fire on the Redcoats. The British navy blasted away at the American guns in Cambridge throughout the night, only to discover in the morning that they had been bluffed; the cannons were now pointed down at them from Dorchester Heights. The British

Commander General William Howe remarked, *"My God, these fellows have done more work in one night than I could make my army do in three months."*

Howe sent troops to assault Dorchester Heights and capture or destroy the guns, but a "Providential" snowstorm stopped the attack cold (pun intended). Fearing a brutal bombardment and destruction of "his majesty's ships," the British opted for "Plan B" and chose to leave Boston. On March 17, 1776, known afterward as "Evacuation Day," 11,000 Redcoats and hundreds of Loyalists left the city by boat.

Washington marched into Boston on March 18, but this wasn't the time to celebrate. It was immediately evident to General Washington and the American leadership that the British departure from Boston was only a temporary break in the action. The British headed for Halifax, Nova Scotia, for some "R and R" (in this case, to regroup and reinforce) and plot their revenge. The new strategy: capture New York City, a major commercial center, key to the Hudson River, and home to a large Loyalist population.

Just as Washington expected, the British Navy sailed into New York Harbor in late June and occupied Staten Island by July 2. Not long after, John Hancock, the president of the Continental Congress, sent Washington a copy of the Declaration of Independence "right hot" off the press! It was to be read to every regiment of the Army. Washington had the men assemble on the parade grounds in Lower Manhattan. At 6 o'clock on the evening of July 9, the reading began. As the stirring words were read to the troops and the people, the Army gave several loud "Huzzahs!" The people of New York raced down Broadway, tore down the statue of George III, cut off the head and posted it on a spike, and melted down the remainder for musket balls, HOO-zzah!

Washington issued "general orders" (to the entire army from the Big HQ) intended to inspire and "Steel his Soldiers Hearts" (from Henry V, Washington loved Shakespeare and read often from his plays and sonnets) that fear may not "unman" them: *"Let us therefore animate and encourage each other, and show the whole world that a Freeman, contending for liberty on his own ground, is superior to any slavish mercenary on earth."*

General Order, Headquarters, New York (2 July 1776)

> *"The General hopes and trusts that every officer and man will endeavor to live and act as becomes a Christian soldier defending the dearest rights and liberties of his country."*

General Order, Headquarters, New York (9 July 1776)

> *"The time is now near at hand which must probably determine whether Americans are to be freemen or slaves... The fate of unborn millions will now depend, under God, on the courage and conduct of this army. Our cruel and unrelenting enemy leaves us only the choice of brave resistance, or the most abject submission. We have, therefore, to resolve to conquer or die."*

Then reality set in. The British had over 30,000 troops (42,000 if you counted the sailors and Marines of the Royal Navy) pitted against Washington's 19,000. The Continental Army was still a "work in progress," and facing off against what was probably the best army in the world and their equally qualified Hessian allies was a bit more than many of the young men of the new Continental Army had bargained for. Now Washington and British General William Howe played a dangerous game of cat-and-mouse where Washington attempted to keep his ever-shrinking and dispirited Continental Army together and avoid a major confrontation, while Howe tried to force that Major Confrontation (called a general action in those days) and annihilate the Patriot Army once and for all.

The opening move of the deadly game was the Battle of Long Island on August 27, 1776. For Washington, it was a devastating lesson in the shadow war of espionage and intelligence. With so many troops, Washington was sure that Manhattan (called York Island at the time) was the objective and a landing on Long Island would only be a diversion. So he divided his army, sending the smaller part under command of Nathanael Greene to Brooklyn, and keeping the main force on Manhattan. When it became evident that the main assault was on Long Island, it was too late. The British had already flanked the Continental positions and the rout was on.

Washington came as fast as he could and tried to rally the troops. From Brooklyn Heights, he watched as the "Maryland 400"(actually about 300) led by General William Alexander desperately charged the British lines time and again to allow the other soldiers of the army to retreat to the fortified hill tops in Brooklyn. Washington exclaimed, *"My God, my God! What brave fellows I must lose this day!"* In fact, 297 of the Maryland troops died to give the rest of the army that chance to live and fight another day. General Washington took the loss personally.

After being almost completely surrounded by Howe's Army, Washington made an incredible tactical retreat, removing his entire army of 9,000 men during the night of August 29, before the Redcoats were aware he was gone. He was the last American to leave Long Island alive, on the very last boat, just moments before British scouts arrived at the landing. There was a thick fog that blanketed the Continental positions that night and into the early morning. Some say the fog was miraculous (given that it was Washington, it had to be a Providential intercession). But more miraculous still was the fact that the entire Royal Navy must have been playing hearts or asleep at the helm—because not one ship guarding the East River saw or heard a thing that night!

Washington had saved the army and the Revolution, but the safety of Manhattan was only temporary. General Howe waited two full weeks before he would press his advantage. During the self-imposed British lull, the Howe brothers, General William (commander of the English Army) and Admiral Richard (commanding the Royal Navy), met with a delegation from the Continental Congress that included John Adams, Edward Rutledge, and Dr. Benjamin Franklin, to see if a reconciliation was at all possible. "Not a snowball's chance in hell" of that happening! So the Howes attacked at the Battle of Kip's Bay instead.

For Washington, "intel" was in short supply. The orders of September 13 were to abandon NYC and move north to the more easily defensible

Harlem Heights. During the move on September 15, British marines and assault troops landed at Kip's Bay (about halfway up the island). Unfortunately, the cannonade of the Royal Navy came down on the "very green" Connecticut militia, who were easily routed. The American defenders on Manhattan were in full flight when General Washington appeared and, in his usual manner, tried to rally and lead the troops back to the fight. But today, that just wasn't going to happen. Our hero finally lost his temper and in an almost unparalleled display of anger, did all he could to "motivate and remind" the men of their honor and responsibility as soldiers: He rode hard back and forth among the fleeing troops, he swore (violently and vigorously), he threatened (with saber, crop, and pistol), and finally, in a towering and ferocious rage, he charged the British—*all by himself*—exclaiming, *"Is it with men like these that I am to defend America?"*

Cooler heads ultimately prevailed and Washington's aides and lieutenants "reined him in" and got him away from certain death. Late that night, when General Israel Putnam (commanding the rear guard) finally arrived in camp "without much loss," the men broke out in loud cheers, and when General Henry Knox and the artillery made it in, the celebration got even louder. Washington actually embraced Knox, who he had feared lost or captured. Washington swore to himself that never again would he lose men or a battle due to lack of intelligence. It was from this time that his many covert spy rings would spring up throughout the war.

The very next day opened with the Battle of Harlem Heights. American scouts (called skirmishers) got the better of British columns moving north attempting to continue the pursuit from the day before. It was a minor engagement, but by pushing the British troops all the way back to their "jump off" positions, the Continental Army regained a bit of their pride and confidence.

More than a month later, General Howe succeeded in forcing Washington to abandon the New York City area once and for all at the Battle of White Plains on October 28. Washington's Army suffered another in a string of defeats largely due to the undisciplined nature of the militia (let's face it, these fellas came and went with the changing seasons), but again, the Continental troops showed their mettle and saved the day and the army from a potentially calamitous "general action" with their courage, determination, and by Howe's fondness to "tarry upon the field" rather than pursue and harass the fleeing enemy. Washington again demonstrated his remarkable skill at orderly retreat, and was once again saved by "Providential" weather. This time, it was a torrential downpour that stopped Howe in his tracks when he finally did decide to chase after "Washington and his rabble."

General Howe finally rid the New York Peninsula of all "Continentals" when he laid siege to Fort Washington on November 16. It was the last Patriot stronghold on Manhattan. Washington had reluctantly, and against his own better judgement, been talked into allowing the soldiers at Fort Washington to make a stand against superior British numbers. The hope of his officers was to create another "Bunker Hill" and make the Redcoats pay a high price for showing up. Didn't work out that way and Washington considered himself responsible for the loss of another 3,000 American soldiers. Two days later, Fort Lee was abandoned and the race across New Jersey began.

Over the course of the New York Campaign, Washington had lost almost 3/4 of his army. Some to combat (killed, wounded, or captured), some to sickness, but most were due to summer enlistments running out (in September) and desertion. The Continental Army had survived a string of loses that would have caused the collapse of any other force from any other country, and a number of troops had either headed for home "in the dark watches of the night" or straight out changed sides when they saw things headed downhill fast for the Patriots. So it was with less than 6,000 men that Washington slipped into Pennsylvania. But these 6,000 were the lions of the Revolution; men who would "stand to," as they say, through thick and thin. They had faced adversity and had kept the "army" together. The Revolution would live on. Washington was made for hard times and he had put that "personal stamp" on the Continental Army.

Washington's winter campaign of 1776, including the surprise assaults of Trenton and Princeton, was the stuff of legend, and those victories gave the revolution new life. Washington led the way at every turn. He set the example by "leading from the front." When the Continental Army crossed the Delaware, he went over with the first boats. When the assault went into Trenton, it was Washington at the head of the first wave.

And at Princeton, when the troops needed to be rallied, there was Washington yelling, "Follow me!" And the troops followed, right on to a great Patriot victory. He had an almost mystical sense of timing and history (as well as "Providence" always making sure he didn't die) that made the Continental soldiers look on him with awe and trust and believe in Washington in an almost mystical way. They would follow him into battle and straight into the jaws of hell.

Case in point: After the victories at Trenton and Princeton (Washington's Army had beaten the Hessians and British forces in three consecutive battles for these two cities), almost every soldier's term of enlistment was over or about to run out. The Massachusetts militia—the guys who had piloted the boats across the East River to save the army in August and then crossed the Delaware River to victory at Trenton in December—were almost a full month over their terms. The men were fixing to head home. They had done their duty by the terms of enlistment. Washington was watching his army evaporate without the Redcoats firing a shot!

He called the army "to parade" (means assembly) on the field at Morristown, NJ. As the men stood at attention, Washington rode out on horseback and invited the men to re-enlist or at least to extend their term of enlistment for one month. When none came forward, the General spoke again, with great urgency and emotion, saying, *"My brave fellows, you have done all I asked you to do, and more than can be reasonably expected; but your country is at stake, your wives, your houses and all that you hold dear. You have worn yourselves out with fatigues and hardships, but we know not how to spare you. If you will consent to stay one month longer, you will render that service to the cause of liberty, and to your country, which you probably can never do under any other circumstances."*

He well understood what he was asking. With every day, every minute, every second under arms, these men were risking not only their lives, but their families' security and welfare. Washington then asked who among them loved his country enough to make the sacrifice...and almost every soldier stepped forward. For love of family, of cause, and of country, they stayed. And not least of all, for love of their General who trusted and believed in them, *their* General who had the courage to charge the British—alone if necessary—and still had the tenderness to demonstrate understanding and gratitude for their sacrifices. Again, George Washington had saved the Revolution.

Then came 1777. A year of great victory and brutal hardship.

"All our hopes were blasted by that unhappy affair at Trenton," said Lord George Germain, Colonial Secretary of State of King George III to the British House of Commons, concerning Washington's winter campaign of 1776-77. The English needed a new plan and they needed it NOW. There was already unrest in the House of Commons over the "fortunes of war," and a great deal of sympathy for "the Colonials" from the British people. Germain's new plan was to divide the colonies in half, right down the Hudson River. One army advancing up the river from NYC, the other

army moving south down the river from Canada. Germain sent more troops to the fight. It was a good plan, but the best laid plans oft go awry (meaning some idiot will screw it up) and awry it went. British General Howe had to get even with Washington for the debacle he had suffered at Trenton. He diverted his troops to take Philadelphia, and so much for the English plan for 1777.

Washington's strategy of holding British General Howe by the nose in Philadelphia and sending significant numbers of his troops north to help General Horatio Gates win the battle of Saratoga kicked the English plans right in the britches! After that, France entered the war on the American side and Washington could once again open that proverbial can of colonial "whoop ass," but now on the British, with the help of the French. Kinda ironic, ain't it?

Washington waited out the winter months in the frigid hell of Valley Forge. There, he and the Continental Army came face to face with the "Refiner's Fire." They entered the Valley a ragged, desperate few, and when they came out the next spring, the Continental Army may have been the finest fighting force in the world. Washington called them "his Christian soldiers" because they would endure anything for the cause of liberty and independence, a cause he saw as Heaven's own. He believed that discipline was the heart of an army's success, so he had them trained by the finest officers he could find, including General Baron Friedrich Wilhelm von Steuben (think of him like a Marine Corps Drill Instructor), lately of the general staff of Frederick the Great (think of him like the Eisenhower of his day). Washington believed that the whole shootin' match was in God's hands anyway, so he had church services for "the troops" led by every minister in the region. Attendance was NOT optional. General Washington was deeply devout, so he always prayed for his soldiers and he endured with them every awful moment of that terrible winter encampment.

Over the course of the winter, things had changed for the British, as well. General Howe had resigned and gone home. Becoming trapped in

Philadelphia for the winter and being seen as the cause of Burgoyne's defeat at Saratoga, as well as being faulted for the failure of the entire Strategy of 1777, had badly damaged his pride and public image. General Henry Clinton had been called to take over management of the English cause. He knew that his troops were "hung out," with no real possibility of support. The war had gone global with the European powers now lining up to fight for the Americans and against the British, so the navies and armies of England were being divided up to protect colonial holdings all over the world. That meant Clinton would be expected to do more with less.

When the French were on their way, Washington came down out of the hills of Valley Forge to retake Philadelphia. The Redcoats had departed on General Clinton's orders to return once more to NYC. When the Continentals came again to the nation's capital, they found it in shambles: Independence Hall was a shell, the furniture had been burned for firewood, nothing remained to remember the Declaration of last July. All the non-Anglican churches had been used for stables or slaughterhouses and were filled with animal refuse. Of the American prisoners who had been taken by the British during the Philadelphia campaign, more than 70 percent now lay buried in the "field of the dead" (now Washington Square) in mass and unmarked graves. It was with more than a little bit of anger and passion for the fight that Washington and his army caught up to the Redcoats at the battle of Monmouth Courthouse on June 28, 1778. Washington personally led the men in the dramatic charge that broke the British rear guard and forced Henry Clinton and his army to sneak out after nightfall and make their hurried escape to New York. The once mighty invader was now reduced to the "order of the pick and shovel" as they "dug in" around NYC. The Battle at Monmouth was the last major battle fought in the northern states. The new British plan was to take the war to the South, where they would chase Washington until *he* caught *them*.

Washington would now use his main army to trap the largest English army in New York while also using those guerrilla tactics he learned in the last war to sap the British strength and resolve in the South. At the battles of King's Mountain, CowPens, and Guilford Courthouse, the Continentals drove the British like cattle on the trail and beat them like a government mule! Finally, when the French navy beat the British navy as they tried to resupply and reinforce their army in Virginia, Washington smelled an opportunity for victory. He struck like lightning and defeated the British at Yorktown in 1781.

Washington had been forced to overcome enormous obstacles in pursuit of this victory. The re-organizing and training of the Continental Army at Valley Forge was a miraculous masterpiece of military management in the harshest of situations. Throughout the war, he had found ways to hold his army together as a professional fighting force during the darkest of days—time after time after time. All the while he was trying to work with a demanding and imperious Congress as well as jealous state governments and governors. Washington had to improvise to offset shortages in material and supplies and "rein in" his oft-times impulsive junior commanders. And then to have to deal with the pride of our allies—talk about herding cats! Only a leader blessed with extraordinary foresight, personal integrity, and self-discipline could have provided this all-important leadership. It seems "self-evident" that without Washington, the Revolution would not have succeeded.

But Washington's personal beliefs were more on point:

> *"Glorious indeed has been our Contest: glorious, if we consider the Prize for which we have contended, and glorious in its Issue; but in the midst of our Joys, I hope we shall not forget that, to divine Providence is to be ascribed the Glory and the Praise."*

At war's end, Washington promptly sent his victorious army home, resigned his commission and authority, and once again became a "gentleman farmer." His actions astounded the royal courts of Europe, who fully expected the victorious general to seize power in the now independent colonies. Those people never understood Washington's strong belief in civilian authority over the military. He had made clear his position in March of 1783 when a petition pushing the army to force Congress to restore back pay had made the rounds among the officers at Newburgh, New York. Washington allowed the officers to assemble in order to talk it out. Unannounced, he came to the meeting and asked permission to speak. Of course his request was granted and Washington, the Patriot, verbally opened fire! He called the petition "open treason" and recalled to them that their loyalty should be to their country, not to the Army. To make the point *crystal* clear, he read a letter from a member of Congress from Virginia. Washington struggled through the first part of his prepared remarks, then reached for his spectacles. Pulling them out, he remarked off-handedly, *"Gentleman, you must pardon me, for I have not only grown gray but almost blind in service to my country."*

This disarming hint of vulnerability from our otherwise stoic leader so deeply affected the officers that many wept openly. After His Excellency left, they resolved to present him with *"the unanimous thanks of the officers"* and have "*the officers reciprocate his affectionate expressions, with the greatest sincerity of which the human heart is capable.*"

The chastised officers meekly dispersed, the mutiny had been defeated. Washington had won perhaps his greatest victory of the war with words, not weapons, and most likely saved the republic.

In September of 1783, all British soldiers had left the United States of America. Washington would soon retire from the service. He met his officers at Fraunces Tavern for the final farewell. Colonel Benjamin Tallmadge was an eyewitness to the tenderness and brotherhood of those who had stood together and risked their lives with Washington. He wrote:

> *At 12 o'clock the officers repaired to Fraunces Tavern in Pearl Street where General Washington had appointed to meet them and to take his final leave of them. We had been assembled but a few moments when his Excellency entered the room. His emotions were too strong to be concealed which seemed to be reciprocated by every officer present.*

> *After partaking of a slight refreshment in almost breathless silence the General filled his glass with wine and turning to the officers said, "With a heart full of love and gratitude I now take leave of you. I most devoutly wish that your latter days may be as prosperous and happy as your former ones have been glorious and honorable."*

> *After the officers had taken a glass of wine General Washington said, "I cannot come to each of you but shall feel obliged if each of you will come and take me by the hand."*

> *General Knox being nearest to him turned to the Commander-in-chief who, suffused in tears, was incapable of utterance but grasped his hand when they embraced each other in silence. In the same affectionate manner every officer in the room marched up and parted with his general in chief. Such a scene of sorrow and weeping I had never before witnessed and fondly hope I may never be called to witness again.*

The Adaptable Entrepreneur

They called him "Cincinnatus" after the great Roman patriot farmer who, after holding all power to defeat the enemies of Rome, simply gave it back to the senate and went back to farming. Likewise, Washington, after giving his authority back to Congress, couldn't wait to get home to Martha and Mount Vernon. The American and French Societies of the Cincinnatus are named in Washington's honor, as well as the city of Cincinnati, Ohio. He turned his horse south and headed for home. Upon his return in 1783, he found his business interests worn away like old socks and his cash all but played out. Washington had used his considerable fortune to fund the Revolution. Looked like hard times—but hard times and challenges were what Washington was made for, and this time was no different. His "enterprises" would include fish, lumber, and livestock (beef, pork, and poultry), an extensive stable of the finest horses for stud, and hounds for hunting. But his greatest accomplishments were, perhaps, the changeover of his "plantations" to farmland. No longer would his land grow tobacco and other traditional plantation cash crops, now he would produce wheat, rye, and corn. Washington became the finest (and largest) distiller of whiskey in the United States: over 12,000 gallons monthly, and business was brisk!

Washington also considered how to bring his immense wealth of land and natural resources to market. Deep in the Shenandoah Valley of Virginia, Western Maryland, and Pennsylvania, Washington owned huge tracts of land. Much of this land he opened to lease for veterans of the Revolution; they could farm or use the land as they saw fit. And he imagined a way to bring the natural resource wealth down from the interior to market in Chesapeake Bay. Washington saw the advantage of digging a canal along the rapids and falls of the Potomac River.

To promote the development of his brainchild, Washington hosted a conference of representatives from Virginia and Maryland at Mount Vernon in 1785. Though this meeting failed to resolve the problems that existed for the canal project, it led to a convention in Annapolis the next year and, finally, to the Constitutional Convention in Philadelphia in 1787. Funny how things work out, ain't it? Without Washington's canal troubles, there may never have been a Constitutional Convention at all!

The Pragmatic President

If the economic and political promises of Independence were going to have a chance, Washington saw that the Articles of Confederation would have to go. In fact, his determination and drive to see a stronger union and more effective government were born from his "vision of the West" as he saw it in his day. All this from his days as Surveyor "out yonder" and his experience in the French and Indian War.

Again, when he showed up in Philadelphia, Washington was seen as *the* go-to guy. He was unanimously elected president of the Constitutional Convention. His very presence lent prestige and dignity to the entire operation. He was an important unifying force in every conversation and resolution. Under Washington's careful guidance, the Convention negotiated the compromises needed to "form a more perfect union" and wrote the provisions that created a strong central government. The ratified Constitution led to Washington's inauguration as First President of the United States in New York City in April 1789.

As President, Washington tried to turn the promises of the Revolution and the Constitution into realities. Applying lessons learned in commanding the Continental Army, he set about organizing and forming a new central government. With his special brand of dignity and quiet authority, he tried to balance the competing interests of the "parties" that were gathering around two of his cabinet advisors, Thomas Jefferson and Alexander Hamilton. He handled the demands of dealing with Congress with his typical reserve and resolution. Washington respected its legislative authority, but never hesitated to apply his presidential boot to the backside of any question. In foreign affairs, he insisted on strict neutrality in the continuing war between France and Britain; his economic and domestic policy strengthened and protected the stability of the new nation. He protected the western states and territories through military actions and international treaties. And he zealously defended the authority of the federal government, calling forth state militias to suppress the Whiskey Rebellion (folks who wouldn't pay tax on booze in Western PA and took up arms over the question) without batting an eye. Everything he did set a precedent. And he established a final critical precedent by refusing to accept a third term.

Washington's Farewell Address to the country stirred the American spirit. He not only cautioned against sectional differences, political parties, and foreign entanglements, but put forward the meat of his personal and political thinking. In letting go of the reins of power for the last time, he reminded his fellow citizens that:

> *Of all the dispositions and habits, which lead to political prosperity, Religion and Morality are indispensable supports. In vain would that man claim the tribute of Patriotism, who should labor to subvert these great pillars of human happiness, these firmest props of the duties of Men and Citizens. The mere Politician, equally with the pious man, ought to*

> *respect and to cherish them. A volume could not trace all their connexions with private and public felicity. Let it simply be asked, Where is the security for property, for reputation, for life, if the sense of religious obligation desert the oaths, which are the instruments of investigation in Courts of Justice? And let us with caution indulge the supposition, that morality can be maintained without religion. Whatever may be conceded to the influence of refined education on minds of peculiar structure, reason and experience both forbid us to expect, that national morality can prevail in exclusion of religious principle.*

He was the man of the age. He walked away from power not once, but twice. He rose above the interests of class and section. He always put his country first. He was loved by his men, loved by his officers, and loved by his nation. And at the end of his public service, all he wanted to be was a "gentleman farmer."

After all the things he'd miraculously survived, believe it or not, Washington died of "acute epiglottitis" (a badly swollen gland in the throat), or would have, if his doctors hadn't "bled him out."

On December 14, 1799, at the age of 67, the greatest American Rebel passed away.

We all recall with pride the eulogy given by one of his most devoted officers, Henry "Light Horse Harry" Lee, which concludes, in part, *"he was First in war, First in peace, and First in the hearts of his countrymen!"*

And rightly so. But we should remember that in his will, Washington freed his slaves, and one of these, Mr. Richard Allen, gave a moving eulogy of George Washington to all the former slaves of Mount Vernon at Bethel Church on December 29, 1799. Here it is in its entirety:

> *At this time it may not be improper to speak a little on the late mournful event—an event in which we participate in common with the feelings of a grateful people—an event which causes "the land to mourn" in a season of festivity. Our father and friend is taken from us—he whom the nations honoured is "seen of men no more." We, my friends, have particular cause to bemoan our loss. To us he has been the sympathising friend and tender father. He has watched over us, and viewed our degraded and afflicted state*

with compassion and pity—his heart was not insensible to our sufferings. He whose wisdom the nations revered thought we had a right to liberty. Unbiased by the popular opinion of the state in which is the memorable Mount Vernon—he dared to do his duty, and wipe off the only stain with which man could ever reproach him. And it is now said by an authority on which I rely, that he who ventured his life in battles, whose "head was covered" in that day, and whose shield the "Lord of hosts" was, did not fight for that liberty which he desired to withhold from others—the bread of oppression was not sweet to his taste, and he "let the oppressed go free"—he "undid every burden"—he provided lands and comfortable accommodations for them when he kept this "acceptable fast to the Lord"—that those who had been slaves might rejoice in the day of their deliverance.

If he who broke the yoke of British burdens "from off the neck of the people" of this land, and was hailed his country's deliverer, by what name shall we call him who secretly and almost unknown emancipated his "bondmen and bond women"—became to them a father, and gave them an inheritance! Deeds like these are not common. He did not let "his right hand know what his left hand did"—but he who "sees in secret will openly reward" such acts of beneficence. The name of Washington will live when the sculptured marble and statue of bronze shall be crumbled into dust—for it is the decree of the eternal God that "the righteous shall be had in everlasting remembrance, but the memorial of the wicked shall rot."

It is not often necessary, and it is seldom that occasion requires recommending the observance of the laws of the land to you, but at this time it becomes a duty; for you cannot honour those who have loved you and been your benefactors more than by taking their counsel and advice. And here let me entreat you always to bear in mind the affectionate farewell advice of the great Washington—"to love your country—to obey its laws—to seek its peace—and to keep yourselves from attachment to any foreign nation." Your observance of these short and comprehensive expressions will make you good citizens—and greatly promote the cause of the oppressed and shew to the world that you hold dear the name of George Washington. May a double portion of his spirit rest on all the officers of the government in the United States, and all that say my Father, my Father—the chariots of Israel, and the horsemen thereof, which is the whole of the American people.

Amen and amen!

President, General, Father of his country; George Washington was respected by all, even his enemies. King George III said of him that he was the man of the age, the most noble of men. Dr. Benjamin Franklin said that Washington was the indispensable man of the Revolution and the truest example of the American character. His motto was, "Deeds, not words." And he lived by the creed, "For God and Country."

He is buried as a "country gentleman" in the Washington family plot at Mount Vernon, Virginia—America's first and most favorite son.

Washington's Farewell to His Officers

Dr. Franklin was the mind behind American Independence . . . and almost everything else in the 18th century!

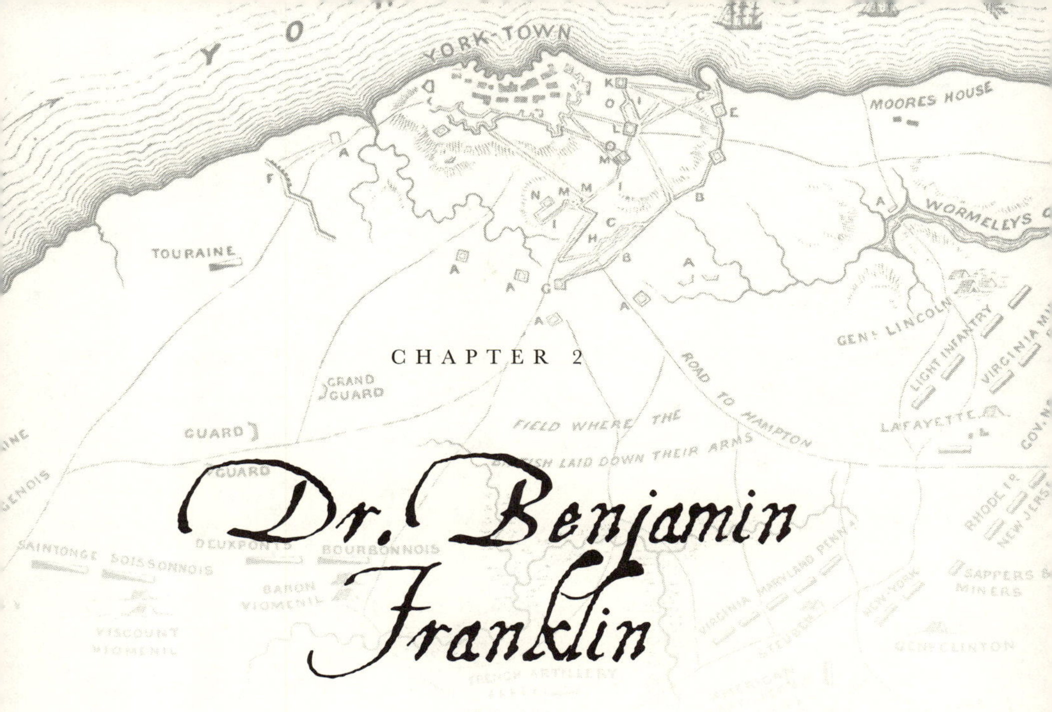

CHAPTER 2

Dr. Benjamin Franklin

Bodacious Philosopher of Liberty and Independence

Boston, Massachusetts, was the birthplace of a patriot who dedicated his life to service. Doctor Benjamin Franklin was a real human being. A man who worked to improve every aspect of himself every day. He never believed that he was perfect, but he definitely believed that striving for perfection was what made us most human and that the goal of living should be to become a complete human being. His ideas on liberty and freedom sprang from his dedication to improve society and the community every day, as well. Come to think of it, that's how he got involved in the American Revolution.

Franklin excelled at everything to which he set his hand and his greatest accomplishments came after he was 55 years old. Franklin believed he had a responsibility to do good to his fellows and every aspect of his life demonstrated his commitment to that idea. His philosophy of "*being excellent to himself and others*" makes him one of the most celebrated founding fathers in American history.

Read All About It!!

It was on a cold January day in 1706 that Benjamin Franklin was born on Milk Street in Boston. His life would become one of the most storied in history. He's the son of a blue-collar guy and Franklin learned a blue-collar ethic. You know, take your lunch pail in early and stay until the job is done. Early on, he was apprenticed as a typesetter to his brother, James, who was a printer in Boston. In time, Franklin wanted more of the business. Typesetting was cool and all, but young Ben saw there was money to be made. James wasn't gonna part with a penny that he didn't have to. In fact, he wouldn't even let his young apprentice submit a letter to the editor for publication! So…Franklin secretly started writing op-ed pieces under the name of fictional widow "Silence Dogood." The widow's letters were the talk of the town. An example of the good that "widow Dogood" did came when James was jailed for three weeks in 1722 for publishing material unflattering to the governor. Young Benjamin took over the newspaper and had Mrs. Dogood proclaim: "*Without freedom of thought there can be no such thing as wisdom and no such thing as public liberty without freedom of speech.*" All good things come to an end, and so it was with Silence Dogood. When the "good people" of Boston found out that Silence Dogood was actually the typesetter at James Franklin's printing shop, almost everyone was "slap yo' granny" stunned. They thought the writing and the ideas coming out of Silence Dogood were amazing. She said so many things that were wise and valuable. But Ben's brother was madder than a wet cat! His little brother (and the apprentice) stole the limelight, and Franklin, B. was a "media darling." So big brother became Cain to little brother's Abel…and brother James began to be very short with Ben. He actually beat him. That's when Ben figured it's time to "beat feet" and move it a little farther on down the road. Franklin ran away to New York in search of a new life and new opportunities.

Unable to find work in New York, Franklin decided that Philadelphia (the English empire's third largest city at the time) was where it was at and headed toward the city of brotherly love. Franklin had learned that he could get a job in Philadelphia working for a printer named Andrew Bradford. Nothing came easy for young Franklin, who ended up walking for 18 miles across New Jersey. When he finally reached the Delaware River, he got caught in a heavy thunderstorm, during which he saved the life of a drunken Dutchman who nearly drowned. The Dutchman offered him a ride to Philly.

When he finally arrived at the Market Street Wharf on October 6, 1723, it was a damp, rainy morning. Franklin barely had money enough to buy breakfast, so he bought himself a warm bun and met the girl of his dreams, Deborah Reed. In time, she took him home and the rest is history. Franklin would end up staying with his "fiancée" and her family for the next few years. As things turned out, Bradford had no work for our aspiring hero, but he did introduce Franklin to Samuel Keimer, recently released from a debtor's prison in London, who now was opening a new print shop in Philly. Keimer hired Franklin on the spot. After a few months, while working in the Keimer printing house, Franklin was convinced by Pennsylvania Governor Sir William Keith to go to London to acquire the equipment to establish another newspaper in Philadelphia. Turns out the Governor was full of empty promises. No cash on arrival in London, no supporters waiting at the dock, and no way home! Franklin was again on his own. Reaching into his inexhaustible bag of optimism, personal initiative, and resourcefulness, he found work as a typesetter in a printer's shop. And within a short two years' time, he found a way to return to Philadelphia in 1726: on the dime of Thomas Denham, a merchant who employed Franklin as clerk, shopkeeper, and bookkeeper in his business.

When he returned to America, Franklin learned that Governor Keith had lost his job and was now a common citizen. Keimer offered Franklin a manager job on his return, which Franklin at first declined so he could continue working for Denham in his goods store. But, when Denham died,

Franklin took over at Keimer Publishing and "put his printing house in order." He became a full-fledged workaholic, making a mold for duplicate types and spending all hours of the day at the presses. Sometime later, Franklin agreed to take over at the Keimer printing house when it went bust and used it to begin a new newspaper with printing supplies (often called cuts and types) that he had brought from London. Through Franklin's great industry, his new publishing venture avoided bankruptcy.

During these days, Franklin published volumes and volumes of "great American writings." Poor Richard's Almanac, The Way to Wealth, and many "broadsheets" (means one-page articles). He also became the official printer for the Pennsylvania Assembly, the colonial government, thanks to his connections with a Mr. Hamilton whom he met onboard a ship to England. Franklin began to make a substantial amount of money which he used to pay off all the debts he ever incurred, plus interest. In 1729, Franklin expanded the operation. A debate arose in the government over paper money and Franklin printed a pamphlet entitled "The Nature and Necessity of a Paper Currency" (can you say promoting self-interests?). When the House voted in favor of paper currency, they hired Franklin to print it, which brought him endless income. He was later hired to print even more government documents. Now Benjamin, government contracts in hand, was set for life. Franklin's appetite for owning newspapers—and for controlling their content—became insatiable. By the time he retired from the printing business at the age of 43, Franklin owned, or had controlling interest in, 75 percent of the newspapers in the colonies. Ben Franklin was now uniquely positioned to create the opinion of the American colonist. Talk about your media moguls… William Randolph Hearst had nothing on Ben Franklin.

Philosopher, Do-gooder, and All-Around Nice Guy

While he was growing his media empire as a businessman and entrepreneur, Franklin was also deeply concerned with and involved in improving his community. In 1727, Franklin, age 21, created the Junto, a group of "*like minded aspiring artisans and tradesmen who hoped to improve themselves while they improved their community.*" The Junto was a discussion group for issues of the day. Their discussions gave rise to the "fire department" as well as "fire insurance" and a "lending library." Reading was a great pastime of the Junto, but books were rare and expensive. The members created a library, initially assembled from their own books. This wasn't good enough, so Franklin conceived the idea of a subscription library which would pool the funds of the members to buy books for everybody to read. This was the birth of the Library Company of Philadelphia, which is now a great scholarly and research library with 500,000 rare books, pamphlets and broadsheets (remember those one pages), more than 160,000 manuscripts, and 75,000 graphic items (illustrated satire, read artsy-fartsy cartoons). It was at this same time that Franklin joined the FreeMasons, and he would become the Master Mason of the American nation.

When Franklin retired from business in 1743, he devoted himself to being an inventor and philosopher. The first thing he did was found the American Philosophical Society so that he could sit around and philosophize with "his brother wizards." Among other pursuits, Franklin threw himself into the study of electricity, which catapulted him to international fame. He was named a fellow of the British International Society of Philosophy, a title he held even during the years of the Revolution. He received Honorary degrees from Harvard, Yale, the University of St. Andrews in Scotland, and Oxford. He worked on theories concerning natural laws, he mapped the Gulf Stream and air currents (like the jet stream), and invented spectacles, the lightning rod, and his famous stove (among other things). He began to understand that if there are "natural laws" that govern relationships in the natural world, then there must be "natural laws" that govern the inner workings of humanity, as well as human interaction. He set his mind on figuring out, observing, and studying those laws.

Franklin's philosophical life led him to become deeply involved in politics. He is the guy who first proposed what we now call "the Albany

Plan for Union" where he advocated that the colonies come together and be one nation, instead of 13 separate entities. He thought there was more strength in that position. In fact, the first political cartoon ever printed in a newspaper was Ben Franklin's "Join or Die!" That cartoon was about joining the Union because it was good for the common defense and good for the common welfare.

Franklin went to England again during the French and Indian War to represent Pennsylvania, Massachusetts, New Jersey, and Georgia, and he became quite well-known in the English political circles. He was named the minister plenipotentiary (meaning full of possibilities) for the several colonies to the Crown. While he was there, he toured Ireland and saw the horrific effect of British policies on the economy there. He also released the private letters of Lieutenant Governor Hutchinson of Massachusetts. Hutchinson had apparently been playing both sides of the fence, telling the colonists in Massachusetts one thing while presenting a very different face to the British Crown in a "governing for profit" arrangement. The revelation would cost Hutchinson his job and propel Franklin into the forefront of the patriot movement. You see, the king's privy council (the guys closest to George III who were most likely "in" on the shenanigans) commanded Franklin's appearance at a closed session of the council to explain his actions. There, the famous and world renowned Dr. Benjamin Franklin was "dressed down" like a school boy! He realized that he (and his American countrymen) were regarded as no more than the Irish. Franklin walked into this hearing kindly disposed to justice and the American colonist argument for protection of their rights as "freeborn Englishmen" and left an ardent, radical, and realistic Patriot for American independence!

We Must, Indeed, All Hang Together Or, Most Assuredly, We Shall All Hang Separately

Franklin's political life during the Revolution was filled with excitement. As soon as he got home from England, Pennsylvania elected him part of the 2nd Continental Congress. He was looked upon as the wisest and oldest of statesmen due to his age and experience, and still as one of the youngest men in the congress due to his habits and behavior. He *lived* every day to the *fullest*. His counsel always weighed heavily in debate, or at least drew the loudest laughter—often both. And it was thought to be imperative (means without a doubt necessary) that he be appointed to the committee to write the Declaration of Independence. Because he was the "inimitable and high esteemed" *Doctor* Benjamin Franklin, the noted philosopher of the Age of Enlightenment, the committee wanted his input. And Franklin had many ideas, but he left it to other men to write while he edited heavily. We don't know which words are his and which words are Jefferson's (or Adams' for that matter). What we do know is that he was pro-independence and wanted the turkey to be the symbol of the new nation as the bird that sustained our pilgrim forefathers in their days of want.

After the Declaration was signed, Franklin was sent by Congress to France as the American Minister Plenipotentiary, along with others (Silas Deane and Arthur Lee—John Adams would come over in 1778) in hope of negotiating an official relationship. Franklin fully enjoyed his notoriety in Paris. He went about town dressed as a "frontiersman" in buckskins and furs. He gave the appearance of the rough and ready American while being the soul of discretion and political savvy. He began a masonic lodge in France and "invited" many of the French ministers into the brotherhood. In fact, Franklin so much impressed the French King and his court that when the American Victory at Saratoga was announced, it was like "shootin' fish in a barrel" to negotiate a full-on treaty. Franklin also sent to Gen. Washington the young and idealistic Marquis de Lafayette as a soldier and ally (not to mention boatloads of French troops), as well as Baron von Steuben (late of the Prussian Staff and at the time "best in the world") to teach and train America's army, and he acquired the ships needed for American "Privateers" like John Paul Jones to harass British shipping across the Atlantic. Benjamin Franklin was the only Founding Father to sign all four "important" documents of the day: The Declaration of Independence in 1776, The Treaty of Alliance with France in 1777, The Peace Treaty that ended the war with England in 1782, and The U.S. Constitution in 1787.

"I Believe it is a Rising Sun"

Truth be told, had Dr. Franklin been involved in writing the Articles of Confederation, the Constitutional Convention of '87 probably would never have been necessary. But, as we've read, he was needed in France. Funny how Providence works things out. When Franklin returned from foreign service, he was almost immediately elected "President" of Pennsylvania. And he saw, just as quickly, how bad the Articles of Confederation were. He was involved in arranging the meeting in Annapolis that ultimately led to the Constitutional Convention in Philadelphia in May of 1787. As the "Sage of the Age," he again had much to contribute, but used his wit and wisdom to move and motivate others to action. Cases in point:

1) He moved that the convention be opened with prayer—every session—so that we remember our humility, gratitude, and equality before God.

2) He urged that Gen. Washington be elected to preside over the proceedings and also pushed for Washington to be the first American president.

3) He engaged the youthful James Madison in political discussion almost every evening because he saw promise in the young man.

Franklin was a "cagey" old guy. He was involved at every step with what was going on. At the conclusion of the Convention, he said to the delegates, *"I have often`in the course of the sessions…looked at that sun behind the President* (carved on Washington's chair) *without being able to tell whether it was rising or setting. But now at length I have the happiness to know it is a rising and not a setting sun."*

As Dr. Franklin was leaving the assembly hall when it was all over, he was asked what they (the convention) had given us (the nation), a republic or a monarchy? To which he replied, "A republic…if you can keep it!" He not only knew, but expected that the full participation of every citizen to "*secure the blessings of liberty for ourselves and our posterity*" was a necessary and vital part of the success of the new adventure to which we had set our hands.

Franklin always had a jovial streak. It is said that when he and Gen. Washington met again for the Constitutional Convention, he (the doctor) invited him (the general) to dine. While at dinner they both asserted that the other had been the principal mover of events to found the new nation, and that the other was the "quintessential American" (means you da man!). At the conclusion of the dinner, Franklin, in a very humorous way, asked Washington to join him in a toast, saying, "Let us toast ourselves with this tea, and agree that the world is infinitely better off for *our* having been here!"

Franklin was a man's man. He was strong and broad, capable and confident. He had near boundless energy both physically and intellectually. He was successful in every venture to which he applied himself. As Postmaster General, he even made the post office profitable! He was generous and kind and always an advocate for the public good. He was loved and respected across the colonies, the nation, and overseas. Printer, inventor, philosopher, Master Mason, Revolutionary, and America's home-grown Sage, still, he remained humble and painfully human. He even wrote his own epitaph:

> *Here lies the body of B. Franklin, Printer;*
> *Like the Cover of an old Book,*
> *Its Contents torn out,*
> *And stript of its Lettering and Gilding,*
> *Lies here, Food for Worms.*
> *But the Work shall not be wholly lost:*
> *For it will, as he believ'd, appear once more,*
> *In a new & more perfect Edition*
> *Corrected and amended*
> *By the Author.*

Ben Franklin would die April 17, 1790. More than 20,000 people attended his funeral at a time when Philadelphia was a city of about 50,000. To honor him, the entire city shut down for the week.

They called him "The Last Puritan."
In truth, he was the driven and
relentless Apostle of Liberty
and Independence!

CHAPTER 3

Samuel Adams

"Say You Want a Revolution?"

Samuel Adams was born in Quincy, Massachusetts, the son of prominent landowner and brewer, Samuel Sr. (so it ought to be Sam Sr. beer). Sam Jr. was cousin of and political mentor to John Adams. He's a Harvard man, B.A. class of '40, and Master of Arts in '43…1743. After college, he studied law, but gave it up to family pressure to get into business. Adams took a position as a clerk in the counting house of Thomas Cushing, one of the colony's leading merchants. Samuel Adams was *not* a success in business and soon left Cushing to begin a series of his own short-lived ventures.

In spite of his "storied" lack of success at business—failing as a clerk, small business owner, malter, newspaperman, and tax collector, as well as burning through a 1,000-pound sterling inheritance like it was kindling, the seeds of future success had been sown. Adams showed real genius in the world of politics. Samuel excelled in political discussion and debate, political writing, and especially the art of political maneuver and strategy. Politics became his passion and he pursued his political ends with a religious zeal and singleness of purpose rarely seen in those colonial days. But Samuel Adams was the right man for the right time and in the right place.

He Could Preach "Hot Hell" in Freezing Snow

Why was Samuel Adams so virulently anti-English? Here's the story: His Dad was a wealthy man who was popular in the community. His father was also one of the speculators in the Massachusetts Land Bank, which gave people the wherewithal to borrow money to improve their situation based on land value (the British didn't want too much money being in the hands of "the provincials"—that's us). The British Parliament wasn't happy that someone had found a way to create more wealth in the colonies than they were comfortable allowing, So, the king's council decertified the Land Bank and left the principals holding the bag. Sam Adams Sr. died in poverty, and for the rest of his own life, Adams Jr. fought off lawsuits pertaining to the Land Bank, which created in him a deep and bitter feeling towards the British mercantile system, the King, and his Privy Council. Adams often joked that the king's council *should* meet in the "privy" (outhouse) if all they were producing was crap—or words to that effect.

Samuel Sr. was also a deacon in the Congregational Church, made up of puritans and separatists who weren't fond of the British from the get go. Adams Jr. was raised in a deeply religious home (his folks wanted him to be a minister), and Adams was a man who was profoundly affected by the Great Awakening. He had heard the preaching, its equality, diversity, and democracy, and it had resonated deep within him. He, like Richard Henry Lee, was a devout Christian. In fact, his nickname with most of the patriots was "the last Puritan." It's when he enters politics that he finds his "ministry." This is the pulpit from which he will launch his anti-British/pro-American political "awakening!"

Adams saw his unsuccessful business efforts as "Heaven-ordained" learning opportunities that were pointing him irresistibly to some unforeseen end. He felt not only drawn, but "called" to preach a political gospel of revolution, liberty, and independence. Samuel's newspaper, *The Independent Advertiser*, called for resistance to the British and supported revolutionary thought. The paper was published during the French and Indian war, so Adams was seen as unpatriotic (at least), and got a reputation as a "rabble rouser" for his efforts. Next, he became a tax collector for the Crown. His thought was to take the position so the taxes wouldn't get collected; he never had any intention of collecting them because he thought they were illegal. His position gained him fame, popularity, and widespread support for his ideas and positions. It also created a huge personal debt; the British wanted the tax money and sued Adams. To this day, he still hasn't paid up.

In 1764, Adams was elected to the General Court (the legislature of the time) of Massachusetts, representing the town of Boston. His "unique skill set" was recognized by the men of the court and he soon rose to be one of the leaders. He was offered positions by royal officials that would have brought him great wealth, but he refused them all and remained *chronically* in debt.

Adams was an effective unifier; he was able to bring together three rival revolutionary groups to form the "original" Sons of Liberty. He was one of the most forward organizers of the protests over the Sugar Act (1764), the Stamp Act (1765), the Declaratory Act (1766), and the "Townshend" Act (1767). The last act was named for Edward Townshend, the King's minister of money and keeper of the royal wallet. The intent was to have the courts in the colonies always rule in favor of "cash for the king" (hugely unpopular). Adams' constant, loud, and insistent criticism of Parliament's policies incited public outrage, which erupted into confrontation and violence at the Boston Massacre in 1770. After that, Adams began working with "committees of correspondence," which exchanged ideas with "like-minded" men in other colonies who opposed British rule. Adams was perhaps at his finest as a principal player in planning and executing the Boston Tea Party.

The Sons of Liberty and the Boston Tea Party

Three ships loaded with tea sat anchored in Boston harbor, the *Dartmouth*, the *Eleanor*, and the *Beaver*. The "Sons" were determined to prevent the tea on these ships from being landed on American soil, because if it were, a tax would have to be paid—and we weren't falling for that! You see, Parliament had passed a new law, the Tea Act of 1773, which kept a small tax of three pence (means roughly 3/10ths of a penny) on all English tea brought into the American colonies. This shipment of tea was special; it was from the East India Company (that meant the king), and it would be made available to Boston merchants, selected by the East India Company, who were loyal to the British government—extremely loyal. The Company knew they would make sure that tax got paid. Point was, if we paid the tax on the tea, then we accepted the argument that Parliament could rightly tax the American colonies without our consent. We were still very much convinced that the idea was "dead ass" wrong!

November 28, 1773, the *Dartmouth* was the first of the tea ships to arrive at Griffin's Wharf in Boston harbor. The tax on the tea had to be paid within twenty days, making the deadline for payment December 17. Colonial Boston had become the home of revolutionary and radical thought. Thousands of people came from Boston and the "towns round about" to meet and discuss the "tea crisis." On Monday, November 29, a meeting was called at Faneuil Hall, the usual place for town meetings, but so many people showed up—better than 4,000—that the meeting had to be moved to the Old South Meeting House, the largest building in all of colonial Massachusetts and the site of Boston's largest revolutionary gatherings.

The resolves from the meeting were signed "The People" (see democracy working here) and the meeting became known as "The Body of the People" (has to do with that Congregational Church heritage). The massive crowd at the Old South Meeting House included those not normally allowed at official town meetings, such as men from surrounding towns and those without voting privileges (oh, the Pilgrims would be proud!).

This was truly the voice of the People. Royal Governor Hutchinson described these meetings as including "*the lower ranks of the people...the poor, and the rabble*" (means wicked and disreputable folks). The meeting voted to put a guard of 25 men (Sons of Liberty all) on the tea ships to ensure that the tea would not be landed (means taken off the ships).

For almost three weeks, there was a growing animosity between "the People" and the Governor. The deadline was coming soon. The Sons of Liberty were determined that the tea would *never* be landed. They sent a message to the Royal Governor asking him to let the ships leave Boston Harbor still laden (means loaded) with tea. The Governor told the "Sons" to pound sand.

On December 14, another meeting of "the People" was called at the Old South Meeting House. Samuel Adams called on the Committees of Correspondence from surrounding towns to "*be in readiness in the most resolute manner to assist this Town in their efforts for saving this oppressed country.*"

The neighboring towns responded by sending resolutions of support and representatives to Boston. Without governmental permission, the tea ships would be fired upon from Castle William, the armed fort at the entrance to Boston Harbor, if they left for England. The owners weren't going to risk their ships and cargoes being destroyed. So there the tea ships sat, anchored at Griffin's Wharf in Boston Harbor.

At 10 o'clock in the morning on December 16, 1773, thousands of colonists gathered at the Old South Meeting House for a final meeting. Over 5,000 people (more than a third of Boston's entire population at the time) crowded into the meeting house. The place was packed! Representatives came from all over the colony, making it the largest political meeting Boston had ever seen. The "Sons" sent a final message to the governor, who was now guarded by regulars (means British troops) in the countryside, far from Boston and potential personal harm. They asked him to give permission for the tea ships to leave harbor, cargoes intact. The message wasn't returned until late in the evening; the governor refused the request and would order the unloading of the tea "on the morrow."

So there you have it, all attempts at diplomatic negotiations with the royal government had failed. The "Sons" had exhausted all legal means of keeping the tea from being unloaded. Hearing the news, Samuel Adams declared: *"This meeting can do nothing more to save the country!"* as a pre-arranged signal to the Sons of Liberty to put "the plan" into action. Members of the Sons of Liberty left the Old South Meeting House, gathering their brothers outside the meeting, and made their way down to Griffin's Wharf. They were joined on the way by still other brothers who had been getting ready in taverns and homes along the harbor road. These fellas were "thinly disguised as Mohawk Indians" with their faces blacked out with soot and were wearing heavy coats.

Meanwhile, back at the Old South Meeting House, the crowd could not be contained and the meeting was adjourned. Hundreds of people rushed to the docks to see what was happening. About 50 men remained at Old South Meeting House, among them Samuel Adams, John Hancock, and Joseph Warren. Leaders of the Sons of Liberty and the larger Patriot movement, these men could not risk being accused of being part of the destruction of the tea. That evening, it took 150 men nearly three hours to dump more than 340 chests of tea into Boston Harbor…And a good time was had by all! Well, all the Sons of Liberty at least. The day after the Tea Party, John Adams wrote: *"This destruction of the tea is so bold, so daring, so intrepid and so inflexible, and it must have so important consequences and so lasting that I can't but consider it an epoch in history."*

Turned out to be just the case. The incident had inflamed the embers of rebellion. The Boston Tea Party became the precursor of Revolution and a turning point in American History.

On to Independence

To organize a revolution meant you had to build unity and obtain the cooperation of the thirteen colonies. The Tea Party had created unity among the colonies and King George's reaction would further cement that bond. Now the question Adams faced was how to get everybody thinking together. Remember, just a few years back, Adams had been part of the formation of Committees of Correspondence by which all towns in Massachusetts maintained open communication. The Sons of Liberty, Virginia Chapter, proposed that each colony should form a committee and that they should be brought together in one location. There was the epiphany (means an a-ha! moment)! All that had to be done was to bring representatives of all 13 colonies together and "evangelize" Adams' particular gospel of liberty and independence. With this result in mind, the First Continental Congress was held in Philadelphia in the fall of 1774, where the first independent revolutionary government was created.

Back to King George and his "historic" over reaction—we call them the Coercive Acts. They were a series of laws passed by Parliament (at the king's direction) that would "get even" with the colony of Massachusetts for that "damnable Tea Party!" These acts closed the port of Boston until the king was repaid the over two million lost by the tea destruction, dissolved the Massachusetts assembly and replaced them with royal appointees, outlawed prosecution of royal representatives in the colonies for any crimes committed—only the king could discipline "his boys"—and the *Quartering Act*...Parliament ordered that the colonists of Massachusetts would house, feed, and clothe the British Regulars who had been sent to keep order—on their own dime! This was last straw sort of stuff and the Quartering Act was adding insult to injury. The king had sent over two thousand more troops to "restore order" in Boston, and WE were going to pay for it? Now Samuel Adams and the Sons of Liberty had their devil against whom they could preach—King George III (sometimes the king was a devout dunce).

Samuel Adams attended the First Continental Congress in a suit of clothes paid for by his friends and brothers in the Sons. Samuel, as we have noted, was chronically in debt (sometimes he was too poor to pay attention) and his "Sunday best" simply wasn't good enough to represent Massachusetts among the other colonies. He was accompanied by his cousin John Adams and the two became well respected for their oratory skills and passionate support of independence. After hearing Samuel speak, Congress decided to boycott British goods until the Coercive Acts were repealed.

When Adams returned to Massachusetts, he became part of the outlaw Massachusetts Provincial Government and immediately reformed the armed militia. The "minutemen," the express riders, the town and provincial militias, had all existed since the days of the French and Indian War—Adams just made sure that now they were loyal to the Sons of Liberty and the "outlaw" congress. Stirring up trouble has its rewards—and its downside—and it wasn't long before trouble was again answered with trouble. In April 1775, the crown offered a reward to anyone who could capture Samuel Adams and his partner in mischief, John Hancock (wealthy businessman and smuggler extraordinaire). Soon Gen. Thomas Gage, the military governor, issued an order to capture and arrest them as they were the "main instigators of unrest."

Adams and Hancock, both residents of Boston, were hiding out in Lexington (at Hancock's Grandfather's home) directing the provincial government and the colonial mayhem. On the night of April 18, Paul Revere was sent on his now famous ride (he made several) to warn the patriot militias that the regulars were out (meant the British were coming!) and meant to confiscate their ammunition, powder, and arms…oh, yeah, and to warn Adams and Hancock that their arrest warrants had been signed. They needed to "get outta Dodge" and fast! That night, Revere helped them pack their gear and get on the road. They "hit the trail" none too soon. In fact, Revere made it out of Lexington only moments before the British came to town and ended up arrested just minutes later. Later that day, someone (no one really knows who) fired a single shot on the Lexington Green, and so began the American Revolutionary War. There was no going back now.

Samuel Adams was elected to the Second Continental Congress, as well, and became one of the driving forces behind the movement for independence. He made a speech at the Second Continental Congress supporting independence and the Declaration of Independence. He said, *"If ye love wealth better than liberty, the tranquility of servitude than the animating contest of freedom, go from us in peace. We ask not your counsels or arms. Crouch down and lick the hands which feed you. May your chains sit lightly upon you, and may posterity forget that ye were our countrymen."*

Samuel Adams served on military committees, economic committees, political committees, and did all he could for the American fighting man. He did all he could to keep the nation strong. Adams was a real visionary; he considered himself a citizen of the United States before he was a citizen of Massachusetts. The nation was more important to him than his colony.

Adams remained active in politics for the rest of his life. He frequently served as the moderator of the Boston Town Meeting. He was elected to the state senate. He very carefully considered the arguments both for and against the Constitution before deciding to support ratification. Even with the support of Hancock and Adams, the Massachusetts convention narrowly ratified the Constitution by a vote of 187 to 168. He served as the Lieutenant Governor. When Hancock died, Sam Adams served as Governor of Massachusetts.

The great patriot died at the age of 81 on October 2, 1803, and is buried next to many of his Patriot brothers in the Granary Cemetery in downtown Boston. Samuel Adams Jr. can lay claim to the title of America's Revolutionary.

Short, balding, fiery, and obnoxious, Adams was still the man who moved mountains in pursuit of Independence and Victory.

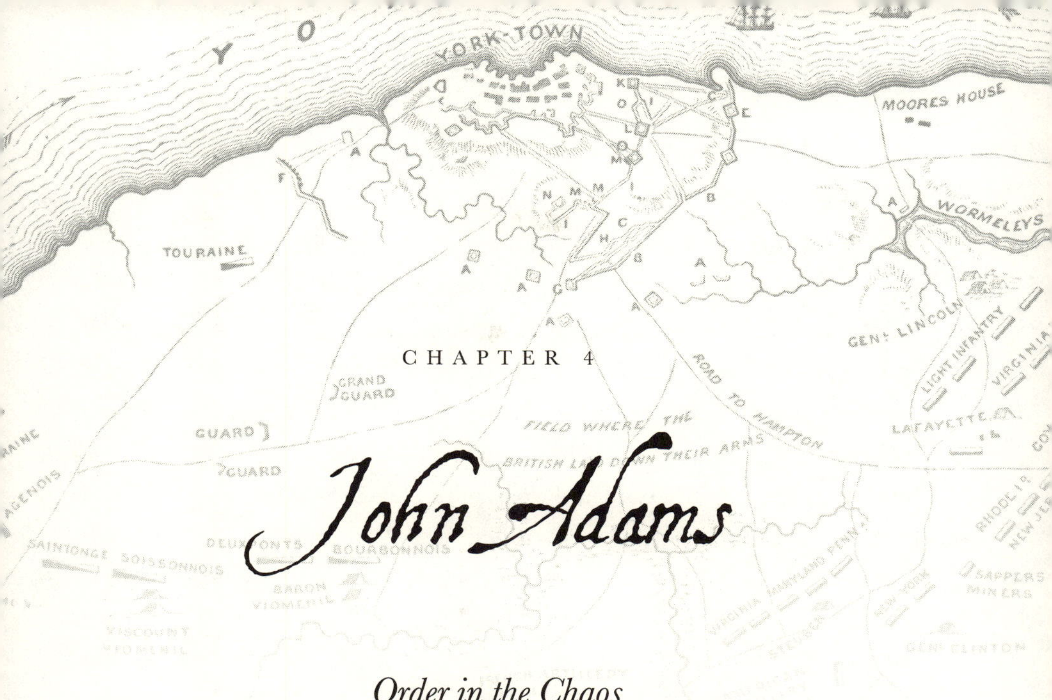

CHAPTER 4

John Adams

Order in the Chaos

If Samuel Adams was the loud and insistent voice of rebellion and independence, then John Adams was the legal champion. Together they were the Revolution's apostles to the people of Massachusetts. Samuel converted the working folks and John appealed to the professionals. Samuel might have been "first in the fire," but once John jumped in, he was no less insistent and inflammatory.

John Adams was born into a very religious home. His father was a strict Congregationalist (Puritan), a deacon, and a Selectman. John's family saw religion and politics as going hand in hand. They weren't a wealthy family, but were raised with a strong heritage. That heritage was generation after generation of Puritans. Pioneers facing the wilds, they saw themselves as a city on the hill, setting an example for everybody. John Adams grew up looking at these people as the bearers of freedom, the founders of this idea of Liberty, and he felt a deep need to walk up to their example. Their example had a holiness and purpose. To him the Puritans were heroic and he would honor their legacy with his actions.

The Prudent Patriot

Adams was stocky and athletic. Early on, John just didn't see the need for school. He was more of a Huck Finn sort of student. When John Adams Sr. confronted his son about his "truant and reckless" ways, he learned it was more the school master and not the studies that stood in the way of his son's success. Change of schoolmasters and "presto"—it wasn't long before young John saw the value of a good education. John Jr. would attend Braintree Latin school and then on to Harvard. Seems them Adams boys were "Harvard men" (remember back then, Harvard was the best Community College around—it had yet to adopt its now famous pomposity). After graduating in 1755, Adams passed the bar and opened a law practice. In his first year, he had one client. He didn't win a case for three years. But by 1764, he had a thriving practice, so much so that he might have been carrying the biggest caseload in Boston. Now that his practice was flourishing, he started courting Abigail Smith, the daughter of a Congregationalist minister. John and Abigail were married and five children later, he was the most successful attorney in Boston. In fact, after the Boston Massacre, it was John Adams who was prevailed upon (by the Sons of Liberty) to defend the British soldiers and ensure they got a fair trial. Adams won the cases and kept all but two of the accused soldiers from punishment. He firmly believed that every man deserved a fair trial and felt that his defense of the British soldiers was *"one of the most gallant, generous, manly and disinterested Actions of my whole Life, and one of the best Pieces of Service I ever rendered my country."*

It was the fame and reputation as the best legal mind in Massachusetts that threw Adams' political career into high gear. When everyone in America started protesting the Parliamentary policies, the Sugar Act, Stamp Act, etc., Adams was initially reluctant to get involved. He had a young family and a thriving law practice—he knew he had a lot to lose. He knew that Parliament had messed up, but he was also worried that the Sons of Liberty had a hidden agenda. He didn't trust his own cousin Samuel because *that* Adams was all about independence from the "get go" and he figured *that* idea was driving the train. John saw it initially as being about maintaining their rights as "Freeborn Englishmen." Nevertheless, his cousin and others put pressure on him and he started to write articles to newspapers (anonymously) that turned into big political impact pieces. He began to change his tune as he saw Britain stripping the colonies of their autonomy. In 1765, he drafted the instructions for the Braintree representatives in the Massachusetts legislature. Plain and simple, these instructions were an explanation of how Puritan virtue and the ethics of the city on the hill, righteousness and independence, had to be coupled with resistance to the acts of Parliament. Adams was saying that Parliament was violating: 1) Tenets of English law. Under royal charter, all of the colonies were autonomous. They were still loyal to the king, but Parliament had NO jurisdiction in the colonies. We had our own assemblies, thank you. 2) The things we hold most sacred. We (the Pilgrims and the Puritans) came to America seeking opportunity and religious liberty, and now they (the British) were trying to deprive us of those things. We're not going to stand for that. Y'all drove us out of England to Holland, and then from Holland to here…so how far away do we have to go, anyway? And now here you are again figuring you can kick us around some more…AIN'T gonna happen!

Adams wrote, "*On the tenets of our pilgrim forefathers we stand against your acts or attempts to deprive us of our autonomy.*" Later in '65, he gave a speech before the governor and the council where he was the first to say "no taxation without representation." Adams explained that the opposition of the colonies to the Stamp Act was because the Stamp Act deprived the American colonists of basic rights guaranteed to all Englishmen. In 1774, because of his strong and outspoken resistance to the Stamp Act (and other acts of Parliament), Adams was elected as one of the delegates to represent Massachusetts in the First Continental Congress.

Massachusetts sent Adams to the first *and* Second Continental Congresses. Adams felt strongly that the "conservatives" of the First Continental Congress (those who favored staying loyal to Great Britain) were no better than the royally appointed "robbers" sitting in governorships across the colonies. He wrote to his wife, Abigail, that *"Spiders, Toads, and Snakes, are their only proper Emblems."*

As a delegate to the First Constitutional Congress, Adams renewed his push for the right to a jury trial. He felt that *"Representative government and trial by jury are the heart and lungs of liberty. Without them, we have no other fortification against being ridden like horses, fleeced like sheep, worked like cattle, and fed and clothed like swine and hounds."* The man had a way of speaking his mind.

By early 1775, Adams felt that Congress was moving in the right direction—toward independence from Great Britain. *"Reconciliation if practicable,"* was his public view, but privately he agreed with Benjamin Franklin's conclusion that independence was desirable and inevitable.

In June 1775, he nominated George Washington of Virginia as commander-in-chief of the Continental Army. Adams had figured that the many militias (there were quite a few) that had come from a number of colonies to surround Boston and lay siege to the British Army could be unified under an experienced leader, especially if he held a "national" rank. And a leader from Virginia would ensure unity and support from the southern colonies. Adams was insightful and shrewd and Washington's commission was approved unanimously. So, while General George Washington worked on the military solution to independence, Adams would use his clout and momentum in Congress (along with his boundless energy and drive) to create the political reality of the American Nation. By the fall of 1775, it was John Adams who was driving the train of America's separation from Great Britain through Congress.

The Power of the Printed Word

John Adams was a man with a quick, powerful mind and *very* strong opinions. His thoughts on government were sound and solid and sought out by many of the delegates to the Continental Congress. Every colony was now anticipating becoming a state and they each wanted his advice about forming a new government. Adams' views and observations were so convincing that he was asked to write them all down. He did so by writing letters to the representatives of the different colonies; each a bit longer and more in depth than the last. Richard Henry Lee of Virginia was so impressed that he had the most thorough letter printed and circulated (with John's approval, of course). It was published—anonymously—in April 1776, and was simply titled "Thoughts on Government: a Letter from a Gentleman to his Friend." It seems that none of Adams' other writings rivaled the lasting importance of this effort. His ideas have had an enduring influence on almost every state government, not to mention the U.S. Constitution.

Adams thought that government should be created "with the end in mind" to achieve desired results; those being the liberty, happiness, and security of the greatest number of people. He wrote that, "*There is no good government but what is republican. That the only valuable part of the British constitution is so because the very definition of a republic is an empire of laws, and not of men.*" His writings also supported a two-body legislature (called bicameralism) as a check and balance against the weaknesses of a single body legislature. AND he suggested that there should be a separation of powers between the Executive, Judicial, and Legislative branches. He still further voiced the opinion that if a continental government were to be formed, then it must "be confined to certain enumerated powers." If you've been following along closely, then you see that John Adams built the framework of the later Constitution more than a decade before it was written!

Declaration of Independence

In the 1776 session of Congress, Richard Henry Lee of Virginia put forward the Resolution for American Independence on June 7. John Adams readily seconded the resolution, which stated, *"These colonies are, and of right ought to be, free and independent states."* Adams co-championed the measure until it was adopted by Congress on July 2. Once the resolution passed, independence became inevitable, though it still had to be declared formally. The commitment was now all or nothing.

John Adams and Thomas Jefferson were appointed by the Second Continental Congress, along with Benjamin Franklin, Roger Sherman, and Robert R. Livingston, to write a Declaration of Independence from Great Britain. Here is Adams' account of how Jefferson became the writer of the initial draft:

> *The subcommittee met. Jefferson proposed to me to make the draft. I said, "I will not."*
> *"You should do it."*
> *"Oh! no."*
> *"Why will you not? You ought to do it."*
> *"I will not."*
> *"Why?"*
> *"Reasons enough."*
> *"What can be your reasons?"*
> *"Reason first, you are a Virginian, and a Virginian ought to appear at the head of this business. Reason second, I am obnoxious, suspected, and unpopular. You are very much otherwise. Reason third, you can write ten times better than I can."*
> *"Well," said Jefferson, "if you are decided, I will do as well as I can."*
> *"Very well. When you have drawn it up, we will have a meeting."*

Adams handed the task over to Jefferson, expressing his admiration of Jefferson's "superior" writing skills. Adams said that the young Virginian was *"unmatched in his eloquence and penetrating mind"* (if that's not kissing some serious butt, I don't know what is!). And he regretted not writing the document to his dying day. In reality, Adams and Franklin edited the document heavily using Richard Henry Lee's Westmoreland Resolves as a guide. After a lot of congressional wrangling and compromising, the Declaration of Independence was adopted by the Second Continental Congress on July 2, 1776. Adams wrote of the day:

> *The Second Day of July 1776, will be the most memorable Epocha, in the History of America. I am apt to believe that it will be celebrated, by succeeding generations, as the great anniversary Festival. It ought to be*

> *commemorated, as the Day of Deliverance by solemn Acts of Devotion to God Almighty. It ought to be solemnized with Pomp and Parade, with Shews* (shows)*, Games, Sports, Guns, Bells, Bonfires and Illuminations from one End of this Continent to the other from this Time forward forever more.*

Yeah, I know. We celebrate Independence Day on July 4 because that's when Congress ratified what they had "adopted," but you get the idea!

John Adams served on more committees than any other congressman—ninety in all—and he chaired twenty. He was the head of the Board of War and Ordnance, the congressional committee that oversaw the operations of the Continental Army. He was also a driving member of the committee that prepared the "Model Treaty" (read basic outline of our hopes and dreams) that gave the folks Congress sent to France the ideas and language necessary to secure foreign trade and military aid.

In 1779, Adams was one of those American diplomats. He was sent to negotiate the Treaty of Paris, which brought an end to the Revolutionary War. After the war, Adams remained in Europe, and from 1784 to 1785, he arranged treaties of commerce with several European nations. In 1785, he became the first U.S. minister to England. He was well-received by the king, but most of the "nobles" despised him.

In 1788, Adams returned home after nearly 10 years in Europe. In 1789, he was placed on the ballot for America's first presidential election. As expected, George Washington received the highest number of electoral votes and was elected president. Adams was elected Vice President. In time, Adams would become the President, as well, serving for one term before being ousted by his sometimes friend/sometimes not, Thomas Jefferson. But that's a story for another book.

John Adams retired to his home in Braintree, Massachusetts, where he spent his days farming, writing, and giving reams of good advice to those who asked for it. He and Jefferson had fallen out with each other during their days in the Washington administration, and it had only gotten worse during their presidential campaigns. But in 1812, mutual friend Benjamin

Rush (another signer of the Declaration of Independence) encouraged both men to bury the hatchet. Their reconciliation brought about many great letters, historic observations, and political insight that otherwise would have been lost forever.

John Adams passed away at the age of 90 on July 4, 1826, fifty years to the day of the signing of the Declaration of Independence and the same date of the passing of Thomas Jefferson. Adams and Jefferson, Jefferson and Adams, no matter how you say it, those men are synonymous with Liberty and Independence.

Jefferson believed that the Declaration of Independence was his most important accomplishment.

CHAPTER 5

Thomas Jefferson

The Man with Two Brains!

Here was buried Thomas Jefferson, author of the Declaration of American Independence, of the statute of Virginia for religious freedom, and father of the University of Virginia. Born April 2, 1743–Died July 4, 1826.

This is the epitaph of one of the greatest Founding Fathers of our nation, written by him in hopes of expressing what he had been privileged to give to the people and not what the people had given to him. Make no mistake, the inscription on his tombstone does not do justice to the incredible life of Thomas Jefferson. He spoke five languages fluently and could read two more, he was a member of the House of Burgesses, a master Architect, a representative to the Continental Congress and the Virginia Congress, Governor of Virginia, U.S. minister to France, Secretary of State for President George

Washington, and President of the United States. He was a philosopher, scientist, historian, planter, author, inventor, husband, father, and voice of our revolutionary generation when he said, "*We hold these truths to be self-evident, that all men are created equal, that they are endowed by their Creator with certain unalienable Rights, that among these are Life, Liberty and the pursuit of Happiness.*" He was the author of the heart of the American Spirit—that government is the servant of the people, not the master. This man with incredible intellect, this consummate gentleman, was a country boy at heart who loved nature and wandering in the woods and hills of his homeland. He was, from top to bottom of his 6'2" frame, all American.

The Piedmont Prodigy, or The Woodland Wizkid

April 29, 1962, President John Kennedy addressed the year's Nobel Prize winners at a White House dinner with the words, *"I think this is the most extraordinary collection of...human knowledge that has ever been gathered together at the White House, with the possible exception of when Thomas Jefferson dined alone."* Kennedy was sharing a commonly held sentiment: Thomas Jefferson was an unsurpassed genius.

Jefferson was born to an affluent family. His first memory, however, was of a fifty-mile journey on horseback into the wilderness to set up shop in a faraway plantation because his father was the executor of another man's estate. Being in the wilderness was a big thing for Thomas. It gave him time to read books, ride horseback in the woods, wander, and wonder. These things were important to the young Mr. Jefferson. In books, he found reason. In nature, he found himself. As a young boy, he was privately tutored by the wisest men in the ministry, both Anglican and Presbyterian.

At the age of 16, Jefferson was accepted to William and Mary College, the finest college in the colonies at the time. Upon arrival, the future architect said of the buildings there, "*But for roofs, they may have been taken for brick kilns*" (the ovens where bricks are baked). Jefferson was not a fan of the building style of the day. He did, however, love the forward thinking of the teachings at William and Mary; he studied math, science, rhetoric, and literature. Jefferson learned from Professor William Small who brought the "true" Enlightenment teachings to Williamsburg from his native Scotland. This was the age of Enlightenment, when "enlightened men were thinking enlightened thoughts," and the age of reason, where men doubted all that could not be proven by science. This kind of thinking suited Jefferson right down to the ground. Even in matters of religion, Jefferson concluded that he was *"a sect unto himself,"* having a personal creed that may best be described as a "reasoned" Christianity.

Because he was now in the heart of the colony, and in no small part due to his genius and reputation as a prodigy, Jefferson was often invited to dine with the governor (of Virginia) and other political notables of the time. So, Jefferson's intellect connected him to the brightest minds in the area (and of the era) and that's how he met up with George Wythe. Wythe taught ideas about independence and free will, and Jefferson thought these ideas were an intellectual revolution. He also found that they fit very nicely with his own ideas of "natural law." Jefferson thought that it was natural for man to want to be free. Under Wythe, Jefferson pursued the study of law. And under Wythe's guidance, Jefferson became perhaps the nation's best-read lawyer and was accepted to the Virginia bar in April 1767.

For Jefferson, the study of law was more than just a means of earning a living. He felt that in legal issues, he could consider many aspects of society. As a young country lawyer, Jefferson practiced law on a circuit, following (and arguing before) the colonial court as it traveled to various district seats throughout Virginia. While he was on the circuit, he met 23-year-old Martha Wayles Skelton, a wealthy widow and daughter of a prominent Virginia lawyer and landowner. Her first husband and infant son had died two years earlier. Martha and Thomas married on January 1, 1772, moving into a stark one-room brick house on Jefferson's 5,000-acre Virginia plantation, which he called "Monticello." It wasn't much to look at when they moved in, but wow, how he made it grow!

As a lawyer, Jefferson would represent a lot of slaves who were seeking their freedom, because in Virginia at the time, there were many laws about manumission (being given your freedom). Jefferson took the case of Samuel Howell. Samuel was saying that because he was part white he should be freed right now and not wait for the age of emancipation which was 33 (most slaves in VA were given their freedom at that age). Jefferson's argument was one of "natural law"—that *"everyone comes into the world with a right to his own person and his own will…This is what is called personal liberty, and is given him by the author of nature, because it is necessary for his own sustenance."* This was Jefferson's first known public comment on the idea of natural law as an argument for independence and liberty. It's also an idea that he later included in the Declaration of Independence.

Radical, Rebel, Revolutionary

As a member of the Virginia House of Burgesses (the Virginia assembly) from 1769 to 1774, Jefferson played an active role in the organization of the Virginia Committee of Correspondence (he was a Son of Liberty, too!). Colonial anger against Britain was set to boil over, and committees like this one represented an "underground" of political agitators who worked to oppose British control of the colonies. When Jefferson wrote his argument, *Summary View of the Rights of British America*, it propelled him onto the center stage of American politics. He became known as a man of "immeasurable abilities in articulating the colonial position for independence." Before long, he was standing with Patrick Henry as one of the leading radicals who argued that the British Parliament had no authority at all to make laws for the colonies. Following the passage of the Intolerable Acts by Parliament in 1774, Jefferson wrote a set of resolutions against the acts, one of which was called "The Day of Fasting and Prayer resolution" that asked colonists to appeal to the Almighty for protection and resolution of the present crisis, and…a boycott of all British goods. That otta show 'em!…and it did!

Jefferson was ill and missed the Virginia Assembly meeting to decide what to do about the Coercive Acts recently passed by Parliament in retaliation for the Boston Tea Party. His *Summary View of Rights of British*

America drew a hard line in the sand and with it, he showed himself to be an unashamed rebel agitating for independence. He was not chosen to attend the First Continental Congress (where we were hoping for reconciliation with the crown), but he was sent to the Second Congress when (to Virginians, at least) independence was inevitable.

When he arrived in Philadelphia, he quickly became friendly with the Adamses (both John and Samuel) and an intense supporter of Richard Henry Lee and the Virginia Resolution for American Independence.

He was chosen to serve on the "committee of five" that was charged with writing and presenting a Declaration of Independence. He thought the mind of John Adams should write the basic document, but Adams felt otherwise. Adams was convinced that a Virginian should be "at the head of the business" and Jefferson was THE Virginian on the committee. Adams felt that Jefferson wrote ten times better than any man in congress (including himself), and finally, Jefferson was liked by almost everyone, while John Adams, in his own words, was "obnoxious, suspected, and unpopular." So, there you have it, Jefferson set to work.

Jefferson said of the great work:

> *The object of the Declaration of Independence... Was not to find out new principles, or new arguments, never before thought of, not merely to say things which had never been said before; but to place before mankind the common sense of the subject; in terms so plain and firm as to command their assent, and to justify ourselves in the independent stand we had been compelled to take. Neither aiming at originality of principle or sentiment, nor yet copied from any particular and previous writing, it was intended to be an expression of the American mind, and to give to that expression the proper tone and spirit called for by the occasion.*

The Lee resolution was put before Congress on June 7, 1776, the Declaration was submitted on June 28, unanimously approved on July 2, and adopted on July 4. For Thomas Jefferson, his work with the Continental Congress was over. He was headed home to Virginia and his young wife, Martha.

From 1776 to 1779, Jefferson served as a member of the Virginia House of Delegates. He helped end the traditional link between religion and government by authoring the famous Virginia Bill for Establishing Religious Freedom (which prevented government from using—establishing—a state religion, kind of like an exclusive club) which was finally passed into law thanks to the efforts of Jefferson's friend James Madison. During the rest of the Revolutionary War, Jefferson served for two years as Virginia's governor. When the British forces (under the command of the traitor Benedict Arnold) overran much of Virginia, the government was forced to abandon the capitol at Richmond. Jefferson tactically retreated from his home at Monticello after taking breakfast with several delegates who were then in his care. It was a touch and go escape, to be sure, but Jefferson knew his "backyard" well and eluded capture by a British raiding party led by the notorious British officer Banastre Tarleton (the butcher of the battle of Waxhaws) to rejoin his wife and children at his hideaway known as Poplar Forest, outside of Lynchburg.

Unfortunately, political opponents portrayed Jefferson's actions as a cowardly refusal to stand his ground. The charge followed him for the rest of his public life. Feeling rejected, embarrassed, and desperately concerned about the health of his wife, Jefferson retired to Monticello.

November 6, 1782, was a black day for Thomas Jefferson. His Martha died in childbirth. Pregnancy had always been rough for her, and this was her sixth. Martha's mother had died young, and as a girl Martha endured two stepmothers. Just before her death, Martha told Thomas that she could not bear to have another woman raise her children. She pleaded with him to promise never to marry again. Jefferson gave his dying wife his solemn word and never remarried.

Jefferson was sent by Congress to Europe to join Benjamin Franklin and John Adams to negotiate trade agreements with England, Spain, and France. Since the death of his wife, his closest friends knew of his deep depression and feared that Jefferson might be suicidal. They believed that sending him to France would give his mind something new to do and prevent him from harm. During the voyage, Jefferson taught himself how to read and write Spanish. Jefferson and Adams' friendship became even closer while serving as ambassadors to France and England. John and Abigail Adams felt Jefferson was part of their family now, and Abigail said Thomas Jefferson was *"the only person with whom my companion could associate with perfect freedom and reserve."* Jefferson found Abigail to be the first woman he could talk to as an intellectual equal.

Joseph Ellis wrote about them in his book *Founding Brothers: The Revolutionary Generation*:

> *They were an incongruous pair, but everyone seemed to argue that history had made them into a pair. The incongruities leapt out for all to see: Adams, the short, stout, candid-to-a-fault New Englander; Jefferson, the tall, slender, elegantly elusive Virginian; Adams, the highly combustible, ever combative, mile-a-minute talker, whose favorite form of conversation was an argument; Jefferson, the always cool and self-contained enigma, who regarded debate and argument as violations of the natural harmonies he heard inside his own head. The list could go on - the Yankee and the Cavalier, the orator and the writer, the bulldog and the greyhound. They were the odd couple of the American Revolution.*

A country gentleman who was a rebel through and through. He saw the need for American Independence before almost everyone else!

CHAPTER 6

Richard Henry Lee

The Original Rebel

Richard Henry Lee had the good fortune of living during one of the most exciting and crucial times in American History: the struggle, birth, and childhood of the United States of America. He stood against the British Crown with such men as Patrick Henry, John and Samuel Adams, Benjamin Franklin, and George Washington. Lee's vision, drive, force of spirit, and "eloquence of oration" (means he could talk like the angels of heaven) had a lasting effect on the outcome of the American Revolution and the course of all American History, as well.

Tall and imposing with reddish hair and a strong sense of confidence, Richard Henry Lee would outlive two wives, become the father of 11 children, and emerge as one of the most famous members of the "first" family of Virginia. The Lees were more than just a family, they were an international corporation before such things existed. With plantations and land interests in America, business offices in Virginia and London, and shipping firms and contracts travelling to almost everywhere, the Lee family "moved and shook" colonial America. Lee was always fiery and passionate in defense of freedom and independence. And always the gentleman in both word and deed, except where George III was concerned. Then he could swear like a stable boy and act like an angry hillbilly. He was the author of the Westmoreland Resolution—the precursor to the Declaration of Independence—and the Virginia Resolution on Independence. That's the one that really got the whole thing rolling. Lee was a lifelong public servant in the Virginia Legislature, the Continental Congress, and the Virginia militia, as well as to the President of the United States. Richard Henry Lee was the Thunder and Lightning in the Tempest of the American Revolution.

A Bolt of Lightning Across a Clear Blue Sky

Richard Henry's career began, like many, by his birth into a famed old family of Virginia, the Lees. He was born on the 20th of January 1732 at his family's plantation near Stratford in Westmoreland County. He was the second of five brothers, Thomas Ludlow (the eldest), Richard Henry, Francis Lightfoot (Frank), William, and Arthur. Lee grew up at Stratford Hall, an enormous tobacco plantation. His parents, Thomas (a one-time royal governor of Virginia) and Hannah Ludlow Lee, hired Scottish ministers (great awakening type fellas) to tutor their children. The boys were not always allowed to sleep in the Great Mansion House (Mom and Dad affectionately referred to the boys as "mischief, mayhem, chaos, and havoc") so, on school days at least, they slept above their school room in a separate building. Often, classes started before breakfast and ended at 5pm (that oughta show 'em). Thomas and Hannah felt it was important to send their children to England to educate them and teach them customs and law. When Richard Henry was 16, he and his older brothers sailed to England on a Lee tobacco ship. He never saw his parents again: both died in 1750. Richard Henry finished his schooling at Wakefield Academy in Yorkshire and took a brief European trip (a tour of the Continent) before he sailed home to Virginia.

His oldest brother, Philip Ludwell Lee, inherited the Stratford Hall plantation while Richard Henry inherited land in northern Virginia and in the "overmountain" region. Richard Henry chose to stay at the Great House and leased his inherited land to tenant farmers. The Lee children also inherited company shares planned to speculate on the land in the Ohio River Valley. Richard Henry continued to study ancient classics and modern history, later quoting both in his speeches and his writing.

At age 23, Lee raised a military company to support British Gen. Edward Braddock during the French and Indian War. Fortunately for Lee, Braddock refused the support before he was killed in the summer of 1755. In time, Lee learned that his leadership would be needed both for military and public service. Two years later, Lee was appointed justice for Westmoreland County. At 25, he married Anne Aylett, and leased land about three miles away from Stratford Hall from his brother Philip. They designed and built a three-story, 10-room home named "Chantilly-on-the-Potomac." Richard Henry was ready to take his place in Virginia society. The Lees of Virginia had a fine tradition of public service, and Richard, in 1758, followed in the footsteps of his family, entering the Virginia House of Burgesses. Thus, he began seventeen years of continuous services for his colony.

The Lightning Strikes

Richard Henry Lee was confrontational by nature and had a fiery and rebellious spirit to boot. He seemed to challenge authority with almost every breath. Small wonder that he stood in Burgesses and railed against the established norm of slavery. His first speech was against the transportation of slaves to Virginia. He said, *"And well am I persuaded, Sir, that if it be so considered, it will appear, both from reason and experience, that the importation of slaves into this Colony has been and will be attended with effects dangerous both to our political and moral interests."* He suggested increasing the taxes. *"Lay so heavy a tax upon the importation of slaves as effectually to put an end to that iniquitous and disgraceful traffic within the Colony."* This speech was given in 1759 and was arguably the most extreme anti-slavery feeling of the time.

After the French and Indian War, the British decided (in the proclamation of 1763) that all the land "over the mountains"—the Ohio River Valley—was going to go to Quebec. It killed Richard Henry Lee. The major part of his land inheritance was "OVER THE MOUNTAINS" and he was involved in family business deals that were directly connected to investment in the interior (read the Ohio River Valley). This was "last straw" sort of stuff and it put him in direct opposition to the laws and acts that Parliament would pass over the next 12 years. He wholeheartedly agreed when his friend, Patrick Henry, spoke against the Stamp Act on May 29, 1765, in the House of Burgesses, when he lambasted Parliament, denounced the Stamp Act entirely, and raked the king over the coals, ending with, *"Caesar had his Brutus; Charles I his Cromwell; and George III* [cries of "Treason" from the crowd] *may he profit by their example! If this be treason, make the most of it!"*

Lee's relentless opposition to British measures, such as the Sugar Act, the Stamp Act, and the Townshend Acts, placed him in the forefront of defenders of colonial rights. Openly calling the Townshend Acts *"arbitrary, unjust, and destructive of that mutual beneficial connection which every good subject would wish to see preserved,"* Richard Henry was now a standard bearer planted firmly on the colonial side of the argument. Being more than a man of words, in February of 1765, he drew the residents of his home county into the "Westmoreland Association," uniting themselves not to buy any British goods until the Stamp Act was repealed. Lee was, as always, one of the most prominent to move forward the question of American rights. And so he wrote the Westmoreland Resolution of 1766, binding citizens to support *"our lawful sovereign, George the Third…so far as is consistent with the preservation of our rights and liberty."* Lee was supported by 115 men who signed his Resolution. These men comprised Virginia's best and brightest. Many considered the Resolution seditious as Lee challenged the king (frankly, it was open rebellion, but hey, what can ya do?) and placed himself and the colony of Virginia on the path to Revolution much earlier than anywhere or anyone else. Later, his Resolution gave inspiration to Thomas Jefferson while writing the Declaration of Independence.

The year 1768 was tragic for Lee. His wife, Anne, died December 12, leaving four young children: Thomas, Ludwell, Mary, and Hannah. During the winter, Lee went goose hunting, one of his favorite sports. His goose gun exploded in his left hand and he lost four fingers. He actually cut them off with his hunting knife, finished hunting with another gun, and *then* returned home to seek medical attention. He began to use black silk, either wrapping the damaged hand with a handkerchief or using a black glove to cover the scarred and damaged hand. Thinking positively, Lee began to draw attention during his speeches by raising and vigorously waving his injured hand to make a point. It seemed if he couldn't raise and wave that left hand of his, he became mute.

During the summer of 1769, Lee married again: a widow, Anne Gaskins Pinckard, a descendant of three Mayflower pilgrims. She had two children of a previous marriage. The couple later had two sons and three daughters of their own: Anne, Henrietta, Sarah, Cassius, and Francis Lightfoot, bringing the number to 11 children. Over the course of the next several years, Lee found himself facing off against royal and parliamentary measures that he deemed destructive of colonial rights, freedoms, and friendship with Great Britain. Discussions in the House of Burgesses from the time of the Tea Tax to the Coercive Acts were seen as disloyal (if not outright treasonous) by Virginia's royal governor, Lord Dunmore. Dunmore, following the dubious example of Royal Foreign Minister Lord North (the guy who enacted marshal law in Massachusetts), dissolved Burgesses in May of 1774 and outlawed the delegates he deemed disloyal—our hero being one of the first and foremost. Once the House of Burgesses was no longer legal, the members moved to Richmond and became the "outlaw" Provincial Congress. And with that change, the Virginia government was now in full-on rebellion. As a result, the Virginia militias that previously answered to the governor of Virginia—and now were made up of "Sons of Liberty" to a man—were loyal ONLY to the Provincial Congress. So much for royal government in Virginia.

Richard Henry had been among the first men to propose a system of intercolonial committees of correspondence. These committees were set up to coordinate the efforts of the colonies against the British. The committees directly led to the forming of the First Continental Congress, with Virginia appointing Richard Henry Lee, Patrick Henry, and George Washington. On September 5, 1774, these men with others such as John Jay and John Adams met in Carpenters Hall in Philadelphia for the first meeting of the Continental Congress.

Lee's speeches in Congress were often powerful, passionate, and sometimes spontaneous. *"The great orators here,"* wrote John Adams, *"are Lee...and Patrick Henry."* Lee and Adams became a powerful team, often meeting with Adams' cousin, Samuel, at Lee's sister Alice's house in Philadelphia. Alice had married physician William Shippen, Jr., who would become America's chief medical officer in the Revolution.

And the Thunder Rolls

The year 1775 was significant. Lee's brother Philip died on February 21, and Richard Henry was the executor, taking on the care of his brother's family as he did for most of his siblings. He traveled extensively from home to Philadelphia and to Richmond, VA. Lee was at St. John's Church in Richmond on March 23 when Patrick Henry gave his classic *"Liberty or Death"* speech. On April 20, 1776, Lee wrote to Patrick Henry, urging Virginians to lead the colonies to force independence. He quoted many of the words from Shakespeare's Julius Caesar, with few changes. *"There is a Tide in the Affairs of Men, Which taken at the Flood leads on to Fortune—That omitted, we are ever after bound in Shallows."* Means you best be ready to catch the boat when it's time to go on to greatness.

Even more aggressive now than before, Lee was pushing for stronger action against the British. With the issue of independence stalling in Congress for the better part of a year, a shrewd political move was needed to push the dream of independence into a reality. Richard Henry's openly rebellious views for independence from the British Crown led to his being chosen as the man to move the issue of independence in Congress.

On June 7, 1776, he stood in Congress and spoke with a voice like thunder introducing a resolution that would forever change the course of American History: *"Resolved: That these United Colonies are, and of right, ought to be, free and independent States, that they are absolved from all allegiance to the British Crown, and that all political connections between them and the State of Great Britain is, and ought to be, totally dissolved."*

John Adams seconded. Congress postponed a debate until July 1, allowing a committee to write a proposed declaration of independence based on Lee's Westmoreland Resolutions. The draft was presented June 28, debate was held July 1, and the Declaration of Independence was "unanimously" adopted. Everyone voted "aye" with the exception of the New York group. They abstained, courteously.

The British papers went wild. *"Richard Henry Lee and Patrick Henry have at last accomplished their object: The colonies have declared themselves independent of the mother country,"* was published.

Pressure was building from Virginia. Letters poured in to Lee at home. *"I wish to divide you, and have you here…and in Congress,"* wrote Patrick Henry from Williamsburg. Another Virginia delegate wrote, *"Would to God you could be here."* George Mason, the author of Virginia's Bill of Rights, wrote, *"We are now going upon the most important of all subjects—government!…Let us see you here as soon as possible…We cannot do without you."*

Lee was very aware of being needed in two political worlds at once. Both Virginia and the new U.S.A. needed him. He was shuttling back and forth from Richmond to Philadelphia, then to Williamsburg and on to Chantilly over and over again. He wasn't present for the vote on the Declaration of Independence, but he did return with his brother Francis Lightfoot for the signing in August—Lee was sure that Virginia would not vote against her own Resolution. He had been called back to Williamsburg to help with the formation of the new state government and there was family business with the "overmountain" investments that needed some looking after.

Richard Henry remained in Congress until 1779, retiring due to ill health. He returned home to Virginia where he was almost immediately elected to the Virginia Legislature. Then when military leadership was required to protect his home, family, and property, Richard Henry was quickly re-commissioned a colonel in the Virginia militia. During the spring of 1781, the British burned houses and tobacco warehouses along the Potomac River. Observing three British ships approaching the Stratford wharf, Lee called up the militia. As the British disembarked, the Americans fired the first of several volleys. At least one British soldier was killed and several others were wounded as the British retreated. *"I am at present lamed by my horse having fallen on me in a late engagement with the enemy who landed under cover of heavy cannonades from three vessels of war upon a small body of our militia were posted,"* wrote Lee to Samuel Adams, *"After a small engagement we had the pleasure to see the enemy, tho superior in numbers, run to their boats and precipitately re-embark* (means hastily skedaddle) *having sustained a loss of killed and wounded."*

With the American victory in 1782, Lee returned to Congress and was soon chosen president of the United States and Congress Assembled (that was the title of the president of the U.S. Congress under the Articles of Confederation). He remained two more years in Congress, where he played an important part in the passage of the Northwest Ordinance. From 1785 to 1787, Lee worked with George Washington to develop and fund the Potomac Company, an effort to build canals that would connect the Ohio and Potomac Rivers. In large part, due to the frustrations of that effort, the discussions began and continued over the failures of the Articles and resulted in the proposed adoption of a new Constitution. Though he saw the obvious advantages of the new Constitution, Lee found himself on the side of the Anti-federalists, the men who opposed the formation of a stronger central government. He personally believed that the states were giving up way too much for what they were getting from the new

document. And as for the citizen, Lee felt that a Bill of Rights was absolutely necessary. Nevertheless, the Virginia gentleman was gracious in defeat and accepted an appointment as senator for Virginia in the new Federal Government. Lee used his position and influence to ensure the adoption of the Bill of Rights in 1789, especially the 2nd Amendment to keep and bear arms and, most importantly, the 10th Amendment (States' Rights).

In 1792, Lee retired from public life and went home to Chantilly-on-the-Potomac. On June 19, 1794, just as summer thunder passes into a warm and pleasant rain, Richard Henry Lee passed away peacefully in his home: The lightning bolt of liberty, the thunder of the Revolution, and Virginia's Original Rebel.

*Nathanael Greene was a "gimpy" Quaker kid
who rose through the ranks
from private soldier to general,
and became Washington's War Horse.*

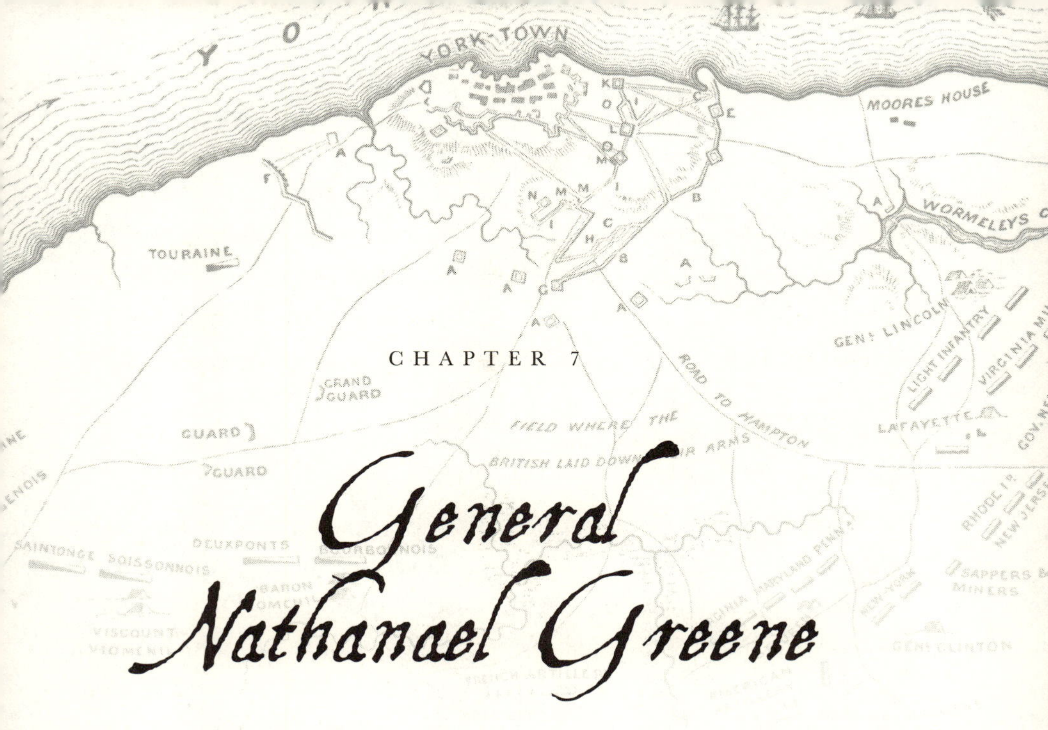

CHAPTER 7

General Nathanael Greene

"One Fist of Iron, the Other of Steel…"

He was called the Fighting Quaker, Savior of the South, and Washington's War Horse. Nathanael Greene started the Revolutionary War as a private, yet became Washington's most trusted lieutenant and second in command of the entire Continental Army. Greene's calculated risk-taking and his bold strategy and tactics make him comparable to Napoleon and Robert E. Lee. He began life as a "gimpy" Quaker kid from New England (he had a serious limp from a joint injury or illness as a child) who was seen as "unfit" for military service, but became a heroic son of the South through his daring exploits to save "Dixie" from the British during the war. Greene had British General Lord Charles Cornwallis jumping through his own tail trying to figure out how and where to fight this "mad military genius." His "Southern Campaign" from Savannah to Yorktown destroyed English hopes of ending the war on their terms. Greene forced the Redcoats to chase his army over hill and dale, across swamp, rivers, forests, and field until he caught them and ended British ambitions in America. He was part stoic New Englander with a dash of the cavalier southern boy and 100% Patriot. Nathanael Greene was one of America's greatest soldiers and Sons of Liberty.

Shakin' the Quaker Thing

Nathanael was born on July 27, 1742, in Potowomut, Rhode Island. He was named for his father, a respected minister of the Society of Friends (Quakers) and foundry owner. Because of his father's Quaker beliefs, Greene was taught only the basics: reading, writing, and business math. He would later say of his early life, *"I lament the want of a liberal Education."* But he found a way to achieve on his own—he studied in secret. He made miniature toys to sell in Newport for money to buy his own books. Seems he was "destined" for some great work. Greene got a "leg-up" in his self-education project from two "well-lettered" men, Lindley Murray, a young lawyer working for John Jay's law firm in New York (this guy later wrote the book on American grammar-literally!) and Ezra Stiles, the future president of Yale—enough said.

Just a note about Quaker beliefs in the 18th century: The Society of Friends had flourished during the Reformation and was perhaps the most radical expression of leaving all things Catholic behind. All the sacraments of the Universal Church were abhorrent to the movement. They accepted personal revelation as current and THE true and relevant guide to worship. They were a highly moral people, pacifists, generally opposed to holding public office, but always willing to do good to and for others. While not as extreme as some sects (like the Amish), Quakers nevertheless believed in living a simple life and marrying within the sect. A simple education was all that was taught in most Quaker homes and military service, let alone military studies, were a strict taboo. You see the conundrum young Nathanael was facing: Stay true to "the faith" or true to his own heart—tough business, even today. Fortunately for us, he chose to follow his dreams.

As Greene grew to manhood, relations between England and thirteen of her colonies in North America were in the process of falling apart. Nathanael was caught up in the fiery zeal of resistance and rebellion (sort of different for a Quaker boy). And after attending a military parade in Connecticut, he became an avid student of all things military, even more unusual for a Quaker boy. Every military book, paper, and treatise was enthusiastically digested by young Nathanael. He became a master of military history, strategy, and tactics, at least on paper. Greene was "ready" and determined, if the call ever came, "*to defend my rights and maintain my freedom or sell my life in the attempt.*" Outta his mind crazy for a Quaker kid! The seizure of one of the Greene family's ships by a British revenue schooner (the H.M.S. Gaspée) made matters personal. Greene was as good as "gone to war" right then. This and his affinity for military studies got him quietly cashiered out of the Society of Friends faster than you could whistle "Yankee Doodle."

Still, Greene was a well-rounded man. He remained active in the family iron business, as well as Rhode Island politics, and he was anxious to start a family. On July 20, 1774, he married Catharine Littlefield. Caty, or Kitty, as she was known by her friends, was extremely attractive and vivacious; the attraction was immediate, spontaneous, and the couple ultimately had six children together. During the war, she visited her husband as much as she could and was very charming and popular. She proved to be a favorite of all and an excellent hostess (she was General Washington's favorite dance partner when Martha was unable to continue—Washington loved dancing). Martha Washington and Caty Greene would become life-long friends.

In August of 1774, the Sons of Liberty, East Greenwich county chapter, formed a Patriot "minuteman" militia company, which they later called the Kentish Guards. Greene was a founding member. His membership in the group was challenged, however, because of his limp. The episode hurt him deeply and was only dropped when an influential (and undoubtedly wealthy) member of the Guards and a close friend, James Varnum, threatened to resign if Greene was forced out. Varnum may have mentioned that he would take his money and the uniforms with him. The Kentish Guards still wear those dress blues today.

In April of 1775 came the news of battles at Lexington and Concord. The Kentish Guards went to Boston, and with them went Private Nathanael Greene. The lowest rank in the service, but Greene stood proudly, shoulder to shoulder, with his Patriot brothers besieging the British. At this same time, the Assembly of Rhode Island met at Providence to establish an "Army of Observation" made up of the several militia groups from Rhode Island and Connecticut. On May 8, Greene was commissioned a brigadier general and given command of RI state troops (see how that "staying active in politics" worked out well for Nathanael?). He led his troops to Roxbury just outside of Boston, where he demonstrated a flair for keeping his troops well-supplied and for unifying the intercolonial militias. On June 22, 1775, he was commissioned as the youngest brigadier general in the Continental Army. He took command of Prospect Hill overlooking Boston during the Siege. He missed the action at Bunker Hill on June 17, but in a letter describing the battle, he exclaimed, "*I wish we could sell them another hill at the same price we did Bunkers Hill.*"

Two weeks later, on July 3, General Greene was selected to present the newly formed Continental Army to the freshly arrived Commanding General, George Washington. Even during their first meeting, Washington saw something special in Greene. Within a year, he thought of Greene as the best of his generals and most prepared to succeed him in case of his death or capture. It was a mutual admiration society: Greene named his firstborn son George Washington Greene in honor of his friend and his first daughter Martha Washington Greene to honor "Lady" Washington, as she came to be known. Over the next eight months, Greene stood by and supported every decision that Gen. Washington made, up to and including the placement of artillery on Dorchester Heights. When British

General Thomas Gage saw the Patriot cannon on the "high ground," he chose the better part of valor (discretion) and decided to "beat feet" out of Boston. After the British evacuated, Greene took command of the city.

Out of the Frying Pan and Into the Fire

In early April of 1776, the Continental Army moved to defend New York from an impending British invasion. The Howe brothers, General William and Admiral Richard, brought 400 ships and 32,000 British troops and Hessian soldiers for hire (men from a mid-sized German state whose ruler was George III's cousin) to take New York and end the war. They landed on Staten Island, all 32,000 of them. Washington wasn't sure where the British would attack—Manhattan or Long Island? So, he divided the army. Half remaining on Manhattan island under his command, General Greene took command of the other half posted on Long Island. He was promoted to the rank of major general in early August, but was hospitalized back in Manhattan with severe fever during the Battle of Long Island on August 27. Greene's first major action of the war was at the Battle of Harlem Heights on September 16. This was the first actual "victory in the field" of the war for the Continental Army. General Greene had been sent by Washington to lead the pursuit and make sure things didn't "go too far." Washington wanted to be sure that a limited engagement (controlled skirmish) didn't become a general action (major battle, end of the war type of thing). After the battle, Greene was sent to command the American forces guarding New Jersey at Fort Lee. It was here that he made his worst mistake of the war. He still hoped for another Bunker Hill (to force the Redcoats to pay a high price for what they gained), so Greene "encouraged" (or ordered) his lieutenant to hold Fort Washington, on the opposite side of the Hudson, at all costs. Fort Washington was strategically important for the Continental Army, but impossible to defend. The garrison was severely outnumbered and outgunned. Overmatched, the fort and her three thousand men fell to the British without any real resistance. This was Bunker Hill in reverse, too many lost for nothing gained. The Continental Army could not fight the war using that equation.

Even though the disaster was under Greene's watch, Washington still put great faith in him, and Greene would figure prominently in the retreat of the Continental Army across New Jersey. He commanded the right wing of Washington's surprise attack at the Battle of Trenton on December 26, when the Continental Army delivered some more of that "colonial whoop ass" on the Hessian allies of the British. He commanded a section of Washington's main column in the Battle of Princeton on January 3, 1777, where that can of "whoop ass" was opened up on the British. The results of these two battles were: 1) Americans believed we could win this war again, 2) the British abandoned New Jersey and fled back to the safety of New York City, and 3) Washington was now seen as a military genius. General Greene had seen and learned much from the experiences of 1776.

Double Duty

General "Gentleman Johnny" Burgoyne, the newly commissioned commander of half the British Army was no "old Campaigner." He brought his featherbed—headboard and all—as well as his entire household to charge through the rough terrain and forest of the northeast. As he and General Howe attempted to split the Continental Army in two, Greene's involvement became vital. Howe had to move quickly, he fiddled his orders and now meant to take Philadelphia (the rebel capital), capture the rebel congress (thus ending the war), hurry back to NYC, move up the Hudson to rendezvous with Burgoyne, and be back in England in time for tea! His dreams of victory and triumph were mired down by Washington's strategy, Greene's brilliance, the American soldier's love of liberty, Howe's own pride, and no small measure of the Grace of God.

It began when the Continentals faced off with Howe's Redcoats along the Brandywine River and hoped to turn back the British invasion. At the Battle of Brandywine on September 11, things quickly went downhill for our side. Outnumbered and outmaneuvered, it took more than just "courage under fire" to save the Continental Army from rout and destruction. Greene led his division four miles in under fifty minutes through broken country to set up a defensive line that allowed Major General John Sullivan's division to retreat. Then, he closed his lines and held the British at bay until nightfall, which gave the main force time to withdraw from the field. Greene and his men had saved the day; these men were real heroes.

You have to understand that everything that happened at this time was part of a much bigger strategic picture. Remember there are two British armies attacking, Howe's Army near Philadelphia and Burgoyne's Army "rampaging" southward in upstate New York—all part of Germain's grand strategy. Washington had divided his army by thirds, 2/3 under his command, and the remainder he sent north to reinforce the "northern department" of the war facing Burgoyne. Washington's hope was that he could pin Howe in Philadelphia (the 3rd largest city in the empire at the time), While General Philip Schuyler, C.O. of the U.S. Northern Army, could kick "the Brits" right in the pants somewhere north of Albany, NY. *That* can of "whoop ass" was opened up at the battles of Saratoga in early September 1777 and went down pretty much as Washington had planned. Howe never got out of "Philly" and "Gentleman Johnny" surrendered his entire army at Saratoga! Washington's strategy won the day, but it was a hard road gettin' there.

The Victory at Saratoga was welcome news. It changed the war. The French would now become our allies and...well, we'll get to all that later. For now, Washington's Army still had to contend with the British who controlled Philadelphia. At the Battle of Germantown on October 4, 1777, General Greene led the left wing of Washington's attack. The strategy was very similar to the surprise attack on Trenton almost one year before, but in the fog and weather, a friendly fire exchange spelled defeat for the Continentals, and the Americans withdrew. The British would spend the winter, warm and cozy, in Philadelphia. For Greene and the soldiers of Washington's Army, it was a very different story.

Across the potential battlefield of Whitemarsh, Washington's Army glared at the Redcoats through the icy rain and mists of a late Pennsylvania fall. There would be no fighting, Washington wouldn't come down off the high ground. And for his part, General Howe had no desire to "come up" and face the Continentals on ground that they had chosen. So for two weeks, General Greene and his boys peered out of their fortified positions on the hills overlooking Philadelphia. Then the orders came to move into the winter encampment at Valley Forge.

The first order of business was to get the men under cover in some sort of shelter. It was Greene who supervised the building of hundreds of huts in the rolling Pennsylvania hills. Three advantages to the soldiers doing the work themselves: 1) It kept the men busy (and out of trouble), 2) The physical work kept the men warm, and 3) It got the job done, fast! While the men worked and slept outdoors, so did the officers.

On Washington's orders, all would share the same hardships. By January 1, the army had a "roof over its head" and the officers moved into their headquarters. Many of the men were without shoes or boots. Coats and jackets were threadbare to say the least, and blankets were few and far between. As winter set in, the problems got worse. Along with the shortage of adequate clothing, there was a terrible lack of food. The only real fighting during those winter months was when American and British foraging parties (soldiers looking for supplies in the countryside) ran into each other. The post of Quartermaster had been held by Gen. Thomas Mifflin, but he got involved in some political intrigue (more about that later) that took time away from his duties. With the QM absent, things had gone from worse to awful. Washington was at his wit's end. Finally, there was a stroke of "inspiration" that not only solved the problem, but changed the momentum of the war.

On March 2, 1778, Washington appointed Greene the new Quartermaster General of the Continental Army. The supply situation was a disaster and the new Quartermaster had to put in a lot of long hours just to keep the army operational. This new assignment was not his choice, but he knew it was necessary. He made the statement, *"Nobody ever heard of a Quartermaster in History."* Greene only accepted the job on condition that he kept his command in the field, thus the two hats. Washington would still consult him on matters of strategy and tactics and he still attended every council of war. Suddenly the troops at Valley Forge had food, clothing, blankets, and a renewed spirit! Greene's business skills, honed in the family iron works, were a big part of the mighty change that was taking place in the Continental Camp. They may have entered the winter encampment "a rag-tag bunch," but they were now forged into the finest steel. The Continental Army of 1778 was a war machine! And they were anxious to prove themselves. That would be at the Battle of Monmouth on June 28.

As explained in the chapter on George Washington, that winter was hard on the British, too. General Henry Clinton was now in charge and had to "make do" with what he had, just like the Continentals did. He ordered a withdrawal from Philadelphia. The Redcoats were headed back to New York. Clinton figured he would consolidate his troops in safety and then redirect his effort. He was also well aware that Washington's Army was a different animal now; lean, powerful, and hungry.

When the Continental Army came down out of the hills around Philly, the first thing they did was retake the capital. The Redcoats had left it a mess. So it was with a burning desire to prove themselves and an even hotter fire for revenge that Washington's Army attacked the British rearguard at Monmouth, New Jersey. At first things were going well, then General Charles Lee (we'll discuss him later) decimated the attack by ordering his men—the guys leading the charge and doing the attacking—to retreat!!

Washington came up with the main force and fired Lee on the spot, rallied the troops with a hearty "follow me!" and charged the British line. General Greene was in charge of the right wing, and had taken position on a high hill. He and his men had "flanked" the British position (meaning they got around to the side). The British broke and fell back. Everyone slept on the battlefield that night. We expected to take up right where we left off, but sometime during the night, the Redcoats "skedaddled" and moved quickly (ran!) back to the safety of NYC. General Greene and his boys, again, were heroes of the day. It was the last major battle in the northern part of the United States during the revolution.

On June 7, Greene commanded the front line that stood tall against a fierce British attack at Connecticut Farms in New Jersey. Two weeks later, he led the force that again repulsed the British at the Battle of Springfield on June 23. Greene resigned as Quartermaster General on July 26. He then presided over the military court that convicted Major John André of espionage in September. André was the British officer who was involved in Benedict Arnold's treason. A month later, Washington gave Greene command of West Point, a strategic position on the Hudson River. The former commander, that same Benedict Arnold who betrayed the American cause, had gone AWOL (absent without leave), and was now a commissioned British officer (we'll discuss him later, too). Greene only held command of West Point for a couple of weeks. When Major General Horatio Gates snatched defeat from the jaws of victory while facing the British Army at the Battle of Camden on August 16, Washington appointed Greene the new Southern Commander.

Lessons Learned

After the disastrous defeat of Gen. Gates at Camden, the British had unchallenged control of the deep south, with a path clear of American forces into North Carolina and Virginia. The British commander, Lieutenant General Charles Cornwallis, went on to establish a chain of outposts across South Carolina in an effort to secure his lines of supply and communication and to rally the many Loyalists who the British believed would "flock to the banner of King and Country." Greene fought Cornwallis in areas that to any "normal" commander would be a nightmare; Mountains that cut supply lines, swamps and bayous that seemed impassable, as well as forest and grassland that stretched across distances that European armies would find impossible to handle. But Washington had sent Nathanael Greene, and Greene was a guy who got the job done. His first priority as Southern Commander was to rebuild and "fire up" an army that was outnumbered, poorly equipped, and badly demoralized.

Let's take a minute to put things in perspective. We are moving from 1778 to 1780, and from upstate New York to the Carolinas. Here is a quick "sit rep" (situation report) of how things have been going in the South: *bad*, really bad. Congress had first appointed General Robert Howe to command in the South—he lost his entire army AND the city of Savannah, GA. Then Congress sent General Benjamin Lincoln, who promptly lost his army and the city of Charleston, SC (not entirely his fault—the city fathers feared the slaves more than the British), and last, Congress sent the famously inept (but politically well-connected) Gen. Horatio Gates, hero and victor of Saratoga. He was a bumbling and timid maladroit who had been blessed with highly talented and aggressive subordinates at that battle. Gates lost the better part of the almost 4,000 men sent to retake the southern states in less than 90 minutes of battle at Camden,

South Carolina. Gates himself rode away at high speed, covering the 60 miles back to Charlotte, NC, before supper.

And so it was that Nathanael Greene came to the South. Congress had finally allowed General Washington to appoint "an appropriate officer" for the task. Without hesitation, Washington sent his best. When Greene arrived, he found the situation every bit as dismal as described, yet he took hope, for there were still many men resolved to fight: the guerrilla warriors of Francis Marion, Andrew Pickens, Elijah Clarke, and William Campbell, as well as almost 2,000 regulars who had not been captured at Camden. All told, Greene was facing Cornwallis with his 4,100 Redcoats and 2,000 Loyalist troops with his own 1,500 Continental reinforcements brought from the North, 1,900 Continentals and militia who had escaped the debacle at Camden, and almost 1,200 irregular troops under command of the renegades previously mentioned.

Greene split his force in two in the face of superior British numbers by sending a "flying army" (a highly mobile cavalry and "fast" infantry) under the command of Brigadier General Daniel Morgan to harass Cornwallis and raise local militia support. By dividing his army, he was making the most of the limited resources of the land while keeping the several "commands" close enough to unite in order to fight. He would avoid a major engagement with the British, attack their weaknesses, and basically "run them from pillar to post" until he had the advantage and could take the fight to them!

The situation began to change with the Battle of King's Mountain in 1780. Patriot "Irregulars" under Colonel William Campbell engaged and destroyed a Loyalist force under Major Patrick Ferguson. How destroyed you ask? The entire British force was captured or killed (100% of all British forces)—that's tapping the "whole keg o' whoop ass!"

Cornwallis reacted by sending "Tarleton's Legion," a mixed force of cavalry and light infantry that was highly mobile under the command of his most vicious officer, Lieutenant Colonel Banastre Tarleton. Tarleton was out after the Patriot militias and especially Morgan's Army, with the thought of crushing him between the two British forces. When Greene learned of Tarleton's pursuit of Morgan, he wrote to Morgan, *"Col. Tarleton is said to be on his way to pay you a visit. I doubt not but he will have a decent reception and a proper dismission."* The result was the Battle of Cowpens on January 17, 1781. Morgan "shellacked" Tarleton in the greatest Patriot victory of the war in the South. Ninety percent of Tarleton's Legion was killed, wounded or captured (Whole Keg!). Cornwallis was now down 2,000 Loyalists, as well as some very fine British cavalry and light infantry. Now Morgan's troops reunited with Greene's main force and the flight to the Dan River began for real. Even though Cornwallis had lost his "eyes and ears" with Tarleton's defeat, he gave chase to Greene's reunited army. When Greene's scouts reported that Cornwallis was in hot pursuit, Greene exclaimed, *"Then he is ours!"*

The "Race to the Dan" showed the superior mobility of the American Army and the tactical genius of its commander. In one month's time, Greene's Army marched 200 miles through North Carolina and into Virginia, evading British pursuit in some of the toughest weather of the war. Greene's ability to use local geography and plan for contingent operations and maneuvers left Cornwallis in the dust. Greene succeeded in escaping and exhausting the British Army and forced them to overextend their supply lines all in one move.

Cornwallis returned to the Carolinas to recruit more Loyalists to fill his depleted ranks and to acquire badly needed supplies. Greene re-crossed the Dan River and shadowed him for days. The two armies collided head-on at the Battle of Guilford Courthouse on March 15. Cornwallis succeeded in driving Greene from the field (that was how they determined victory in those days), but he literally got "shot to pieces" in the casualties column: 25 percent killed or wounded in action—nobody wins a war like that.

Weakened, Cornwallis withdrew to Wilmington, North Carolina, and eventually on to Yorktown, Virginia, where he was defeated by General

Washington, Le Comte de Rochambeau, and soldiers from the United States, France, and Canada.

General Greene now led his army back down to South Carolina and began the "War of the Posts." Troops under his command, along with those rascally irregulars, simultaneously attacked several exposed outposts in the now vulnerable British line of forts. Greene led his main army in three more battles, Hobkirk's Hill (April 25, 1781), the Siege of Ninety-Six (May 22—June 19, 1781), and Eutaw Springs (September 8, 1781), one of the bloodiest engagements of the entire war. Although he never achieved a single tactical victory, Greene completely destroyed British power and authority in the southern states. His lack of success in winning a battle is best summed up in his own words, *"We fight, get beat, rise, and fight again."*

In less than two years, Greene succeeded in capturing all the British outposts, taking 3,500 prisoners, and splitting the British Army in half, bottling them up in Charleston and Wilmington. When the Treaty of Paris was signed, the British controlled only those cities—the rest was controlled by Greene. A major element in his success, and one he was quick to point out, was an outstanding group of supporting officers including his Marylander division commanders, Otho Holland Williams and John Eager Howard, two cavalrymen, William Washington (second cousin of George Washington) and Henry "Light-Horse Harry" Lee (father of General Robert E. Lee), and his Polish engineer, Thaddeus Kosciuszko.

After the war, Greene moved his family to his new estate, Mulberry Grove, just north of Savannah, Georgia. He attempted to settle down to the life of a Southern planter while refusing all attempts by prominent Georgians to involve him in local politics. Tragically, he died at the age of 44 on June 19, 1786, of a stroke, possibly caused by overexposure to the sun. It will never be known to what great heights he would have risen had he lived a longer life.

Washington's War Horse, the Savior of the South, and the best damned soldier in the Continental Army, Major General Nathanael Greene.

Dan Morgan was bred for war.
In fact he was blood kin to the
bear that bit Daniel Boone's butt!

CHAPTER 8

Daniel Morgan

The Boozin', Brawlin' Leader of the Virginia Rifles

Major General Daniel Morgan was the most successful field commander of the American Revolution—and maybe the least remembered. History has been less kind to the *"Old Wagoneer"* (as his soldiers came to call him) than to other leaders of less ability but more political connection. The tales of this great Patriot and those who served under him at the siege of Boston, the assault on Quebec, the destruction of the British Army at Saratoga, and his annihilation of Banastre Tarleton's British legion at the Battle of Cowpens are all but forgotten.

Daniel Morgan was a big man. He stood over six feet tall and was built like a rock. His indomitable spirit, quick wit, and good-natured humor made him a favorite among the frontier people with whom he lived and worked. They said of his cousin, Daniel Boone, *"Boone is a man who walks like a bear,"* but of Morgan himself they said, *"Dan Morgan is a bear that walks like a man!"* Many of the folks from Winchester and the Shenandoah Valley looked up to Morgan as a natural leader. He enjoyed a good joke, loved a good brawl, was fond of a good game of cards, and could "hold strong liquor" better than any man alive (never met a beer he didn't like either). He was a fast and sure friend, as well as a devil of an enemy. But if you looked at young Daniel Morgan, it would be hard to believe that God had cut him out for anything other than trouble. You wouldn't be far wrong.

Not much is recorded about the early life of the great General. He was born in 1736 to Welsh immigrant parents in Hunterdon County, New Jersey. His early life was that of a tough frontier family. He left home at 16 after a fierce argument with his father. He travelled up and down the Great Wagon Road from Philadelphia to the Yadkin River in the Carolinas before deciding to settle in Winchester, Virginia. He worked on a farm and in a saw mill, but was offered a job as a teamster (a wagoneer) and found that the outdoor work suited him right down to the ground. Six months later, Morgan had saved enough money to buy his own cart and team and was running his own "outfit" along the Great Wagon Road. The wagon was the truck and railroad of the day and in the 1700's, they were the only way to get products from the "over yonder" back to market in the "big city." Morgan's experience along the Great Wagon Road, being the highway of the day, and his first-hand knowledge of southwest Virginia and the Carolina "hill country" undoubtedly contributed to his overwhelming destruction of the British at Cowpens and the ensuing panicked pursuit by Cornwallis in a vain effort to catch him—an effort that weakened the British, led to their defeat at Yorktown, and brought about the end of the war.

The Wagoneer

Morgan served as a civilian teamster during the French and Indian War with his cousin, Daniel Boone. After returning from the advance on Fort Duquesne (Pittsburgh) and the defeat at the Monongahela with General Braddock's command, he ran afoul of one British lieutenant who struck him with the flat of his sword. The rough, tough Morgan, who didn't take crap off of anybody (kinda like John Wayne toilet paper), damn near sent the officer on to the "promised land" with a single blow of his huge right fist. He was court-martialed and sentenced to 500 lashes. One of his favorite stories to tell was that the British miscounted and gave him only 499 and they owed him one more—seemed no one ever tried to finish the task. This punishment had been known to kill lesser men, but didn't have the desired effect on Morgan. The lieutenant publicly apologized to Morgan. As was his way, Morgan wholeheartedly forgave him, but from that day, Dan Morgan held a lifelong hatred for the British Army.

In 1758, he was commissioned an ensign in a company of Virginia rangers. When he and two escorts were returning from the back country with a dispatch for the commanding officer at Winchester, Indians ambushed them. The escorts were killed and Morgan was seriously wounded by a bullet that hit him in the back of the neck, knocked out all the teeth in his left lower jaw, and exited his cheek. Morgan would take some time to completely heal, but if 499 lashes couldn't kill him, what chance did a musket ball have?

After the frontier grew quiet, Morgan returned to his work as a wagoneer. He also continued his rough and rowdy ways. In a frontier full of hard drinking, street fighting tough guys, he was top dog! Daniel Morgan was the Alpha male of the buckskin crowd. But he had a good mind for business, he always saved his money, and in 1759 he bought a fine house in Winchester.

In 1763, Morgan was taken with Abigail Curry (truth be told she was as taken with him) and the two set up housekeeping and had two daughters before Daniel made Abigail an honest woman. Their daughters Nancy and Betsy both grew up to marry Revolutionary War veterans. Abigail settled Daniel down and taught him to read and write. By 1774, when Daniel and Abigail finally married, he owned 255 acres, was a prosperous farmer, a captain of militia, and a respected citizen in the community. His marriage to Abigail changed him from a loud and unruly hothead into a "high spirited" gentleman, eager to improve his mind and live a more admirable life. As a captain of riflemen in the Virginia militia, Morgan served in Governor Dunmore's War of 1774-75, a conflict between local native tribes and Virginia settlers over the Appalachian Mountains. His company took part in raids on Shawnee villages in the Ohio Valley. Upon returning from the conflict, Morgan and his men heard of the Battles of Lexington and Concord on April 19 and swore they would *"stand by the people of Boston and take up arms in their defense."*

Morgan's Riflemen

After the American Revolutionary War began, the Continental Congress created the Continental Army on June 14, 1775. They called for the formation of 10 rifle companies from the "middle colonies" to support the Siege of Boston, and late in June, Virginia agreed to send two. The Virginia Assembly chose Daniel Morgan to form one of these companies, and as Captain, be in command. Morgan recruited 96 men in just 10 days and in just 21 days, marched them from Winchester, VA, 600 miles to Boston, MA, arriving on August 6. His company of marksmen was nicknamed "Morgan's Riflemen." These boys stood out in a crowd. They were all proficient "Indian fighters" (they were back-woods warriors), they wore buckskin "long shirts," breeches, and moccasins rather than the blue and buff uniforms and boots of the Continentals. They also carried tomahawks and long, thick, vicious looking hunting knives—apparently for "stickin' pigs" and taking scalps. But what really gave Morgan's company a significant advantage over other soldiers of the day was that instead of the smooth-bore muskets used by most British and American companies, his men carried rifles. They were longer, lighter, and easier to fire, and because of the rifled barrels (rifling spins a bullet so it travels faster, farther, and straighter), those guns "put iron on target" at over 400 yards. Not bad when the musket soldier *hopes* for a hit at 50 yards, but the disadvantages were that the rifle was slower to load and couldn't be fitted with a bayonet. To complete the "edge" that Morgan's company would use throughout the war, these country boys played by a different set of rules—"frontier rules" some called them—that were just common sense to Morgan and his men. The Rules, in order of priority: 1) If they ride a horse, shoot them first (take out the officers), 2) If they're directing traffic, shoot them next (Indian and Loyalist guides, sergeants, and officers on foot), 3) Anybody with a flag, bugle, or drum, shoot them as possible (take out command and control), and 4) Artillerymen, kill 'em all (silence the big guns).

The Rules worked really well and gave Morgan's men a huge psychological advantage. The British Army considered these "backwoods tactics" to be dishonorable, especially the targeting of officers, but they caused chaos and mayhem within the British ranks, so say what you will.

Later that year, the Continental Congress authorized the invasion of Canada. Colonel Benedict Arnold (yeah, THAT Benedict Arnold, but at the time he was still a Patriot) convinced General Washington to start an eastern assault in support of the main thrust of the invasion going up the Hudson Valley, led by General Richard Montgomery. Washington agreed to send three companies from his army at Boston, but they had to be volunteers. Every company volunteered. Morgan's company was one of the chosen few. Arnold selected Captain Morgan to lead the three companies as a battalion. The expedition set out from Fort Western (Augusta, ME) on September 25, with Morgan's group "walking point" (out front).

The expedition started with about 1,000 men, but by the time they reached Quebec on November 9, those numbers had been cut down to 600 fit to fight. When the main group arrived, they launched a joint attack. The Battle of Quebec began in a fierce storm on the morning of December 31. The Patriots attacked in two columns, commanded by Montgomery and Arnold, and attempted to encircle the city's defenders.

Arnold's column attacked the lower city from the north, but Arnold suffered a leg wound early in the battle. Morgan took command of the force and successfully overcame the first rampart (fortified wall) and got into the city. Montgomery's column started their attack as the blizzard got worse and he and many of his troops were killed or wounded in the first attack. With Montgomery down, his column broke apart. The British commander was now able to lead hundreds of the Quebec militia in surrounding the men of the second attack. The British were also able to bring cannons to bear behind Morgan's attack.

Surrounded and fired upon from all sides, Morgan's troops soon surrendered. Morgan handed his sword to a French-Canadian priest, refusing to give it to a British General (who hates the British Army?). Morgan became one of the 372 men captured. But being an officer, he was quickly "paroled" (meaning you promise not to fight until you are technically "exchanged" for an officer of equal value—those were different times) and he remained a "prisoner of war" until he was finally "exchanged" in January 1777.

When he rejoined Washington, Morgan was happily surprised to learn he had been promoted to colonel for his bravery at Quebec. He was ordered to raise and command a new infantry regiment, the 11th Virginia of the Continental Line.

On June 13, Morgan was given command of a brand-new unit: the Provisional Rifle Corps, an elite light infantry force of 500 riflemen (basically infantry on horseback) chosen from Pennsylvania, Maryland, and Virginia regiments of the Continental Army. Many were from his own original regiment. Washington sent them to harass General William Howe's rear guard and baggage train. Morgan and his men did that with gusto during the winter months and the Continental withdrawal across New Jersey.

Saratoga

Remember that during this time, the British were attacking from both north and south and Washington had split his army in an attempt to gain and maintain some control. General Philip Schuyler was attempting to defeat the British in upstate New York and a detachment of Washington's Army, commanded by Morgan, was reassigned to the army's Northern Department. On August 30, he joined General Horatio Gates, new commanding officer of the Northern Department, to put an end to Burgoyne's offensive. Gates was a guy who couldn't pour piss out of a boot with directions on the heel, but he had many friends in Congress. Schuyler and Gates hated each other and Gates would use his "congressional connections" to get command of the Northern Army.

The British had captured Fort Ticonderoga, then blundered as the Hessian cavalry had been destroyed at Bennington, Vermont, by "the Green Mountain Boys" now commanded by John Stark. With that defeat, away went the warriors of the first nations to "sit this one out" and side with the winner. Still with an army of almost 8,000 soldiers, Burgoyne came to Saratoga. He would run into a Patriot buzz saw at Freeman's Farm on September 19.

Dan Morgan and his riflemen would play a huge part in one of the most important victories in American history. Morgan's corps, with the added support of Henry Dearborn's 300-man New Hampshire infantry, was the sharp tip of the Continental spear. They ran headlong into General Simon Fraser's wing of Burgoyne's advancing army and the fight was on! Every officer in the British advance party died in the first exchange of fire (those Backwoods rules!) and Fraser's advance guard "skedaddled."

Morgan's men rushed on in pursuit, but the charge fell apart when they ran into the main Redcoat column. Benedict Arnold arrived and he and Morgan reformed the American lines. As the British began to form up on the field at Freeman's Farm, Morgan's men broke them up with heavy doses of accurate rifle fire from the woods on the far side of the field. The British couldn't move forward—their officers, sergeants, and artillerymen were almost completely annihilated! Morgan's men rallied when they were joined by another seven regiments of Continentals, and for the rest of the afternoon, American fire stopped the British cold. But repeated American charges did no better when we constantly ran into a forest of British bayonets.

At sunset, recall was sounded and the American lines melted back into the woods and returned to their fortified positions on Bemis Heights, just a mile or two away. It seemed that the Redcoats had won the day (remember—he who holds the field), but Burgoyne's Army was in a world of hurt. The British supply lines were WAY overextended and would soon be cut by American troops retaking Lake Champlain and there was no possibility of any reinforcement or relief as General Howe was now stuck fighting for Philadelphia. "Gentleman Johnny" was on his own out in the deep woods. The news of the day wasn't any better. Over 600 casualties, mostly officers, sergeants, and artillerymen (over 75 percent of his artillerymen). Burgoyne held the field, but his army had been cut to ribbons to do so. All in all, a very bad day.

Over the next few weeks, the American Army swelled to better than 12,000 men, Burgoyne's Army was now down to less than 7,000 with daily desertions on the rise. The Redcoats had to find a way out of the hole they were in. Burgoyne decided to attack (like nobody would expect that!) and break out toward Albany. The result was the Battle of Bemis Heights on October 7. Morgan now commanded the entire left (or western) flank of the American Army. Benedict Arnold had been relieved of command by General Gates (seemed Gates didn't like anybody who stepped into HIS spotlight) and Burgoyne's plan was to turn the left American flank, attacking with 1,500 of his best men remaining. This pitted Morgan's brigade against General Fraser's troops one more time for all the marbles!

After scattering the British picket line (made up of Loyalist Canadians and what was left of the "First Nations" fellas) to the four winds, Morgan's sharpshooters then went straight for the Redcoat light infantry commanded by General Fraser. They had Fraser's boys trapped in a crossfire between themselves and Dearborn's New Hampshire regiment. The Redcoats broke and began to run, but there was General Fraser, trying to rally them, encouraging his men to hold their positions when Benedict Arnold arrived. Remember, Arnold had been relieved of command by the very jealous General Gates, but Arnold refused to be "benched" for what he felt was the single most important battle of the war so far. Damned if he wasn't right! So off to the battle he galloped, spotted Fraser, and called to Morgan: "*That man on the grey horse is a host unto himself and must be disposed of—direct the attention of some of the sharpshooters amongst your riflemen to him!"* Morgan reluctantly ordered Fraser shot. Morgan called on one of his best, Timothy Murphy of Pennsylvania, and said: *"That gallant officer is General Fraser. I admire him, but it is necessary that he should die, do your duty."* Murphy scaled a nearby tree, took careful aim at the tough but "doable" distance of 300 yards, and fired four times. His first shot (called a ranging shot) was a close miss, the second grazed Fraser's horse, and with the third, Simon Fraser tumbled from the saddle, shot through the stomach. General Fraser died that night. The last shot found British officer Sir Francis Clerke. He was General Burgoyne's chief aide. He had galloped onto the field with a message for Fraser. Murphy's fourth shot killed him instantly. Some historians aren't certain that "the facts" of this affair are completely accurate, but one thing's for sure—with Fraser down and dying, the British light infantry was routed. They fled back into and through the redoubts (make-shift fortifications) occupied by Burgoyne's main army (or what was left of it).

Morgan was one of those who then followed Arnold's furious lead to turn a British counter-attack from the center. After that, Arnold and Morgan led the assault on the British redoubts. At the hottest moment of the fight, Arnold went down, shot through the leg and through his horse. Morgan rallied his men to avenge the "fallen" Arnold and within moments, the battle was over. The Americans had won the field and the day! If Benedict Arnold had been killed during the assault on the redoubt, he would have been a hero of the American Revolution. As things turned out, he committed treason and today is considered almost as bad as Judas Iscariot. With his hopes of victory (or escape) shot to hell and about 500 men down from the fight, Burgoyne "retired" from the field and "hunkered down" in his main fortifications. Later that night, the British withdrew to the village of Saratoga on October 13.

Throughout the next week, as "Gentleman Johnny" and his men kept digging in, Morgan and his men moved north of Saratoga. The ability of Morgan's Riflemen to cut up any patrols sent in their direction convinced the British that retreat was impossible. Surrounded, desperate, and outnumbered 3 to 1, Burgoyne surrendered his army on October 17. The world had changed and Col. Daniel Morgan and his rifle corps were a big part of why.

Following the victory at Saratoga, Morgan's Corps re-joined Washington's main army near Philadelphia. Throughout 1778, Morgan attacked and harassed British columns and supply lines in New Jersey, but didn't play a part in any major battles. He wasn't involved in the Battle of Monmouth, but aggressively pursued the retreating Redcoats and stymied British efforts to regroup and reorganize by capturing many prisoners and supplies. It was evident, to Morgan at least, that he was ready for his own command. And when the Virginia Line was reorganized on September 14, Morgan became (once again) the colonel of the 7th Virginia Regiment (that's the 11th Virginia, reorganized).

Morgan became increasingly dissatisfied with his role in the army and was completely frustrated with Congress. He had never been a politically-motivated rebel (to Dan Morgan, it just came sorta natural) or ever tried to cultivate a relationship with Congress. And so he was repeatedly "passed over" for promotion to brigadier general, those opportunities going to men with less "practical" combat experience and leadership skills, but better congressional ties and political connections. Besides all the frustration, his health wasn't what it used to be. His legs and back were in constant pain from years of rough living as a wagoneer and the abuses of captivity from the Quebec Expedition. But the final straw came when he was passed over for command of the newly formed Light Infantry Corps. This was the kind of unit Morgan was born to lead! This was the kind of "wild ride" and "hell for leather" fighting at which he was already known to be the best! Colonel Daniel Morgan submitted his resignation, which was refused, but Congress finally placed him on "indefinite furlough" as of June 30, 1779. And just like that, it seemed his fightin' days were over, so he went home to Winchester.

SECOND HELPIN'

While the Colonel was "on leave," the war had changed. It had gone global. After the victory at Saratoga, France had entered the war as an American ally. France *and Spain* were now fighting the English for control of their overseas empire, as well. Truth be told, this was the second world war in 20 years (funny how those things always come like that). The British were "obliged" to redistribute their army and navy to protect "British interest" world-wide. British General William Howe had resigned and gone home, which placed General Henry Clinton in command in America. He would be asked to do more with less and somehow win the war. Clinton's new strategy was to take the war to the southern states. He thought he could find new resources and manpower down in Dixie. A) He believed that there were many, many Loyalists in the South who just needed a strong showing from the British Army to "once again rally to the banner of King and Country," and B) He was going to liberate and recruit the slaves in the South to fight for the British cause. This idea seems completely at odds with cementing the loyalty of the southern aristocracy. But, to the South the Redcoats (and their contradictory strategy) would go.

By 1779, General Clinton and his second in command, General Charles Lord Cornwallis, had taken Savannah and the state of Georgia, as well as the great port of Charleston, SC, and were well on the way to taking all of South Carolina. Things were looking grim. Congress (in *its* wisdom) wouldn't listen to General Washington and appointed General Horatio Gates to command of the Continental Army in the "Southern Department." The argument was, "Well, he beat the British at Saratoga, he can beat them in the South." There were many differences in the two scenarios, and we'll discuss a few of them directly.

In June 1780, Morgan was urged to re-enter service by General Gates, but at that time, he was disinclined. Morgan felt that being outranked by many of the militia officers might limit his "strengths" and he wasn't ready to take orders from people who he didn't think knew better. Maybe Morgan just saw things as they were. He had to be concerned with the situation in the South. He knew Gates and realized that without good supporting officers, he didn't stand a chance. He realized that Cornwallis, who had been in the war since the beginning, was no "johnny come lately" like Burgoyne. Whatever the reason, Dan Morgan wasn't going to work for Horatio Gates again. But after Gates' catastrophic defeat at the Battle of Camden, Morgan put all other considerations aside and went to join the Southern command in North Carolina.

He met Gates (who was now on his way out of the service, pending congressional review of his actions at Camden) at Hillsborough, NC, and was (finally!) given command of the light infantry corps on October 2. On October 13, 1780, Col. Daniel Morgan received his promotion to brigadier general, and on October 14, General Nathanael Greene became the official commanding general of the Southern Department.

General Morgan met with his new Department Commander, General Greene, on December 3, at Charlotte, North Carolina. Greene realized that leading the light infantry was THE job for which Morgan was particularly well-suited and didn't change his command assignment, but Morgan did receive new orders. Greene had decided to split his army and use "hit and run" tactics to vex, pester, and plague the enemy to buy time to rebuild his forces. Greene knew Morgan to be just the kind of "hard charging, free-wheeling, screwball old wagoneer" he needed for these kind of "freelance" operations, and he gave Morgan and his men the job of foraging and enemy harassment in the backcountry of South Carolina, *while avoiding direct battle*. It was a war of "hit 'em where they ain't!" and Morgan's Corps hit the British hard, stealing supplies and bedeviling the Redcoat high command to the point where they were fearful of going out into the countryside where they just might meet the Boogey man—and his name was Dan Morgan!

As soon as Morgan's guerrilla war tactics became too problematic, British General Cornwallis sent Colonel Banastre Tarleton and his British Legion to track him down. Morgan talked with many of the militia who had fought Tarleton before. They acquainted Morgan with the "Waxhaws

Massacre" where American militia had tried to surrender, but Tarleton ordered his men to "show no quarter." They saw Banastre Tarleton as the most despicable British officer and referred to him as "the bastard Tarleton." General Morgan spent some time studying Tarleton's battles and tactics and decided to disobey his orders. He would face up Tarleton in a direct confrontation.

Morgan chose to make his stand at CowPens, a well-known and popular pasturing and auction field in north-western South Carolina. The pasture was well watered, the Broad River bordered the field on two sides, and a tall hill bordered the northern edge. Morgan knew his enemy and he knew the terrain. First order of business was to run Tarleton and his "legion" ragged. For several days, Morgan's Corps forced Tarleton to chase them through some of the densest woodlands in western Carolina, then, on the morning of January 17, 1781, they met Tarleton in the Battle of the Cowpens. Morgan's Corps of about 700 had been joined by militia forces under Andrew Pickens (somewhere between 600 and 900 men) and William Washington's dragoons (150-200 mounted cavalry). Tarleton's legion (800 Cavalry and Loyalist infantry) was supplemented with the light infantry from several regiments of regulars (about 400 in all) and two 3-pound cannons.

Morgan knew Tarleton to be "a rambler and a gambler" (a fellow of low morals and high temper and driven by impulse), so he took advantage of Tarleton's tendency for quick action and his disdain for the militia (he absolutely despised the American militiaman), as well as the longer range and accuracy of his Virginia riflemen. Morgan set his men in position from the foot to the crest of the hill that dominated the battlefield. The skirmishers (the sharpshooters) were positioned to the front, then a second line of the militia next, with the regulars at the hilltop. The first two lines were to withdraw to the left as soon as they were seriously threatened, but after inflicting maximum damage. This pretended retreat would invite an untimely and reckless charge from the British. Washington's Dragoons would be hidden to the rear by the hill, and at just the right moment would charge and crush Tarleton's right flank.

The evening of January 16 saw everything put in place. All was in readiness and Morgan's men would sleep in their positions. That night, General Morgan went through the camp to visit with each unit without his jacket or shirt. Many had heard the story of the punishment he had received at the hands of the British, now *all* could see the horrible scars that had been left on Daniel Morgan's back—this tactic had the desired effect. In the morning, Morgan's men would fight like never before. I think the fellas were "fired up!"

For their part, the British were still slogging it out through the woods 'til dawn. Then, exhausted and famished, they came out of the woods to see, through the mornings mists, the Americans on the hill. The order was given. Charge! Row after row of British infantry, bayonets glistening in the morning sun, steadily advanced. Morgan's Virginia rifles opened fire. Within minutes, almost every British officer was down. The rifles reloaded again and again. Soon the sergeants and standard bearers were gone! The riflemen withdrew, as planned.

Now the militia troops opened fire. As the British soldiers continued to advance, the American militia, with their backs turned to the British, reloaded their muskets. When the British got close enough, they turned and fired at point-blank range in their faces. And after two shots, the militia withdrew, as planned. Many of the militiamen were Continental veterans who now regrouped their units and came back around the hill to smash into the Redcoats' left flank.

Into the jaws of death charged Tarleton's legion. Col. Tarleton believed the "flight" of the militia to be the beginning of the rout of the Americans he had expected, and he ordered in the cavalry. The Continental line at the top of the hill stood its ground magnificently. The Dragoons of William Washington crashed into the right flank of the British assault, completely overwhelming the stunned Redcoats, then the militia reappeared to Tarleton's left and crushed the British flank. The door had been slammed shut, there was no escape. The war cries and shouts of victory from Morgan's boys echoed through the woodland! Tarleton, fleeing the field with his bodyguards, could still hear it miles away.

In less than an hour, Tarleton's 1,076 men suffered 110 killed and 830 captured. The captives included 200 wounded. Tarleton may have escaped, but Morgan's men captured all his supplies and equipment, including the cannons. General Daniel Morgan's battle plan at CowPens is universally considered to be *the* tactical masterpiece of the American Revolutionary War and one of the most successfully executed double envelopments of all modern military history.

Cornwallis had lost not only Tarleton's legion, but also the light infantry. Gone were his "eyes and ears" in the wilderness. Gone was his ability to react with speed for the rest of the war. It is said that when Col. Tarleton reported the disaster to Gen. Cornwallis, the old man leaned so hard upon his sword that it snapped in two.

The victory at the CowPens was as stunning and surprising as it was brilliant and imaginative. It might have been the only original tactical thinking of the entire war. After all the months of dismal defeats, Morgan had restored hope not only to the Southern Patriots, but to the entire nation. The destruction of Tarleton's legion was the beginning of the end for Cornwallis.

For his heroic actions, Virginia gave Morgan land in the Shenandoah Valley and an estate that he would name "Saratoga." But the cold and damp of the southern winter campaign had taken a toll on the old wagoneer. Morgan's sciatica was now aggravated to the point where he was in constant pain. On February 10, he returned to his Virginia farm for some well-earned R and R. In July, Morgan joined General Lafayette in pursuit of Banastre Tarleton once again, this time in Virginia, but Tarleton had learned his lessons, as well. He wanted no more to do with Dan Morgan and the fox, this time, eluded the hounds.

After resigning his commission, Morgan, now 46, returned home. He had served for almost 7 years. He began investing in land and eventually built an estate of more than 250,000 acres. A part of his settling down was to join the Presbyterian Church and became an ardent "follower of the faith." In 1790, Congress awarded him a gold medal commemorating his great victory at CowPens.

In 1794, Morgan was recalled to service to help President Washington put down the Whiskey Rebellion. He rode out to battle commissioned a major general under General "Light-Horse Harry" Lee. Morgan led one wing of the army into the Pennsylvania outlands. The huge display of power and patriotism ended the protests without the shedding of blood. Morgan commanded the 1,200-man army that stayed in western Pennsylvania until 1795.

Major General Daniel Morgan had always been first to the fight from the days of his youth. There's an old southern saying, "It ain't the size of the dog in the fight, it's the size of the fight in the dog." Dan Morgan won on both counts, but most importantly, he loved liberty and he loved his country. After all the fighting was over, Morgan served in the U.S. House of Representatives until 1799. Daniel Morgan passed away at his daughter's home in Winchester, VA, on July 6, 1802. It was his 66th birthday.

A true 'Yankee Dandy,' this sleek and dapper entrepreneur risked more than most in the quest for Liberty and Independence.

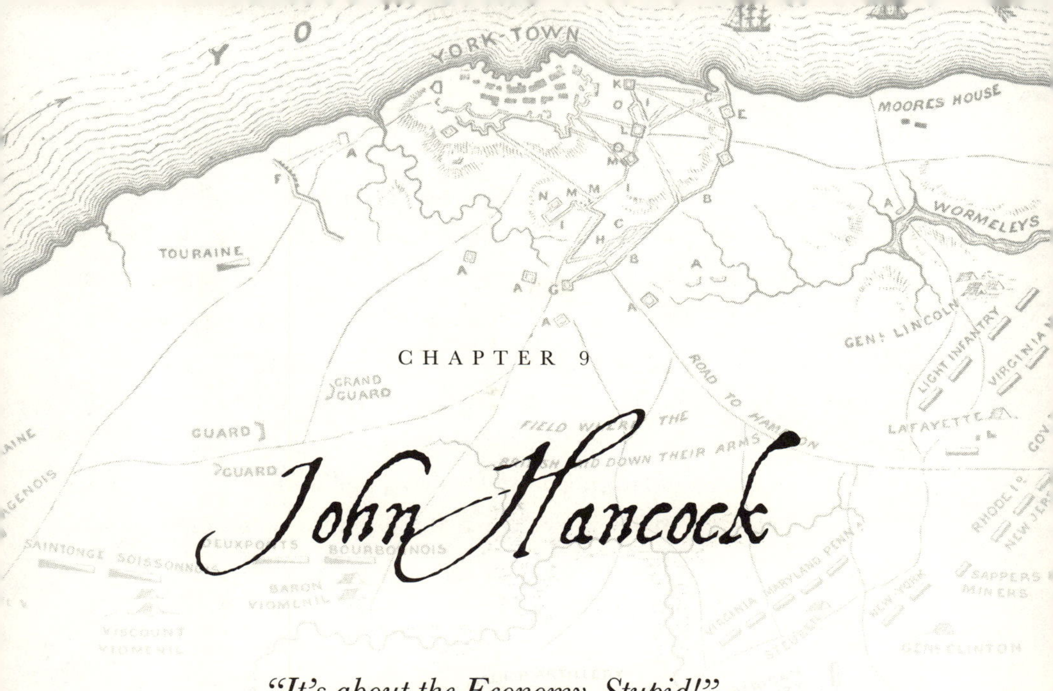

CHAPTER 9

John Hancock

"It's about the Economy, Stupid!"

At the time of the Revolution, John Hancock was still a young man in his thirties. Well-to-do, well-dressed, well-mannered, well-liked, and well-placed to make a huge difference during the war. There seemed to be nothing at which Hancock was not successful: business, outlaw enterprises, even politics. The man was connected. He had friends in every circle. His most enduring friendship seems to have been with Samuel Adams. Even though Adams came from a "different" perspective, the two became close to inseparable. Through his Adams connections, John Hancock became one of the most important Sons of Liberty and an early leader of the independence movement.

The Business of America is Business

Hancock was born January 23, 1737, in Braintree, Massachusetts. As a boy, he became friends with young John Adams who had been baptized by Hancock's father, the Reverend John Sr., in 1734.

Hancock's family lived comfortably, but after the death of his father in 1744, John was sent to live with his aunt and uncle, Lydia and Thomas Hancock of Hancock Manor on Beacon Hill (about as aristocratic as it gets without a title of nobility). Thomas was one of the most successful and wealthy merchants in the colonies, and because they had no children of their own, John became the heir apparent to all his aunt and uncle had to give: love, money, and influence.

Hancock graduated from Boston Latin School in 1750, then enrolled in Harvard College (that's three Harvard men in the ranks of rebellion from Massachusetts—Adams, Adams, and Hancock), graduating in 1754. As the French and Indian War was beginning, he started working at his uncle's mercantile company. The war was good for business. Hancock ships and Hancock shipping were making money hand over fist. Young John was an able and diligent employee. It was evident that he was being groomed for partnership, but he didn't want anything given to him because of family relationship.

Hancock lived in England from 1760-1761 where he developed personal and business relationships with clients, suppliers, and not a few power brokers. When he returned to Boston, he found that his uncle's health had begun to fail, so John became a full partner in the firm. In 1762, he was invited to become a member of the Masonic Lodge of St. Andrews, instantly giving him even more influential connections. When his uncle passed away the following year, Hancock became THE Mr. Hancock of Beacon Hill, owner and proprietor of the full firm, making him one of the wealthiest men in the colonies. Not only did he inherit the firm, but Hancock Manor and all that went with it—several thousand acres of land and a few slaves. The slaves continued to work for John and his aunt, although they were freed upon the death of his aunt to satisfy his uncle's will. John never bought, sold, or traded any slaves.

The House of Hancock, as the business was known, would operate profitably over the next several years despite the growing strain on British-American relations. John Hancock would take his place in Boston society and politics. Not so much because he wanted to, but because his position made it a requirement. Hancock wasn't a political activist—not yet—but he disliked the taxes, not because of "infringement of his personal rights," but because he believed it bad for American business. And just when the tension with Britain seemed to reach its peak, Hancock emerged as a leading activist for independence and a fomenter of rebellion.

The Pragmatic Patriot

In 1765, Hancock was elected one of Boston's selectmen, a post his uncle had held before his passing. Not long after, Parliament passed the Stamp Act and Hancock temporarily stood as a Loyalist. Even though he thought Parliament was way out of line, he hoped the colonists would submit to their king. For him, it wasn't so much about the politics and the debate on rights, it was about business and profit. Peace and the status quo were good for business, and instability threatened that status quo. However, there were things going on that caused a 180-degree change of mind. There were two events that irrevocably put Hancock on the path of the Patriot.

The first of these was his growing friendship with Samuel Adams. Remember that Samuel Adams preached liberty and independence the way a Southern revival minister preaches salvation, and Hancock became evangelized by and filled with "the spirit of American Liberty and Independence" (Say Halleluiah!). The two men were inseparable and their friendship greatly helped to fashion and fund the Patriot movement. In May 1766, Hancock was elected to the Massachusetts House of Representatives. Hancock's political popularity was a direct result of the support of Samuel Adams, who had a lot of clout with the citizenry. Hancock and Adams were an unlikely duo, they were virtually "the prince and the pauper"—Adams with his "well worn" almost antique attire, and Hancock, proud as a peacock wearing the latest and costliest fashionable style. They seemed to have almost nothing in common, but were the best of friends nonetheless. They were both members of the Sons of

Liberty—Mother Chapter, Boston, Massachusetts, and met regularly at the famous "Green Dragon Tavern" to discuss the need for change.

Then there was that smuggling thing. In 1767, the British imposed the Townshend Acts (import duties on just about everything in an effort to restock the royal coffers after the French and Indian War) and created a new opportunity for those who had the "vision" to take the challenge: smuggling. It was a common enough practice for centuries, but now Parliament had gone and made it incredibly profitable for the adventurous entrepreneur to import that which was illegal or so highly taxed as to be "legally" unaffordable (same logic that went into passage of the Volstead Act and Prohibition 150 years later). Somehow, the British Ministry had convinced itself that the "colonists" would accept indirect taxes, such as the tariffs of the Townshend Acts, because it wasn't a "direct" tax…oops! You know the rest, but as for John Hancock, he saw the opportunity and went into smuggling with a full heart and a lusty "Yo Ho Ho!" And he was one of the best. A common joke of the day was "Sam Adams writes the letters and John Hancock pays the postage." A big chunk of Hancock's fortune came from smuggling, but a huge chunk of that wealth went to finance the Revolutionary War, as well.

In the 18th century, Boston was Britain's trading hub in the Americas. She was worth £20 million annually, a huge amount back in the day. Boston was also important for the New England shipbuilding industry: more than 30 percent of all British ships were built in the American colonies, but most importantly, 40 percent of all British exports to the northern colonies entered through the Port of Boston. The British zealously protected their trade "rights" through taxes known as the Navigation Acts. Originally enacted during the mid-1600's and expanded over the following 80 years or so, these acts forbade English colonies from trading with anyone except Great Britain, They couldn't even trade with each other, only Britain. All colonies, all over the world, same limitation, no questions asked! This practice was called "mercantilism" and was a source of enormous revenue for king and country. For years, merchants avoided paying duties by smuggling and/or "buying off" (bribing) customs agents. It was a fairly common practice for customs guys to record part of the cargo and allow the rest to enter the country as contraband, so long as they got a share of the profits or the merchandise. In an effort to protect British commercial interests and pay for an increasing debt, Royal Governor Francis Bernard of Massachusetts requested soldiers in Boston. The American Board of Customs Commission was created in Boston to put a stop to all this "illegal" activity. Smuggling was so widespread that trying to end it was seen as an unfair act in itself. Almost everyone supported smuggling since it allowed merchants to sell their wares cheaper than the legally imported alternative.

In 1733, Parliament passed the Molasses Act in an attempt to control trade between the American colonies and the Caribbean islands. It was an utter disaster that created great wealth for mercantile houses like the House of Hancock. Hancock was a well-known smuggler of molasses, Dutch tea, tobacco, rum, and wine, among other products. He was the richest man in Massachusetts and his radical political views made him a target of the new Board of Customs. In April 1768, customs officials boarded his ship, the *Lydia,* but because they lacked writs of assistance (means a search warrant), they were removed from the vessel before a search could be conducted. No criminal charges were filed.

The "last straw" for Hancock occurred on June 10, 1768, when his sloop, *Liberty,* was seized by the customs office. One month earlier on May 9, the *Liberty* arrived in Boston with a cargo of Madeira wine (a favorite of George Washington, by the way). As usual, it was received by customs agents (called tidesmen) who would make sure all documents were legal and in order and all duties were paid. As the ship was inspected the following day, only 25 caskets of wine were found. Hancock's men were suspected of having unloaded the cargo overnight as the hold of the vessel was roomy enough for four times that amount. The tidesmen testified that none of that occurred during their stay at the vessel. One month later on June 9, one of the men changed his story stating that they were bribed to remain quiet. The following day, June 10, as the *Liberty* was about to leave with new cargo, it was seized by customs officials and towed away to impound.

In response to the seizure of the ship, the Sons of Liberty incited the crowd that had gathered (to watch the spectacle, of course) to protest in favor of the owner of the *Liberty*, John Hancock. The situation was peaceful at first, but turned violent when the *Liberty* was impounded. The mob attacked the customs house and its occupants, one of whom had his boat dragged to Boston Common and burnt. Most of the tax collectors were unharmed and escaped the violence by fleeing to Castle William, out in the harbor and far from the enraged crowd. In effect the incident was smuggling on the part of Hancock versus racketeering on the part of the royal governor. Bernard was using a show of military force to intimidate, punish, and plunder Hancock due to his unsupportive politics. The *Liberty* was confiscated and turned into a revenue boat (a shore patrol boat used to chase down smugglers). She was finally burnt to the waterline by angry Patriots in Rhode Island. As for John Hancock, he was charged with smuggling Madeira wine and for reloading the *Liberty* with oil and tar without giving bond, violating British Acts of Trade. It was determined that Hancock had to pay a fine of £9,000 for smuggling. Hancock retained John Adams as his counsel. Five months after charges were filed, the case was mysteriously dropped due to insufficient evidence.

The "*Liberty* Affair" reinforced the British decision to put down unrest in Boston with a show of military strength. The decision had been provoked by Samuel Adams' Circular Letter of 1768, wherein he hoped to convince other colonies to join in coordinating resistance to the Townshend Acts. Lord Hillsborough, king's secretary for the colonies, saw this as the beginning of open rebellion and sent four regiments of the British Army to Boston to "support" royal officials. He also instructed Governor Bernard to order the Massachusetts legislature to revoke the Circular Letter. Hancock and the Massachusetts House voted "Nay" on rescinding the letter and instead drew up a petition demanding Governor

Bernard's recall to England. When Bernard returned to England in 1769, Bostonians celebrated.

But the British troops remained, and tensions between Redcoats and civilians soon escalated and resulted in the killing of five civilians in the Boston Massacre of March 1770. Contrary to popular belief, neither Hancock nor any of the Sons of Liberty were involved in the incident, but afterwards, Hancock led a committee to demand the removal of the troops from Boston. In a meeting with the *new* royal governor, Thomas Hutchinson, and the British officer in command, Colonel William Dalrymple, Hancock asserted that there were 10,000 armed colonists ready to take action and march into Boston if the troops did not leave. Hutchinson figured that Hancock was bluffing, but realized that the soldiers were between a rock and a hard place as long as they were stationed within the town. Dalrymple agreed to remove the regiments to Castle William. Hancock was the acclaimed hero of the day for his role in the withdrawal of "his majesty's" troops, and his reelection to the Massachusetts House in May was nearly unanimous.

With the repeal of the Townshend duties in 1770, Boston's boycott of British goods ended. Things quieted down in Massachusetts, but "hair trigger" tensions remained. Hancock sought to improve his relationship with Governor Hutchinson, who was also trying to influence Hancock away from Adams' circle of influence. In April 1772, Hutchinson approved Hancock's election as colonel of the Boston Cadets, a ceremonial militia unit whose primary function was to provide escort for the governor and the General Court in an air of pomp and circumstance. In May, Hutchinson thought he finally had Hancock when he approved Hancock's election to the Council (the upper chamber of the General Court, whose members were elected by the House, but subject to veto by the governor). Hancock's previous elections to the Council had been vetoed, but now Hutchinson allowed the election. Hancock declined the office, not wanting to appear to have been converted by the governor to a pro-Loyalist persuasion. But Hancock did use the improved relationship to resolve an ongoing difficulty. To avoid hostile crowds in Boston exerting undue influence upon the legislators, Hutchinson had been convening the legislature outside of town. Now he agreed to allow the General Court to sit in Boston once again, to the relief of the legislators and a positive effect on the populace.

Hutchinson had allowed himself to hope that he could win over Hancock and discredit Adams (he figured he was smarter and cleverer than those "provincial bumpkins"). And it seemed that Adams and Hancock were actually at odds: when Adams formed the Boston Committee of Correspondence in November 1772 to push for colonial rights, Hancock didn't join, creating the impression that there was a split in the Patriot ranks. But Hancock and Adams stood shoulder to shoulder once more in 1773 with the renewal of big political troubles. They cooperated in the revelation of the private letters of Thomas Hutchinson, in which the governor seemed to recommend *"an abridgement of what are called English liberties"* to bring order to the colony (those "provincial bumpkins" had the governor by the stack and swivel!). It seemed the governor was playing both sides against the middle while he attempted to appear supportive of both. The Massachusetts House, blaming Hutchinson for the military occupation of Boston, called for his removal as governor, too. That's two governors down!

Parliament's passage of the Tea Act in 1773 would only bring more turmoil. On November 5, Hancock was elected as moderator of the Boston town meeting that resolved that anyone who supported the Tea Act was an *"Enemy to America."* Hancock and others were working to prevent the tea from being unloaded after three tea ships had arrived in Boston Harbor. Hancock was at the meeting on December 16 where Samuel Adams said to the assembly, *"There is nothing more that this meeting can do for this country."* Hancock then told the crowd, *"Let every man do what is right in his own eyes."* Hancock didn't take part in the Boston Tea Party that night, but he did pull the verbal trigger. He approved of the action, but was careful to never publicly praise the destruction of private property.

Over the next few months, Hancock was disabled by gout, which would trouble him more and more in the coming years. By March 5, 1774, he had recovered enough to give the fourth annual Massacre Day speech at the ongoing annual protest of the causes of the Boston Massacre. Hancock's words denounced the presence of British troops in Boston, who he said had been sent there *"to enforce obedience to acts of Parliament, which neither God nor man ever empowered them to make."* The speech, probably written by Hancock with Samuel and John Adams, Joseph Warren, and other Sons of Liberty weighing in, was published and widely circulated, boosting Hancock's standing as a leading Patriot.

Now Parliament had responded to the Tea Party by closing the port of Boston, part of the Coercive Acts intended to strengthen British control of the colonies and break the Patriot movement—especially in New England. Hutchinson had been replaced as governor by General Thomas Gage, who arrived in May, and was privately friendly to the Patriot point of view. His wife was from New Jersey and he had American relatives, but he also had a job to do: Bring order and enforce British rule.

Gage soon dismissed Hancock from his post as colonel of the Boston Cadets. In October, Gage canceled the scheduled meeting of the General Court. In an act of open defiance, the House reconvened itself in Concord as the Massachusetts Provincial Congress, a new and improved congress independent of British control. John Hancock was elected as president of the Provincial Congress and was an important member of the Committee of Safety. The Committee of Safety created the first minutemen companies, consisting of elite militiamen who were to be ready for action in a minute's notice. You get the idea.

The Fight, the Flight, and the Flame of Independence

In December, the Provincial Congress elected Hancock as one of five delegates to the Second Continental Congress. Before he reported for duty in Philadelphia, the Provincial Congress unanimously re-elected him as their president in February 1775. John Hancock was the political King Kong of New England. His dual roles gave him enormous clout in Massachusetts. Seems he was on everybody's list, good and bad—the English authorities had been thinking about arresting him since early '74. So after attending the Provincial Congress in Concord in April 1775, Hancock and Samuel Adams decided that it was not safe to return to Boston before leaving for Philadelphia. They stayed instead at Hancock's Granddaddy's home in Lexington.

Finally, Gage received instructions from England on April 14, advising him *"to arrest the principal actors and abettors in the Provincial Congress whose proceedings appear in every light to be acts of treason and rebellion."* On the night of April 18, Gage sent out a larger than normal detachment of soldiers on the mission that would spark the American Revolutionary War. The real purpose of the British patrol was to seize and destroy military supplies that the colonists had stored in Concord. This wasn't the first time the Redcoats had gone out on what were known as "powder runs" to try and capture Patriot arms, but this patrol was much larger than most, so "trouble was a brewin'." Many believe that Gage also instructed his men to arrest Hancock and Adams. If he did, the written orders issued by Gage didn't reflect that action. They made no mention of arresting the Patriot leaders. Gage figured that he had nothing to gain by arresting Hancock and Adams, since other leaders would take their place, the colonists would see British soldiers as the enforcers of "tyranny," and the whole shootin' match would go further down the rabbit hole. He sure didn't have to wait long.

Even though Gage had decided against the capture of Hancock and Adams, Patriots initially believed the reports to the contrary. From Boston, Joseph Warren sent his most trusted messenger, Paul Revere, to warn Hancock and Adams that the "regulars were out" and might be trying to arrest them. Revere reached Lexington around midnight and gave the warning. Hancock still considered himself a militia colonel and wanted to take the field with the Patriot militia at Lexington, but Adams and Revere convinced him to stay out of the battle, claiming he was more valuable as a political leader than as a soldier. As Hancock and Adams made their escape, the first shots of the war were fired at Lexington. The long and bloody British retreat from Concord put an end to any speculation—John Hancock and Samuel Adams were wanted men. Following the battles, Gage issued a proclamation granting a general pardon to all who would *"lay down their arms, and return to the duties of peaceable subjects,"* with the exceptions of John Hancock and Samuel Adams. Outlaws, loose and runnin', seemed with the singling out of Hancock and Adams, General Gage had jumped down the rabbit hole head first.

Now with the war underway, Hancock joined the Continental Congress in Philadelphia with the other representatives of Massachusetts. On May 24, John Hancock was unanimously elected President of the Continental Congress, succeeding Peyton Randolph of Virginia. While his storied association with the Boston radicals made him irresistible to the radicals from other colonies, his wealth and social standing gave him a "leg up" with the more moderate and conservative members of the congress. Sounds like he was the perfect man to make thing happen and shake things up, but like every president of the congress, Hancock's authority was mostly limited to that of a presiding officer, you know, "the chair recognizes" kind of stuff, and he had to handle a great deal of official congressional correspondence. So much, in fact, that he had to hire clerks at his own expense to help with the paperwork. On August 1, after Congress recessed, Hancock married his fiancée Dorothy Quincy. The couple had two children who both died very young.

Hancock was president of Congress when the Declaration of Independence was written, adopted, and signed. He is well remembered for his large, flamboyant signature on the Declaration—it stood as the *only* signature on the Declaration for over a month, making him the only member of Congress who had committed treason until August 2, when the other delegates finally signed the finished copy. As president of the Congress, he sent a copy of the Declaration of Independence to Gen.

Washington to be read at his discretion and direction to the troops of the Continental Army. It gave the men something more to fight for during the coming months.

Hancock served in Congress through some of the darkest days of the Revolutionary War. The British drove Washington from New York and New Jersey in 1776, which caused Congress to flee to Baltimore, Maryland. Hancock and Congress returned to Philadelphia in March 1777, but were forced to move six months later when the British occupied Philly. Hancock wrote innumerable letters to colonial officials, raising money, supplies, and troops for Washington's Army. He chaired the Marine Committee (probably his favorite) and took pride in helping to create a small fleet of American war ships, including the USS *Hancock*, which was named in his honor. In October, after more than two years in Congress, President Hancock asked for a leave of absence. He asked George Washington to arrange a military escort for his return to Boston. Although Washington was shorthanded at the time, he still sent fifteen horsemen to protect Hancock on his journey home.

Back in Boston, Hancock was re-elected to the House of Representatives. His generosity had always made him popular, and even though his finances had taken a hard hit due to the war, he gave to the poor, helped support widows and orphans, and loaned money to friends. In December, he was re-elected as a delegate to the Continental Congress AND again as moderator of the Boston town meeting. He re-joined the Continental Congress in Pennsylvania in June 1778, but his time there was as brief as it was unhappy. While he was gone, Congress had elected Henry Laurens of South Carolina as its new president. Hancock had hoped to reclaim the presidential chair—disappointment number one. Hancock was also on the outs with Samuel Adams, seemed Adams was a bit peeved at young John's ostentatious qualities while in Congress—disappointment number two. Most importantly, he desperately missed his wife and newborn son. He was in Congress when, on July 9, 1778, the Massachusetts delegates joined the representatives from seven other states in signing the Articles of Confederation (our first Constitution). The remaining states were not yet up to signing, so the Articles would not be ratified until 1781.

Hancock returned to Boston later in July, motivated by a change of scenery and a chance to finally lead men in combat. Back in 1776, he had been appointed as the senior major general of the Massachusetts militia. Now that the French fleet had come to the aid of the American cause, General Washington had planned for General John Sullivan of the Continental Army to lead an attack on the British garrison at Newport, Rhode Island, in August 1778. Hancock formally commanded 6,000 militiamen in the campaign, but he let the professional soldiers do the planning and issue the orders. Turned out to be a fiasco nevertheless: French Admiral d'Estaing quickly abandoned the operation, then most of Hancock's militia deserted Sullivan's Continentals. Hancock was briefly criticized for the debacle, but emerged soon enough from his short and dubious military career with his popularity intact.

The new Massachusetts Constitution went into effect in October 1780. To the surprise of no one, Hancock was elected Governor of Massachusetts in a landslide, taking over 90 percent of the vote. In the absence of party politics, the contest was one of personality, popularity, and patriotism. Hancock was immensely popular and the unassailable embodiment of patriotism, given his personal sacrifices and his leadership of the Second Continental Congress. Hancock governed Massachusetts through the end of the Revolutionary War and into an economically troubled postwar period, winning re-election by wide margins time and again. He remained governor until his surprise resignation on January 29, 1785.

He was almost immediately re-elected to the Continental Congress. The congress wasn't what it used to be, having lost a lot of importance with the end of the war. Due to his already failing health, Hancock resigned from Congress late in 1786. He was not present at the Philadelphia Constitutional Convention and had misgivings about the new Constitution's lack of a bill of rights and its shift of power to a central government. In January 1788, Hancock was elected president of the Massachusetts ratifying convention, though he was sick and not present when the convention began, and was mostly silent during the salty debates. As the convention was drawing to close, he gave a powerful speech in favor of ratification. For the first time in years, Samuel Adams supported Hancock's position. Even with Hancock and Adams standing once again together, the Massachusetts convention narrowly ratified the Constitution by a vote of 187 to 168. Still, Hancock's support was, most likely, the deciding factor in the ratification.

Hancock spent his final few years as a figurehead governor. His health was finally failing him completely. He died in bed on October 8, 1793, at 56 years of age, and by order of acting governor Samuel Adams, the day of Hancock's burial was declared a state holiday. The lavish funeral was perhaps the grandest yet seen for an American citizen. I guess Adams didn't mind a bit of flash and flair at the funeral of his old friend. I'm certain that it made John Hancock very happy.

He was Washington's favorite mad, dashing cavalryman; "Light Horse Harry" was the original wild eyed Southern boy!

CHAPTER 10

Henry "Light Horse Harry" Lee

The First "Rough Rider"

Henry "Light Horse Harry" Lee was a blonde-haired, blue-eyed, fun-loving southern boy. George Washington called him *"a man of a dauntless heart and energy of spirit that suited him well to the cavalry and to war."* With credentials like that, how could he be anything less than the most wild-eyed, hell-for-leather cavalry officer of the American Revolution? You're right, he couldn't! His skill as a horseman, as well as his temperament, made him a natural "horse soldier." His daring raids and "unconventional style" made him legendary in his day and famous throughout the Continental Army. In fact, his brilliance at "fast moving" and unorthodox battle (the "flying campaign" as it was then known) is what earned him the nickname "Light Horse Harry." By age 23, Lieutenant Colonel Henry Lee had a reputation that was the envy of the Continental Army. His own men loved him, the Redcoats hated and feared him, and officers of both sides were awed and intimidated by his commanding presence and tactical genius. Henry Lee rode fast and fought hard. He was like a hero of Greek tragedy; like an Achilles, made more for combat and conflict, yet sadly conflicted by peace and plenty.

How Unconventional is Unconventional?

It was a dark and stormy night, well it was dark and stormy that January 26, 1756, when Henry Lee II welcomed his first son, Henry Lee III, to a rapidly changing Virginia. It was the time of the French and Indian War. Virginia militiamen stood shoulder to shoulder with "his majesty's soldiers" to defeat the threat of French domination of North America. Well, for Virginia at least, it was to maintain control of the Ohio River Valley, but side by side we stood. Then things changed—by the time young Henry was 10, Virginia was well on the way to open rebellion against King George, and the Lee family was leading the charge! Henry grew up on the family plantation, tutored by the best that his father could provide. He became convinced of the righteousness of the American cause early on, and after attending Princeton (class of 1773), events hurried the young Patriot to a career under arms.

With the outbreak of the Revolutionary War, Lee became captain of the Virginia Dragoons, attached to the 1st Continental Light Dragoons. Just to keep up, Dragoons of this time were fast cavalry units that could operate behind enemy lines in a recon and raider role or ride like cavalry, dismount, and fight as infantry. Lee demonstrated a "happy affinity" for raiding and reconnaissance and by 1778, he was promoted to major and given the command of his own corps (consisting of cavalry and light infantry). They became known as Lee's Legion. It was with these men that he earned his reputation as the most spectacular leader of light troops for the American side. Starting in '78, Lee's highly mobile group of light cavalry provided valuable service to Washington's Army, not only during major battles, but also by conducting recon and surveillance, engaging and disrupting enemy troop movement during long marches, destroying, stealing, and delaying delivery of supplies, the standard "raiding and skirmishing," and organizing expeditions that would go behind enemy lines and last for days or weeks at a time. Today we call these tactics guerrilla or maneuver warfare. Move fast, hit hard, disappear to hit again somewhere else! Light Horse Harry was a master at this kind of war. In September, Lee led a detachment of his dragoons in a mauling of a Hessian regiment at the Battle of Edgar's Lane. It was just a warm up.

In August 1779, Lee led part of his Legion in a daring raid on the British fortifications at Paulus Hook in New Jersey. Inspired by the success of General "Mad Anthony" Wayne's attack on the British-held fort at Stony Point, Lee led his men in a bold nighttime assault of the Redcoat fort at Paulus Hook. The plan for battle came apart early in the evening when almost half of his men were slowed down by an "unreliable" guide. So with less than 400 men, "Harry" adapted to the changing situation, improvised a new plan—on the go—overcame obstacles (a flooding swamp and unfordable river), and attacked before sunrise! Lee took almost 160 prisoners and killed or wounded 50 British soldiers, at least a dozen of whom were officers. The Legion lost two men killed, 3 wounded, and 7 MIA. While they were not able to hold the fort or destroy the cannon (seems there were British and Loyalist women and children being housed in the areas where "blowing things up" would have caused collateral damage, and that wasn't part of Lee's personality), they did steal away loaded down with valuable supplies and intelligence, as well as stealing a great deal of British Pride.

The victories at Stony Point and Paulus Hook gave the Patriot cause a huge boost in morale. So much so that on September 22, 1779, the Continental Congress voted to present Lee with a gold medal, a reward given to no other officer below a general's rank for the Legion's actions during the Battle of Paulus Hook. Lee was promoted to lieutenant colonel and, for his daring and tactical brilliance, was offered a position on

Washington's staff. Harry declined the "honor" and instead chose to go with his legion to the Southern Department of the war.

In January 1781, Lee's Legion raided the British outpost of Georgetown, South Carolina, with General Francis Marion's irregular militia, defeating and scattering the 200-man garrison while capturing all of the officers. Lee and his men were vital in screening the American Army of General Nathanael Greene from the British Army of Lord Cornwallis during their Race to the Dan River the following month. Lee reunited with General Francis Marion's militia, as well as the Continentals and militia of General Andrew Pickens, in the spring of 1781 to capture British outposts in South Carolina and Georgia. From Fort Watson, Fort Motte, Fort Granby, Fort Galphin, Fort Grierson, and Fort Cornwallis in Augusta, Georgia, (you can still find them running down a line from South Carolina to Augusta, GA), Lee and Marion cut a swath of success, victory, and innovation that had the British high command jumping through their tails trying to figure these two out!

They conducted a successful campaign of terror and intimidation against Loyalists in the South, highlighted by an encounter with Loyalist militia that is known as Pyle's Massacre. Seems that Lee's Legion had uniforms that looked an awful lot like the uniforms of the British outfit, Tarleton's Legion. As things work out, while Lee was chasing Tarleton, hopefully to the latter's utter destruction, they encountered a force of Loyalist militia almost 400 strong led by Dr. John Pyle. Light Horse Harry rode right into Pyle's camp without being challenged because of the uniform similarity, then all hell broke loose. The Loyalists lost almost 100 men killed and over 250 wounded while the remaining few fled to the hills. Pyle himself lost three fingers and an eye before being captured. The legion's losses again were unbelievably light: One horse KIA and a Patriot POW shot by the Loyalists before he could escape. This one-sided battle lasted less than 15 minutes. The chase lasted longer than the shooting, but that was less than an hour. For his part, when Banastre Tarleton heard the commotion, he saddled up the troops and hauled ass away from the shooting as fast as his horse could go.

Lee and his legion would go on to serve at the Battle of Guilford Court House, the Siege of Ninety-Six, and the Battle of Eutaw Springs. He was present for the surrender at Yorktown of the Army of Charles Cornwallis.

Lee resigned his commission after the British surrender at Yorktown and returned to Virginia a war hero and country gentleman. He would marry his 3rd cousin, Matilda Ludlow Lee. The wedding took place at Stratford Hall and was well attended by Lees from all over, as well as Harry's companions in arms from the service, including his friend and American icon General George Washington. During the war, Washington had become an ardent admirer of Lee for his spirit, dash, and relentlessness. It had grown into a fast friendship. Mr. and Mrs. Washington had contributed several pipes (that's almost 400 gallons) of their best Madeira wine to the festivities and a good time was had by all! The bride was "given away" by her uncle, Richard Henry Lee. She was called "the divine Matilda" because of her beauty, grace, and kindness. She had inherited Stratford Hall from her father and would live there with her new husband. It would have been nice to say "and they lived happily ever after," but that was not to be.

The daring and rugged young horse soldier was not a farmer. He was born for adventure and conflict, and without a war to fight, Lee found expression in politics. This led to Harry's election to the new Virginia House of Delegates. Tragically, after only eight years of marriage, Matilda passed away in 1790, leaving three young children and a broken-hearted husband. He would throw himself into his work to conceal his grief, and two years later, Harry was elected Governor of Virginia, serving three one-year terms. It was while living in Richmond that Lee met and fell in love with Ann Hill Carter of nearby Shirley Plantation. They were married in 1793. Leaving the governorship behind him, he took his new bride to Stratford.

In 1794, Lee was called to arms by President George Washington to put down the Whiskey Rebellion in western Pennsylvania. Lee commanded the 12,950 militiamen sent to crush the rebels, but the rebellion fizzled when faced with a stern military response and the rebels peacefully surrendered. In 1798, Light Horse Harry Lee was appointed a major general in the U.S. Army for the possible war with France. After all he had done, Lee is probably best remembered for his eulogy at the death of President George Washington. He was asked by Congress to deliver the final tribute for his beloved general, defining him for generations:

> *First in war, first in peace, and first in the hearts of his countrymen, President George Washington was second to none in humble and enduring scenes of private life. Pious, just, humane, temperate, and sincere; uniform, dignified, and commanding; his example was edifying to all around him as were the effects of that example everlasting.*

After the death of his hero and the turn of the century, Harry's fortunes began to change for the worse…and fast. Supporting a family of six, coupled with disastrous land investments, brought him to the edge of financial ruin. Lee was much better with bullets than with "greenbacks." He actually tried to find another war to fight, thinking he could "sign up" as part of the French Revolutionary Army. But his connection, the Marquis de Lafayette, had been imprisoned, ending that adventure. He was still fighting to keep the wolf from the door, when on January 19, 1807, in the large upstairs room at Stratford (where so many Lees had come into the world), Ann gave birth to their fifth son, Robert Edward. Yes! Robert E. Lee. Seemed Light Horse Harry's legacy of military genius and tactical brilliance would live on, no matter what!

Henry Lee III was re-commissioned as major general by President Thomas Jefferson in 1808, fearing war with Great Britain again. Lee organized and commanded the Virginia militia. He sought a commission at the outbreak of the War of 1812 from President James Madison, but was unsuccessful. As part of that effort, he published his *Memoirs of the War in the Southern Department of the United States* in 1812, where he summarized his military experiences during the Revolutionary War. Lee was deeply in debt and hoped the publication of his life's best work would change the tides of fortune (he had actually spent time in debtor's prison). With the money from his book and an inheritance from Ann's father, the family moved to Alexandria, where a new, more modest life was begun. Harry's eldest son, Henry IV, became master of Stratford, if you were wondering.

"Light Horse Harry" was a warrior for the rights of the American citizen. Well into his 50's, he stood almost alone against a mob as he defended a friend and freedom of the press in Baltimore. The man's newspaper had published unpopular articles concerning the war of 1812 and Lee had been beaten senseless by the mob that attacked the printer's business. The internal injuries and damage left him in constant physical pain. In the warm climate of the West Indies, he thought he might find healing, but his health continued to fail. Harry tried to get back home, but died on Cumberland Island, Georgia, in the home of the daughter of his former commander, Nathanael Greene.

Henry Lee III left a legacy of honor and military genius that would live on in his young son Robert Edward Lee. He was a Son of the Revolution, a son of the New Republic, and a valiant son of the Lees of Virginia. First to the fight, first for the right, and first in defense of his country.

Never judge a book by it's cover; this is especially true of Francis Marion. This small, thin, bookish man is still listed as one of the fathers of American Special Forces!

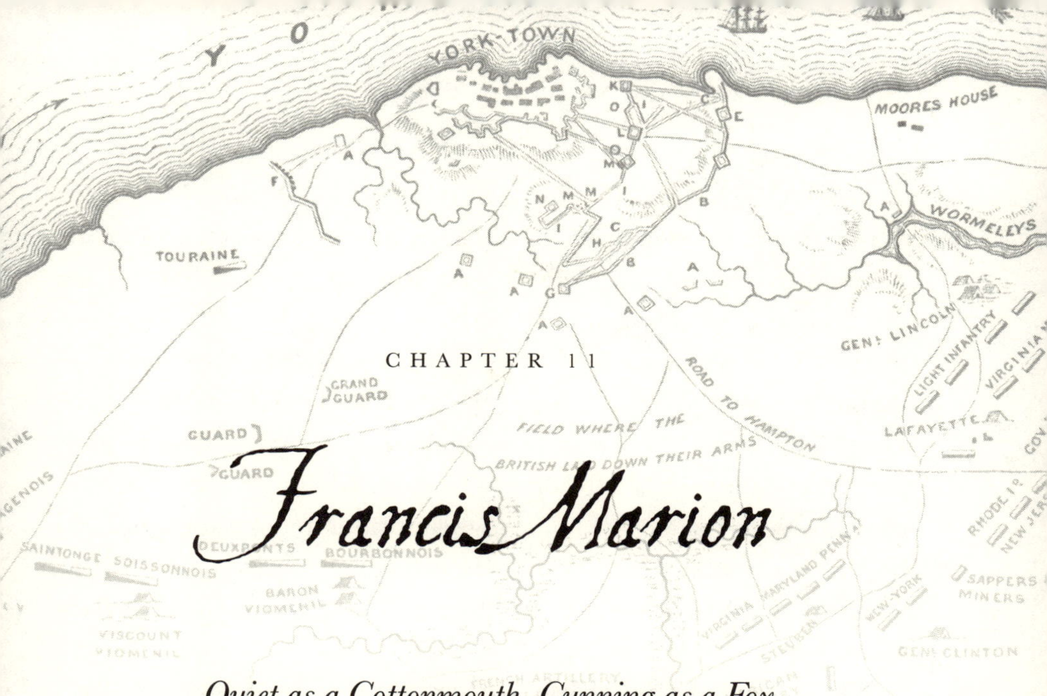

CHAPTER 11

Francis Marion

Quiet as a Cottonmouth, Cunning as a Fox

There they stood, the most raggedy group of rebels in the entire revolution. They were what had been salvaged from the disastrous loss of Charleston. Ragged they were, kinda bent and "dinged up," but these boys were far from broken. Fact was, these fellas were damn near unbreakable. They looked like hell itself, but they were soldiers to a man, and some of the very best. A few had been officers in one of the now defunct South Carolina Continental regiments, including "the boss" Lieutenant Colonel Francis Marion. Just one look would tell you that this boy belonged in the library! Marion was small and scrawny like a runt hounddog, and as plain and homely as an old maid. He didn't say much, but when he did, it was worth a listen. To top it off, this singularly unimpressive gentleman was so crippled by a badly healed broken ankle that he needed help to dismount from his horse. He didn't seem like the stuff of legend, but that's where you'd be wrong. That man was the "Swamp Fox" and his band of soldiers were some of the best guerrilla fighters in history!

When Col. Marion and his "outcast army" of 70 men showed up at the American camp on the Deep River, the Revolutionary cause in the southern colonies was in ruins. The Redcoats had seized Savannah and almost all of Georgia. A British army of more than 10,000, commanded by General Henry Clinton, had surrounded Charleston and trapped the main American army in the South. Led by General Benjamin Lincoln, the defenders of the city surrendered after a six-week siege, and the Patriot cause lost 6,700 Continental soldiers and militiamen. It was the worst defeat of the war. Within weeks, British troops ran roughshod over most of South Carolina. Up on the Deep River in central North Carolina, the Americans were building up strength to stop any further British penetration into the Carolinas and take back what had been lost. 1,400 Continental regulars had been sent by George Washington and formed the veteran core of the new army. They would be reinforced by militia from North Carolina and Virginia. Major General Horatio Gates, the "hero of Saratoga," had been sent by Congress to command.

Onto the scene of hectic preparation rode Marion and his band of refugees. The appearance of what General Gates considered to be the "most slovenly and rustic" mob in all of America brought little hope to the Patriot Army, but was the cause of much laughter. Gates decided there was no place for "these fellows" in *his* army. He happily went along with Marion's suggestion that he and his men be sent back to their native South Carolina to gather intelligence and harass the enemy.

So Marion and his boys (some were teenagers) rode back South...and on into legend. The campaign of the next year proved Marion to be a master at conducting guerrilla warfare and leading irregular troops. Time and again, he defeated larger and better-equipped units with few losses, making him one of America's (if not all history's) outstanding "unconventional" warriors. He was right up there with the best of the "snake eaters" (special forces), probably would have won the Green Beret, and is, in fact, credited as one of the "founding fathers" of US Army Ranger battalions.

Most remarkably, he never lost control of his men or himself, and he did not tolerate those who felt the urge for vengeance. During the war, he and his men were usually hunted and hungry, and always in the shadow of the gallows. Their unconventional style of warfare made them criminals in the eyes of the British—not soldiers. Even when faced with heartbreaking atrocities committed by his enemies (such as the capture and summary execution of his 16-year-old nephew, Gabriel), Marion maintained the highest standards of honor. He was a man who believed that the means must justify the end. American Independence was a high and holy calling, and for Marion, that meant only the best behavior would qualify the nation for those blessings. Whatever else he may have been, Francis Marion was a man of sterling character.

It Ain't the Size of the Dog in the Fight . . .

Born in 1732 and educated as well as his family could afford, Francis Marion was the youngest of seven children of a moderately prosperous Low Country planter. He showed a desire for an adventurous life by shipping out aboard a West Indies-bound merchant vessel at the age of 16. A few days out from Charleston, a whale smashed into the ship, sinking her within minutes. The six crew members drifted in a lifeboat for nearly a week. Two died of thirst and exposure before a passing ship rescued Marion and the other three survivors. Marion took it as a sign from the heavens and *hereafter* he would stick to adventures on land. So he turned to farming. He established a plantation not far from the Santee River about 45 miles north of Charleston. During the French and Indian War, he volunteered for the militia and served as the first lieutenant in a company of light infantry. Even though the Cherokee were British allies during the war, the way they were treated by the British caused them to seek revenge against the colonists. In the fighting that followed, Marion found himself celebrated as a hero.

Relations between Great Britain and her American colonies crumbled to the point of open rebellion in early 1775 and Marion was elected to the South Carolina Provincial Congress. When fighting broke out, he was commissioned a captain and company commander in South Carolina's 2nd Continental Regiment. His ability at molding green recruits into effective and disciplined soldiers was so successful that he was quickly promoted to major and regimental second in command.

Marion participated in most of the major campaigns in South Carolina and Georgia. On June 28, 1776, he was in the thick of things with Colonel William Moultrie and the 2nd Regiment, defending Fort Sullivan, an incomplete fortification of palmetto logs and sand at the entrance to Charleston Harbor. They repulsed an attack by nine British warships. Three years later, in the late summer and fall of 1779, he and his regiment participated in a badly mismanaged French/American expedition to recapture Savannah after it had fallen to the British that turned into a costly and empty frontal assault against well "dug in" British and Loyalist defenders.

Marion would have been among the troops the British bagged when Charleston fell in May 1780 had it not been for a lucky accident. Weeks before the British cut the last roads leading inland from the city, Marion attended a party during which the host locked his guests in to prevent them from leaving while they were "good 'n' drunk." The tea totaling Marion, in attempting to take his leave by jumping from a second-floor window, broke his ankle. He was sent home to heal and escaped capture when the city was cut off and forced to surrender.

As British soldiers ran rampant across the state after the fall of Charleston, Marion was now a wanted man. Ever moving to elude search parties, Marion became a phantom. When he heard of the new American army gathering in North Carolina, he made his way there with a few officers and associates from the 2nd Regiment to offer his services.

During Marion's brief acquaintance with General Gates, folks from the Williamsburg district (between the Black and Pee Dee Rivers in eastern South Carolina) rose up against the Redcoats and sent Marion a message asking him to come home and take command. He eagerly took up the offer. Gates, who was planning his move against the British at Camden (the inland base of English operations), told Marion "go, and quickly" or words to that effect, and gave him orders "*to destroy all the watercraft along the Santee River.*" Gates hoped (but had little confidence) that Marion's small force of insurgents would frustrate British efforts to reinforce Camden and that they could hinder the Redcoat retreat when Gates had, once again, "won the day" with his "brilliant strategy and well-tuned army."

When Marion returned to his stomping grounds, he found that the Redcoats had completely obliterated the pacification and occupation effort of their recent conquest in the backwoods and swamps of the Carolinas. Patriot soldiers had been assured and reassured that they need only "*lay down their arms, give their paroles, and take up their previous employments to return to good standing with the king.*" Later it came out that once men renewed their "allegiance to the Crown," the British command expected them to join the fight against their former brothers in arms! Putting that together with the looting and plundering by the Redcoats occupying the region and the revenge-minded actions of local Tories, and well...you can see where this was going! Guerrilla bands sprang up all around the state: Marion in the South, Thomas Sumter, "the Gamecock" as he was called for his defiant and combative personality, in the West, and the "Wizard Owl" Andrew Pickens in the north. For having so deftly hammered an American army "in the field," it seemed now the British had bitten off more than they could chew...or swallow.

At the outset, Marion commanded four companies of Carolina irregulars. Following his orders from Gates, Marion took 50 men and went to cut the British line of communications along the Santee River between Charleston and Camden. He was on the upper Santee when he got the distressing news that Gates had been trounced badly by Lieutenant General Charles Lord Cornwallis in battle near Camden on August 16. Half of Gates' 4,000 men were killed, wounded, or taken prisoner, and the remainder of the American army had fled back to North Carolina.

Seemed like Marion and his men were all that stood between the Redcoats and absolute victory.

...It's the Size of the Fight in the Dog!

Now, a man of more wisdom and less fight might have concluded that this was a good time to "go to ground" with his small numbers, but Francis Marion saw things a little bit different than most folks. He figured that sitting on the enemy's main line of communications, the Santee River, presented an opportunity. In the dark hours just before dawn on the morning of August 20, he and his men opened for business. They surprised a detachment of British regulars camped near Nelson's Ferry (the main crossing on the upper Santee). Attacking from two directions, "Marion's Men" (as they came to be known) killed or captured 24 of the enemy and rescued 150 Continental soldiers from a desperate fate as POW's, while suffering only one man killed and another wounded. Two weeks later, Marion and his gang were back in action. A Loyalist (Tory) militia had gathered at Britton's Neck, a spit of land formed by the junction of the Great and Little Pee Dee Rivers. Marion and his men rode through the night and at "dawn's early light," swept through the Tory camp, raising all kinds of hell, killing some and scattering the rest. Next, they moved up the Little Pee Dee to attack yet another Tory militia. When this group met him in greater numbers than he expected and were "ready to rumble," Marion faked a retreat, drawing the Tories out from their fortified positions to chase after him, then BAM! He sprung an ambush, utterly defeating them at a place called Blue Savannah. Marion was truly "open for business" and business was good!

Colonel Marion had shown that he understood the necessity of aggressiveness and audacity in sustaining the morale not only of his own troops, but of the entire Patriot cause in the South (his first and most important mission), and in keeping the enemy off balance. But he was equally clever in knowing when to back off. When Lord Cornwallis sent 800 British regulars and Loyalist troops to hunt him down after the unprecedented early success of his first actions, Marion wisely disbanded for the time being and sent his men to their homes while he rode to North Carolina. For the better part of a year, the Swamp Fox and his brigade roamed the region between the Pee Dee and Santee Rivers in South Carolina and brought mayhem, havoc, and death to the British regulars as they repeatedly defeated larger and stronger forces.

As soon as this first British expedition gave up, Marion returned. He gathered his band of guerrillas, rallied the local patriots, and sent the Loyalists who had come to hold the Williamsburg area packing. Face it, it's just dumb to mess with the dog in his own yard!

On September 24, hearing that a BIG group of Loyalists were building a small fort at Shepherd's Ferry on Black Mingo Creek (the largest crossing north of Georgetown), Marion and his brigade went out on another night attack. When the sound of their horses galloping across a bridge alerted enemy sentries, Marion hurried his men across the stream, splitting them in three, and attacking from all directions at once. But the Tories had had enough warning to form up and their first volley caught one of Marion's squadrons riding over an open field, inflicting many casualties.

A bitter fight followed, ending only when another of Marion's squadrons attacked the Tories from the rear, killing and wounding most and scattering the rest into the swamps. This battle was the last before harvest season and most of Marion's men returned to their homes to bring in the year's crop. As for Marion, for the first time he set up shop at the secret hideout that became part to his legend: Snow's Island. It was located on the west side of the Great Pee Dee, just below where it joins with Lynches River in the southeast part of the state. It was protected by a creek, a lake, broad belts of cypress swamp, and thick canebrakes. If you found your way in, you would never get out—the bugs, snakes, and gators would see to that. For the next six months, Marion used this naturally well-hidden redoubt as a supply depot, recruiting station, and safe haven.

By late October, Marion's brigade was back in business again. His men fought without any expectation of pay, provided their own food, horses, and weapons, and lived off the land and what they could capture from the British. Marion refused to let his men loot or plunder and few ever would. To them, all this was a fight for home and for honor. Hearing that the Tories had set up a recruiting station at a mustering ground close to the Black River, Marion led another lightning strike. He led 150 men, covered 40 miles, crossed three rivers, and struck the enemy position at midnight on October 25. The Tories were taken by complete surprise. Those who weren't killed or wounded beat feet into the nearby Tearcoat Swamp and many who were wounded did the same! Marion's raiders rode off with 80 new muskets and an equal number of horses and saddles.

A fuming Lord Cornwallis now sent his most daring and aggressive officer to capture or kill Marion. Lieutenant Colonel Banastre Tarleton commanded the British Legion, a combined-arms force of cavalry and light infantry that rode hard and fought harder. Patriots called Tarleton "the Butcher" after his cavalry literally cut down a retreating detachment of Virginia Continentals at the Battle of Waxhaws in 1780, killing and wounding many as they tried to surrender.

Tarleton, with the thousand men of his command, came after Marion with guns ablazin'. During the night of November 9, Tarleton's legion and Marion's brigade nearly collided at a plantation near the Santee, each side's scouts locating the "enemy" at nearly the same moment. Marion's scouts were faster, and his force was only half the size of Tarleton's, so clever beat audacious, and he decided to make a run for it. The chase lasted all through the night and on into the following day. After a pursuit of 33 miles through swamps, creeks, bushes, brambles, and forests, Tarleton found himself caught on the banks of one more wretched quagmire (Ox Swamp) with not a sight or sound of his prey. Turning to his officers, he said, *"Come, my boys! Let us go back, and we will soon find the game cock* [Sumter], *but as for this damned old fox, the devil himself could not catch him."* Tarleton had had enough. He had been outrun and out foxed, and Marion had his "nom de guerre" (war nickname), the Swamp Fox.

In December 1780, Lord Cornwallis wrote of his discouragement in a letter to his superior, Sir Henry Clinton, *"Col. Marion has so wrought on the minds of the people...that there was scarcely an inhabitant between the Santee and the Pedee, that was not in arms against us."* In recognition of his meritorious service to the state, South Carolina's patriot governor-in-exile promoted Marion to the rank of brigadier general in the state militia.

You're in the Army Now!

Having been unsuccessful at finding or frustrating Marion and his brigade of raiders in their work, the British turned their attention to protecting the line of communications that Marion was sure to attack. From Charleston to their inland base at Camden and on to the frontier settlement of Ninety-Six (so called because it was 96 miles from the Cherokee capitol at Keowee), the Redcoats built fortified outposts all along the line, including Fort Watson, on the east side of the Santee, and Fort Motte, farther north, all capable of ensnaring Marion's brigade for good.

But things were changing in the South. 1780 had been a hard year. Since September, all that had stood between Washington's Army far to the north and the British War machine had been the Guerrillas of Marion, Sumter, and Pickens. 1781 would be very different. Congress had dismissed Gates and sent Major General Nathanael Greene to command the American army in the South. Greene reached the army's camp near Charlotte, North Carolina, in late November. He absolutely recognized the importance and necessity of coordinating his efforts with Marion, Sumter, and Pickens. Greene once said that one guerrilla was worth 10 militiamen, and he had come with a strategy that would integrate the guerrillas and magnify their effectiveness.

In January 1781, Greene deployed Lieutenant Colonel Henry Lee and *his* Legion (an American force similar to that of Tarleton, made up of both infantry and cavalry) to the Pee Dee with instructions to undertake operations with Marion's brigade. Lee reported that it was only thanks to a chance encounter with one of Marion's foraging parties that he was even able to find the well-hidden guerrilla camp.

Marion and Lee "hunted" together on and off for the next eight months. They made a curious pair. At 25, Lee was the very image of the chivalrous warrior: ruggedly handsome, blonde-haired with piercing blue eyes, tall and strong, dashing and daring, gregarious and sociable. Marion, by contrast, was nearly twice Lee's age, hook-nosed, dark-haired and dark-eyed, socially reserved, and soft spoken. Where Lee would drink with the best of them, Marion drank a weak mixture of vinegar and water; Lee cut the image of the valiant cavalier, and Marion was so indifferent to affecting a martial air that he habitually and loyally wore his old leather 2nd Regiment cap even after it was "somewhat singed" from once being too close to a campfire.

Yep, they seemed as different as night and day, but the two formed a highly effective partnership. Both were audacious and inventive, aggressive without being reckless, and wary and discerning when risking the lives of their men. They understood the age-old adage that you don't win a war by dying for your country, you win it by making the other guy die for his country. They demonstrated this skill and understanding in late January in what may have been their most daring raid of all on the British stronghold of the port of Georgetown. It was an intrepid and complex operation that used a midnight landing from the sea by Marion's raiders, coupled with a simultaneous attack against the enemy defensive works by Lee. Went down like a charm. Early on, the British commandant was taken prisoner and most of the town was overrun. When it became clear that complete victory would require house-to-house fighting and a potentially costly assault on the town's main redoubt, Marion and Lee took their valuable prisoners and "swag" and faded back into the shadows of night from whence they had come…Know when to hold 'em, know when to fold 'em.

After the raid on Georgetown, Lee returned to join Greene's army in preparation for the upcoming battle of Guilford Courthouse, and so Marion was once again flying solo. In March 1781, the British made their third attempt to destroy his command. Colonel Francis Lord Rawdon (now in command of the Redcoats in South Carolina after Lord Cornwallis moved north in pursuit of Greene) planned a double-edged attack on the base at Snow's Island. The main strike force (the Hammer) consisted of 500 Loyalist militia and rangers under the command of Lieutenant Colonel John Watson. They were to move east from Fort Watson (yeah, named after the man) along the Santee River Road north of Nelson's Ferry. A second force (the Anvil) consisting of 300 Loyalists, was sent east from Camden to work down the Great Pee Dee River from the north, cut off Marion's retreat to North Carolina, and be ready for when the hunters drove Marion into their waiting guns.

But, as with previous expeditions against Marion, this outing seemed snake-bit from the start. Informed by locals of Watson's advance, Marion and 400 men were ready and laid an ambush along the Santee River Road at the Wiboo Swamp. When Watson got close, he inadvertently avoided stumbling into Marion's trap, but the Tories caught it straight in the teeth trying to cross the narrow causeway through the swamp. The two brawled again two days later. This time at Mount Hope Swamp, where Marion's men had already removed the bridge over the creek. But on this occasion, Watson's men blasted their way through Marion's defenses by loading their cannons with grapeshot. Watson tried to hoodwink Marion into thinking he intended to continue east along the Santee, but instead Watson went north and headed for the Lower Bridge over the Black River.

Marion figured out Watson's real plans and sent a group of 70 mounted riflemen to race across the open country to beat him to the lone remaining bridge. They arrived in time to destroy that sucker and block the crossing. After Marion's marksmen stymied every attempt by the Tories to ford the river (Watson dejectedly admitted that he'd never seen such shooting in his life), Watson "holed up" at a nearby plantation where there were few trees to provide cover for Marion's men. There he stayed for nearly a week.

By March 15, Watson was in tough shape. He was now so desperate that he requested (under a flag of truce) that Marion allow his wounded to be taken to Charleston—a request Marion granted. By March 20, Watson's troops were utterly exhausted and out of provisions, but Marion's expert riflemen made foraging impossible. So Watson and his men broke out, bolting for the safety of Georgetown 30 miles away. Marion, again, was way ahead of Watson—he had already destroyed the bridge over the Sampit River, the only avenue of escape. When Watson's frantic troops reached the ruined bridge, they plunged into the stream and desperately tried to make the crossing just as Marion's main force came up and shot them up like fish in a barrel. The Tories panicked and fled. 20 were killed and 38 wounded while Marion lost only a single man. Watson's command limped into Georgetown late the following day, its remaining wagons overflowing with wounded.

The humiliating thrashing of Watson's much larger force in what's become known as "the Bridges Campaign" was Marion's most impressive sortie to date. But even as his command celebrated its triumph over Watson, a messenger arrived with shattering news: that "other" regiment (the Anvil) had discovered and destroyed Marion's base at Snow's Island. All the weapons, ammunition, and stores stockpiled over the previous months now lay in ashes from burning or were scattered into the waters of the surrounding swamps, lakes, and rivers.

Marion and his brigade were hot! They set off at once for the Pee Dee, determined to get revenge. But the Tories had already scurried like rats back to Camden, contented with this partial success from an otherwise embarrassing campaign. Right then, when it seemed they were literally "up the creek," riders from General Greene finally caught up with Marion to tell him that the Southern Army, after a hard-fought battle against Lord Cornwallis at Guilford Courthouse, was re-entering South Carolina! Greene sent orders that Marion and Lee were back in business together and they were to attack the line of British forts between Charleston and Camden. First up…Fort Watson. The outpost occupied an old Santee

Indian mound that rose almost 30 feet above the surrounding area. A stockade was at the top of the mound, with abatis (rows of sharpened stakes) driven into its sloping sides. Six weeks earlier, Fort Watson had successfully fended off an attack by Thomas Sumter and his boys, 18 of whom were killed in the fighting. That was then, this was now.

Marion and Lee had no cannons, yet they took the fort after an eight-day siege. One of Marion's officers came up with the idea of constructing a tower made of logs that was taller than the fort. Trees were cut, logs were nailed and roped together, and the tower was raised in a single night. When dawn came and the British discovered that American riflemen could now shoot down into the stockade, they surrendered without further argument.

The war in South Carolina had reached the turning point. On April 25, the Redcoats lost a quarter of their army in a ruinous attack upon Greene's forces at the Battle of Hobkirk's Hill, just outside of Camden. Two weeks later, they set fire to the town and marched south. Marion and Lee were reunited once more to attack Fort Motte, the principal British storehouse and magazine between Charleston and their strongholds farther upstate. Fort Motte consisted of a stockade that encircled the hilltop mansion of Rebecca Motte, a wealthy planter's widow who was a devoted daughter of liberty. General Lee proposed burning out the British by shooting flaming arrows into the mansion's dry cedar roofing shingles. Mrs. Motte was "all in" and even supplied a high-powered bow owned by her late husband. With several well-placed shots from the bow and a few rounds from the cannon brought by a forward-thinking Lee, the roof was on fire and the Yankees were chanting "burn, baby, burn!" The British found it impossible to douse the flames, and Fort Motte surrendered. Two down.

The British position in South Carolina crumbled. In short order, three more British forts surrendered. At the end of May, Marion and his brigade appeared in front of Georgetown and started digging siege trenches. But the British and Loyalists and their local supporters lost hope, boarded three ships, and sailed away to Charleston. By July 1781, the British abandoned Ninety-Six, their last remaining post deep in the interior of South Carolina. Marion's brigade distinguished itself on raids conducted outside of Charleston in July and August, and again when it fought as a regular unit with Greene's army in the Battle of Eutaw Springs. The smaller British army suffered 40 percent casualties, wrecking their combat effectiveness.

Until the British evacuated Charleston for good in December 1782, the fighting was limited mostly to small encounters between foraging parties on the outskirts of the town. Marion would not put his men in harm's way unnecessarily during these final days of the war. "Encouraged" to attack British troops who had landed upriver from Charleston to obtain water, he replied, *"If ordered to attack, I shall obey, but with my consent, not another life shall be lost…Knowing, as we do, that the enemy are on the eve of departure, so far from offering to molest, I would rather send a party to protect them."* That was the quality of Francis Marion.

Politics called again upon Marion. In January 1782, he took a seat in the reconstituted South Carolina state assembly. In the war's final stages and after peace came, he supported measures to foster reconciliation with the state's Loyalists. On one notable occasion, he prevented his men from lynching a notorious Tory commander.

When the war ended at last, Marion returned to a quiet life. His plantation had been badly damaged and burned during the fighting, but in the mid-1780s, he married his wealthy cousin (happened a lot back then) Mary Videau and lived in a comfortable, if more modest way. True to form, when the state legislature granted militia commanders "immunity from civil or criminal liability for actions undertaken by their troops during the war," Marion refused to have his name enrolled. He said, *"If I have given any occasion for complaint, I am ready to answer in property and in person…If, in a single instance, in the course of my command, I have done that which I cannot fully justify, justice requires that I should suffer for it."*

In 1790, Marion served in the convention that drafted South Carolina's state constitution, but after that, he retired from public life. He died at the age of 63 in 1795. The best tribute came in a letter that Nathanael Greene wrote to Marion just after the fall of Fort Watson. Greene noted that Marion, despite fighting against superior foes, had kept *"alive the expiring hopes of an oppressed militia."* Greene continued: *"To fight the enemy bravely with the prospect of victory is nothing, but to fight with intrepidity under the constant impression of defeat, and to inspire irregular troops to do it, is a talent peculiar to yourself."*

Well done, Swamp Fox!

He was as fiery and feisty as a bantam rooster, and a snake-eating son of a gun! He took the war to the British when the only real hope was dying for the cause.

CHAPTER 12

Thomas Sumter

"I'm your Huckleberry!"

Thomas Sumter was an Indian fighter's Indian fighter and a country boy's country boy. He was born August 14, 1734, on the frontier—log cabin on the outskirts of Hanover County, near present day Richmond, but at the time it wasn't much of a "goin' concern." His daddy died while Thomas was still young, and as he grew up tending Mom's herds of sheep and such, he also plowed fields and built fences for the neighbors. That left little time for formal education, but it kept the family fed and going. For recreation, he would wander in the woods and mountains of Virginia, becoming quite the frontiersman (Bear Grylls eat your heart out). While still in his youth, Sumter enlisted in the Virginia militia and was so "wood crafty" that during the Anglo-Cherokee war, he quickly rose to the rank of sergeant. It was the experience and knowledge that Thomas Sumter gained during that war that made him the "greatest plague" in the South to Lord Cornwallis and earned him the nickname "Fighting Gamecock" for his toughness and resourcefulness during the Revolution.

Travelin' Man!

After the Anglo-Cherokee war was over, Sumter embarked on a "peace-making" mission. It was known as the "Timberlake Expedition" and was highly successful. The expedition was led by Henry Timberlake, a Virginia gentleman, and the company consisted of Timberlake's servant, an interpreter named John McCormack, and Thomas Sumter as guard and guide. The purpose was to renew friendship and "old ties" with the Cherokee people of the Overhill district (pretty much eastern Tennessee and Kentucky and parts of Northern Georgia). The journey would last almost 18 months and the travelers had many adventures. Early in the venture, but still late in the fall, the four men explored a cave close to the river. Upon their exit, they found that one of the canoes had drifted almost half a mile downstream. Sumter was obliged to swim the distance in freezing cold water to save the canoe.

Finally, in a freezing drizzle, the company arrived at one of the major Cherokee towns, Tomotley, on December 20, 1761. They were warmly greeted by the town's chief, Ostenaco (Mankiller), who gave them food, warm clothing and blankets, and invited them to a peace pipe ceremony. Ostenaco brought them to a "great council" where all the chiefs of the Overhill Cherokee were in attendance. There, Ostenaco literally "buried the hatchet" (a tomahawk) in the ground to signify the peace that now existed between the Cherokee nation and the colonists. The group attended peace ceremonies in every major Cherokee settlement in the region, which made Mr. Timberlake very ill, but it didn't seem to bother Sumter at all.

When the time came for the expedition to return home, Ostenaco did them the honor of personally accompanying them with 1,000 warriors back on the "Great Warpath Road" through the pass back to the Virginia settlements. Ostenaco and two more of the Cherokee Chiefs went with Sumter and Timberlake to Williamsburg where they were warmly welcomed by the people and the Governor, and a "state dinner" was held in their honor at William and Mary College. In April 1762, Ostenaco said he wanted to meet the king of England. Timberlake arranged the voyage and Sumter again volunteered as guard and guide.

They left from Jamestown in May and arrived in London in early June. The fierce and exotic Cherokee warriors were an instant sensation in England, drawing large crowds wherever they went. They were well received by the government and had a private audience with King George III, who was gracious and highly impressed with the "manners and courteous behavior" of the wild warrior chiefs. Sumter and the Cherokee would return to Charleston, South Carolina, in August, but Timberlake would remain in England. Sumter was in a hard way financially. He was now stuck in Charleston without the means to make it home. He petitioned the Virginia legislature to reimburse him for the costs incurred with both trips, but was refused. And to add insult to injury, Virginia sent sheriffs to arrest Sumter and put him in debtors' prison (can't get out 'til you pay yer dues) for the money he had borrowed to help fund the Timberlake expedition!

Now, Sumter had friends, and one of them, Joseph Martin, heard of poor Tom's plight and came to the rescue. Martin gave Sumter 10 guineas and a tomahawk to obtain his release—I guess Sumter could buy his way out or fight, I'm sure he was game for either one! 30 years later, when Martin and Sumter met up once more, Sumter repaid the amount, in full, on the spot—man of honor, that Thomas Sumter. As soon as he was free from prison, he bid farewell to "ol' Viginny" and settled in South Carolina, ultimately in Stateburg in the hills of the Claremont district (now Sumter). He married Mary Jameson in 1767. Together they opened several dry goods stores, were successful planters, and became pillars of the community. It wasn't long before Thomas Sumter was a man of standing, leading *his own* militia group.

Things were quiet for a time and business was good, then the British parliament started to pass those acts that caused people to be angry about a faraway government meddling in local affairs! Sumter was one of the most agitated in the Carolinas. When the fighting started in Lexington and Concord, Sumter re-upped (joined the South Carolina State Militia), and by February 1776 was Colonel of the 2nd Regiment of the South Carolina Line! He saw fighting at the Battle of Fort Sullivan, when the British first tried to take Charleston and were sent packing with heavy losses. And then, in 1778-79, he fought to repel the British invasion of Georgia, but that one didn't go as well. But it was during this time that Sumter was appointed Brigadier General of all South Carolina troops, a rank he would hold for the remainder of the war. After the fall of Charleston, Thomas Sumter showed his true value to the Patriot cause as one of the greatest leaders of guerrilla fighters in history.

After the fall of Savannah, Sumter's regiment was mustered into Continental service (no longer state, but national troops) and placed under the command of General Benjamin Lincoln. Sumter felt that he was "out of the war" so to speak because he held no Continental rank, but after Cornwallis sent Banastre Tarleton on the rampage through South Carolina, things changed. First, the fall of Charleston and the surrender of Lincoln's entire army, and second, Tarleton and his famous "legion" of Loyalists attacked and burned Sumter's plantation and home. Sumter quickly put together a band of "irregular" militia.

It was a fairly "democratic" operation as far as military standards were concerned, come and go as you please, sometimes his raiders numbered over 1,000 men, and others as few as 500. They marauded and terrorized British columns almost at will. Early on in the guerrilla war, Sumter and his militia had captured 300 Redcoats and 80 wagons of supplies. They were moving north to support the new Continental Army under Gen. Horatio Gates, now moving south from Charlotte, NC, when Tarleton's legion effectively surprised them in an early morning attack. Tarleton's scouts overwhelmed Sumter's sentries before they could raise a warning and Tarleton's cavalry charge threw Sumter's camp into a panic. Sumter (who was, most likely, asleep under one of the wagons) barely evaded capture and made it to Charlotte all by himself. It was called the Battle of Fishing Creek, though it wasn't much of a battle. Sumter had been whooped by Tarleton…it was time to get even. There was a lot to get even for, too.

Cornwallis had soundly trounced Gates at the Battle of Camden. There were no effective American forces between Cornwallis and Philadelphia (still far to the north but completely undefended), Washington's Army (who had their hands full with the British in New York), and a Redcoat victory! The only thing that could (or would) stand between them were the guerrilla fighters of South Carolina. Guerrilla bands sprang up all around the state: "The Swamp Fox" Francis Marion in the South, the "Wizard Owl" Andrew Pickens in the North, working closely with the continental troops, and our boy, Thomas Sumter, "the Gamecock" as he was called for his defiant and combative personality, in the West.

But Sumter had a particular "bone to pick", and he figured the best way to get Tarleton "back in the ring" was to cause the British so much trouble that Cornwallis would have no choice but to send Tarleton after him again. Sumter's militia group caused havoc, mayhem, and chaos all across the Carolina backcountry. Most Loyalists wouldn't venture far from their fortified strongholds for fear of the man. Redcoat supply columns to the line forts were being ravaged by Sumter. Cornwallis was having to use so many "regular" troops to patrol in western Carolina that his options were growing limited for offensive action against the next American army, under General Nathaniel Greene, now mustering near Charlotte.

Sumter's raids and "incursions" against British interests in the South finally became so troublesome to Cornwallis that he sent Major James Wemyss and the 63rd Regiment (plus some Loyalist cavalry) to capture and destroy Sumter's militia. Wemyss was a devout "second teamer," but after the fiasco of Fishing Creek, Cornwallis figured he could handle Sumter while Tarleton was sent to neutralize Marion.

Turned out to be a disastrous decision. Thomas Sumter was nobody's fool and he would long remember the lessons of Fishing Creek. Security was "lock down tight"—especially at night—and there was always a redundant deployment of sentries, pickets, and skirmishers. And last but not least, "if it ain't one of us…shoot it!"

Major Wemyss and his fellas caught up with Sumter at a place known as Fishdam Ford at "zero dark thirty" (means 12:30 am, but is used to say "in the wee hours") on November 9, 1780. Did I say caught up with? What I mean is he thought he had Sumter "dead to rights," so he moved hastily in a surprise attack (hell, it had worked at Fishing Creek) and found himself caught in a crossfire from Sumter's men who, having had appropriate warning, had hidden themselves in the shadows of the woods and now were shooting up Wemyss' entire command. End result was that Major Wemyss was wounded, captured, and forced to surrender. The pursuit had turned into an embarrassing rout for the 63rd and Cornwallis would now send Tarleton out to fix Sumter once and for all.

Time for a quick review. Things had *not* been going according to plan since the victory at Camden for Cornwallis. Major Ferguson's Loyalists had been completely destroyed by Patriot militia at the Battle (more of a turkey shoot) of King's Mountain. Major Wemyss and the 63rd had been shot to pieces at Fishdam Ford. Cornwallis was counting on his most feared and effective officer to turn things around. Banastre Tarleton was hated by the American side for his actions after the battle of Waxhaws where numerous Americans were shot down—while surrendering!—by Tarleton's Loyalists. Now Tarleton was coming for Sumter; no love lost and no quarter given…by either side.

On November 18, 1780, some of Sumter's "crew," now over 1,000 strong, caught up with Tarleton's "legion" as they bathed and watered their horses in the Broad River. The Patriots fired enough shots off to get the Loyalists' and Redcoats' attention and the chase was on! Tarleton waited for evening and crossed the Broad River on flatboats. All 500 men (dragoons and light infantry) moved out stealthily in the darkness. Now, Tarleton had yet to be defeated by any militia forces anywhere, and caution was a foreign thought to the man (give credit where it is due—Banastre Tarleton was the best cavalry officer in the British ranks) and this was the second time he was going up against Sumter. Tarleton figured by the evening of the 20th, he would be two and 0 vs Sumter.

Sumter had been aching for a rematch with Tarleton. He knew the countryside and he figured he knew Tarleton; "charge first, regroup, and charge again. The rest will take care of itself." So Sumter's 1,000 moved to a hilltop plantation house called Blackstock's Farm that offered the best defensive position in the district. Sumter placed his riflemen in partially finished outbuildings (they were log cabins that hadn't yet been chinked so the open spaces between the logs had yet to be filled in) and as skirmishers in the woods. The fields of the plantation had been newly plowed and cleared and offered excellent fields of fire. Tarleton's men would be under fire and in the open for hundreds of yards before they made contact with Sumter's main force. Now all Sumter had to do was wait…and it wasn't for long!

Late in the afternoon, Tarleton's cavalry came upon the plantation. Tarleton refused to wait for his infantry and artillery (kinda like George Custer at the Little Bighorn) and ordered a frontal assault by his leading squadrons. They were shot to bits. Next the light infantry made a bayonet attack and forced the militia line back close to the buildings hiding Sumter's riflemen. Remember those "backcountry rules" we mentioned before? You know, shoot the officers and sergeants first? The officers were down in the first exchange of fire and the rest of the group was ground up like raw meat. Tarleton finally ordered a general retreat and his fellas skedaddled back about two miles. Sumter, who was about as cautious as Tarleton, moved up to watch the retreat and "savor the moment" when a group of retreating Redcoats turned and shot off a last volley at the American officers. Sumter was severely wounded, shot in the chest and shoulder. He relinquished command to his senior colonel, John Twiggs, and would spend most of the next year recuperating.

Even with Sumter being put on injured reserve, revenge against Tarleton and his Loyalists was sweet. The Redcoat legion had suffered 92 killed and almost 100 wounded out of the original 500 men. Sumter had lost 3 men killed in action and 4 wounded—a very one-sided ass whoopin'. Tarleton would "fudge" his report of events to Cornwallis (if he hadn't, he may have been fired), claiming his losses were much less and Sumter's were much more. Tarleton even claimed that Sumter had been finished "for good." Wouldn't do that, ya don't want the ghosts showing up like the devil at prayers, now do ye? But even the wounding of the famous "Gamecock" gave the Patriots an advantage, now command under General Nathanael Greene would be completely united. There were no other general officers who figured they should be heading up the shootin' match down south. Tarleton was the man who gave Sumter his nickname. After the engagement at Blackstock's Farm, Tarleton said of Sumter, "*he fought like a Gamecock!*" Following the destruction of an entire unit, Cornwallis succinctly named Sumter "his greatest plague." So, Sumter got even with Tarleton, Greene got off on the "good foot," and Providence had once again frustrated the British advance.

After Sumter had healed up sufficiently to sit a horse, the war was all but over. He would serve in the new Congress of the U.S. government, as well as the Senate. He lived out his life on his plantation in Stateburg and passed in 1832 while rallying support for the States Rights argument of Vice President John Calhoon during the nullification crisis. He was 97 and the last general officer of the Revolutionary War to pass away. He died fighting, which I'm sure made Thomas Sumter happy to the end.

It wasn't just the message, it was about the delivery as well. Patrick Henry preached Liberty and Independence with the zeal and passion of a Pentecostal minister at a tent revival meeting!

CHAPTER 13

Patrick Henry

Fire Breathin' Lightning Rod of Liberty

An iconic symbol of America's struggle for liberty and self-government, Patrick Henry was a lawyer and Patriot who was always willing to stand alone if necessary, but preferred to be the voice of the young American conscience. He was a ready and willing firebrand in almost every step of the founding of America. Early on, he would sound off about the liberty and rights of the American people. As we shall see, he called for the recognition of religious freedom, personal liberties, and the right to keep and bear arms at a time when few others even understood the struggle that was underway. He dared to stand alone against the king and his bishops, the king and his parliament, and, quite literally, the king and his empire!

The Great Awakening

Patrick Henry was born in Hanover County, Virginia, in 1736, to John and Sarah Winston Henry. He grew up in a "house divided" as his dad was Anglican and his mother was Presbyterian (caused more hell than a little bit). But Patrick had a foot in both worlds, so to speak, from his youth. On the one hand, the world of God, King, and St. George, and on the other, the philosophies of the new Protestantism taught by his mother, her church, and the fire and brimstone sermons of the ministers of the Great Awakening; chief among them, George Whitfield. When Whitfield spoke, it was an "open air revival": outdoors, "calling down the thunder," and very well attended. Literally thousands would gather to hear every sermon. The man was the "rock star" of his day. It's estimated that over 1 million people came to hear Reverend Whitfield preach during his "North American Tour" (that would be the entire population plus the folks who attended twice).

Henry's mother was one of the latter, and young Patrick heard Mr. Whitfield on several occasions. He was deeply impressed by his manner of speaking—theatrical, emotional, powerful—and figured he was going to speak in that way when he got the chance. And he was deeply moved by Whitfield's message of faith, hope, and giving your heart to "the Good Cause." It would forever affect Patrick Henry's way of looking at the world. The Good Cause was Liberty and Henry was "all in."

Patrick's Father, John Henry, who had attended King's College and the University of Aberdeen, took over the education of his young son at home, including teaching him to read Latin. Ultimately, Patrick studied law, but for starters, he opened a business that would quickly fail (seemed his gifts lay elsewhere) and married Sarah Shelton in 1754. They were given a tobacco plantation, known as Pine Slash Farm, by Sarah's wealthy father as a wedding present. The soil had been hit hard by drought that season and by years under tobacco. In 1757, the main house burned down and for a time, the Henrys lived in the large "honeymoon cottage" on the property (really a converted barn, but hey, it was home). The couple and their two children would move to Hanover Tavern where Henry would begin to read (study) the law while helping his father-in-law run the tavern. They sold Pine Slash in 1764 when Henry began to practice law and in

1771, bought Scotchtown Plantation. Not long after, Sarah Henry would become severely mentally ill.

Sarah went downhill fast. Soon she was "a danger to herself and others" and was confined by a "Quaker shirt"—an early version of a straitjacket. Henry's friends, including a prominent doctor, advised him to have his wife committed to the county hospital (asylum). When he looked into the possibility, he was sickened by what he found—if committed, his wife would be chained to the wall of a small one-room cell by a leg iron. There were no windows, no sunlight, and no air circulation. There was only a chamber pot and a filthy mattress for furniture. There was no way Patrick Henry would allow his wife to suffer that fate.

So he built a two-room apartment in the basement of the main house at Scotchtown with big windows and a private garden, lots of sunshine and fresh air. Henry would personally care for his wife's needs every day: bathing, feeding, and taking her for walks in the garden. When he had to travel, Sarah's care was given to only the most trusted servant. She passed away in 1775 and was buried in the garden of her home. The malady she suffered at that time was seen as demonic possession, so Sarah was not allowed burial in holy ground. Patrick planted a lilac tree next to Sarah's grave. It still blooms today.

Henry was devastated by Sarah's death. But the cause needed him, his children needed him, and Virginia needed him. He put his life back together and went on to greatness. During the early days of the Revolution, he met and fell in love with Dorothea Dandridge, Martha Washington's cousin (yes, Patrick Henry and George Washington were in-laws), and the two were wed in 1777. With his two wives, he fathered seventeen children. In family life, as in all else, Henry distinguished himself as a man of great energy.

Layin' Down the Law

In 1760, Henry went to Williamsburg to take his attorney's examination before notables of the time like Robert Carter Nicholas, Edmund

Pendleton, John and Peyton Randolph, and George Wythe (all men who joined the Patriot movement) and from that day forward, Patrick Henry and Virginia history walked hand in hand. He established a respected law firm and began to demonstrate the "oratory skills" he so admired in George Whitfield and became famous for himself.

In 1763, he argued the "Parson's Cause" case in Hanover County. The dispute was whether the price of tobacco paid to "established" (official Anglican) clergy for their services should be set by the colonial government or by the Crown. After the British Parliament overruled Virginia's Two Penny Act (which had limited the clergy's salaries), the right Reverend James Maury filed suit against the vestry (churches) of Louisa County for payment of back wages (like a man of the cloth should do such a thing). When Maury won the suit, a jury was called in Hanover County to determine how much Maury should be paid. Henry was brought in at the last minute to argue for Louisa County. Henry proclaimed that *"a king who would veto a good and necessary law made by a locally elected representative body was not the father to his people, [but] a Tyrant, and forfeits the allegiance of his subjects."* Henry went on in his passionate plea to the jury to make an example of Maury (a cleric who was *"an enemy of the community")* and after five minutes of deliberation, the jury awarded Maury one penny in back wages! Guess Mr. Henry made his point.

In 1765, Patrick Henry was elected to the House of Burgesses from Louisa County. It was as if the hand of God had sent Henry to the House to "shake down the Thunder" against Parliament's Stamp Act of the same year. He would magnify his earlier arguments and legal ideology, coming close to treason in defense of his resolutions against the Stamp Act in the House of Burgesses on May 30, 1765:

> **1.** *Resolved, that the first adventurers and settlers of His Majesty's colony and dominion of Virginia brought with them and transmitted to their posterity, and all other His Majesty's subjects since inhabiting in this His Majesty's said colony, all the liberties, privileges, franchises, and immunities*

> *that have at any time been held, enjoyed, and possessed by the people of Great Britain.*

> **2.** *Resolved, that by two royal charters, granted by King James I, the colonists aforesaid are declared entitled to all liberties, privileges, and immunities of denizens and natural subjects to all intents and purposes as if they had been abiding and born within the Realm of England.*

> **3.** *Resolved, that the taxation of the people by themselves, or by persons chosen by themselves to represent them, who can only know what taxes the people are able to bear, or the easiest method of raising them, and must themselves be affected by every tax laid on the people, is the only security against a burdensome taxation, and the distinguishing characteristic of British freedom, without which the ancient constitution cannot exist.*

> **4.** *Resolved, that His Majesty's liege people of this his most ancient and loyal colony have without interruption enjoyed the inestimable right of being governed by such laws, respecting their internal policy and taxation, as are derived from their own consent, with the approbation of their sovereign, or his substitute; and that the same has never been forfeited or yielded up, but has been constantly recognized by the kings and people of Great Britain.*

> **5.** *Resolved, that the General Assembly of this Colony have the only and exclusive Right and Power to lay Taxes and Impositions upon the inhabitants of this Colony and that every Attempt to vest such Power in any person or persons whatsoever other than the General Assembly aforesaid has a manifest Tendency to destroy British as well as American Freedom.*

In a nutshell, Henry put forward the position that only Virginia's House of Burgesses had the right and authority to tax the people of Virginia. He railed against the king and his parliament, ending with the impassioned words, *"Caesar had his Brutus —Charles the First, his Cromwell— and George the Third—"* At this point, cries of treason rose from all sides, but with hardly a pause, Henry continued *"let him profit by their example!"* Henry had won the Burgesses for the good cause. Five of his resolutions being approved, the new leader in Virginia politics saddled his horse and rode out of Williamsburg westward, into the setting sun. From that day forward, Patrick Henry was a leader in every protest against British tyranny and in every movement for colonial rights.

In response to the call from Massachusetts that the colonies create committees of correspondence to coordinate their activities related to the British, Henry took the lead in Virginia. In March 1773, along with Thomas Jefferson and Richard Henry Lee, Henry led the Virginia House of Burgesses to adopt resolutions providing for a standing committee of correspondence. Each colony set up these committees and they brought about the formation of the First Continental Congress in 1774, to which Virginia sent Henry.

Patrick Henry is probably best known for the legendary speech he made to the now "outlaw" House of Burgesses on March 23, 1775, meeting in Saint John's Church in Richmond, Virginia. The royal governor had "dissolved" the house on suspicion of treason and they were now undecided on whether to mobilize for military action against the soon-to-be enemy British Army. Henry rose and argued in favor of action and arms, ending his speech with words that have since become immortal: *"Is life so dear, or peace so sweet, as to be purchased at the price of chains and slavery? Forbid it, Almighty God! I know not what course others may take; but as for me, give me liberty, or give me death!"*

Henry's call to arms carried over the protests of more conservative patriots and was one of the main causes for Lord Dunmore, the royal governor, to order the removal of some gunpowder from the colony's magazine. Henry mustered and marshaled the militia to force restitution of the powder. Since Henry's action followed the British march on Concord by only a few hours, it is said to mark the beginning of the American Revolution in Virginia.

For Liberty and Country

Patrick Henry served Virginia and the United States of America for more than 30 years. He was a member of the House of Burgesses and the Virginia Committee of Correspondence, a delegate to the Virginia

Convention, and a delegate to the Virginia Constitution Ratification Convention. Henry was commissioned as Colonel of the First Virginia Regiment on Saturday, August 26, 1775, by the third Virginia Convention. He was then in Philadelphia, having been elected by the previous Virginia Convention as a delegate to the Continental Congress. He resigned his position as delegate just as soon as he got word (what son of the South wouldn't do the same?) to return to Virginia to organize his regiment and take part in the shootin'! His was one of the first Virginia regiments to see action during the revolution.

He played a prominent role in the fifth Virginia Convention, which convened on May 6, 1776, and on June 29 was elected the first governor of the Commonwealth of Virginia under its new constitution. Henry served five terms as the first and sixth governor of Virginia. During the Constitutional debate, Henry was a powerful advocate for states' rights and was deeply concerned about the authority vested in the new federal government by the Constitution. But when the Constitution was ratified, he supported and served in the new government. He was twice offered positions in Washington's administration, tactfully declining the first opportunity due to differences of opinion with Mr. Washington, and the second due to failing health.

Patrick Henry, the great Patriot and orator of liberty, warrior of revolutionary ideal and fervor, passed from this earth June 6, 1799, at his home on Red Hill Plantation in Campbell County, Virginia, one of the Commonwealth's most famous sons.

His exploits at sea were the stuff of legend! John Paul Jones struck terror into the hearts of not only of the British public, but Parliament as well!

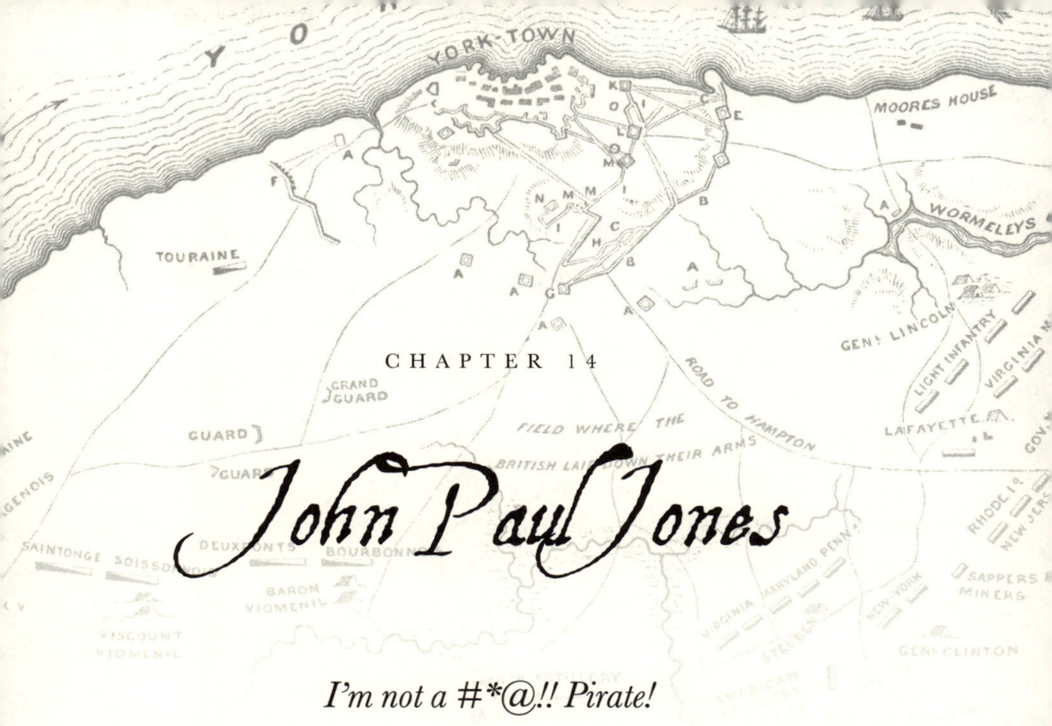

CHAPTER 14

John Paul Jones

I'm not a #@!! Pirate!*

> *The future naval officers, who live within these walls, will find in the career of the man whose life we this day celebrate, not merely a subject for admiration and respect, but an object lesson to be taken into their innermost hearts… Every officer…should feel in each fiber of his being an eager desire to emulate the energy, the professional capacity, the indomitable determination and dauntless scorn of death which marked John Paul Jones above all his fellows.*
> —President Theodore Roosevelt, in an address to the midshipmen of the U.S. Naval Academy, Annapolis, Maryland, 24 April 1906

John Paul Jones was a warrior through and through…all 5'5" of him! He looked more like a woodland sprite or leprechaun than a sea captain at war. But he was hard as nails and tough as a two-dollar steak! He believed in and fought for the ideals of liberty, freedom, and independence, but ruled his ships with an iron fist. He was combative and belligerent, which made him difficult to work with and hell to fight against, but he had the courtesy and manners of the finest of gentlemen when appropriate. He claimed he didn't care for fortune or fame, yet cherished the titles and medals given him by France and Congress. He spent years after the Revolutionary War collecting prize money for himself and his crew. He was a stern master, but fiercely loyal, as well. The British Isles remember him as a marauding pirate and it is still said of him that "*the nurses of Scotland hushed their crying babes by the whisper of his name.*" In America, he is celebrated in heart and fighting spirit as the Father of the American Navy. For his legendary exploits, he was celebrated on two continents, yet he was laid to rest in an unmarked grave for over one hundred years. John Paul Jones: Pirate? Privateer? Or the toughest "Old Salt" of the Revolution?

The Call of the Sea

John Paul (he added the Jones later) was born on the estate of Arbigland, Scotland, on July 6, 1747. He was the fourth child of John Paul and Jean Duff. They had seven children in all, but two died in infancy. His father was the gardener of the estate. Originally the family was from St. Andrew's parish in Eastern Scotland, but John Paul Sr was born in southern Scotland, and William Craik (the owner of Arbigland estate) had met him and hired him to *"lay out his gardens."*

Let's just say that ornamental horticulture did NOT appeal to John Paul Jr, so following in his father's footsteps was out of the question. He went to Kirkbean school with the rest of the "common" children, but spent much of his time at the small port of Carsethorn on the Solway Firth. The Craik family recalls that he "*would run to Carsethorn whenever his father would let him off, talk to the sailors and clamber over the ships,*" and that "*he taught his playmates to manoeuvre their little boats to mimic a naval battle, while he, taking his stand on the tiny cliff overlooking the roadstead, shouted shrill commands at his imaginary fleet.*" Sounds like a boy who's going places.

It was at the age of 13 that he left his quiet, pastoral life behind, set his sights for adventure, boarded the *Friendship* out of Whitehaven, Scotland, and signed on for a seven-year seaman's apprenticeship. His first voyage as ship's boy (errand runner for the cap'n) took him to Barbados in the Caribbean and Fredericksburg in Virginia. He stayed with his older brother William, a tailor, who had emigrated to Virginia and was doing very well. The ship was in port for several months and he spent the time learning navigation and coming to love America.

After his return to Whitehaven, he found that the *Friendship's* owner was in deep financial trouble. John Paul found himself released from his apprenticeship and out of a job. The only position he could find put him straight into the slave trade as third mate aboard the *King George* out of Whitehaven. Two years later in 1766, he transferred as first mate to the brigantine (two-masted ship) *Two Friends* out of Kingston, Jamaica. As soon as they reached port, he quit the slave traffic in disgust, calling it an "abominable trade," and was given free passage home on the *John* of Kirkcudbright. During the voyage, the captain Samuel McAdam and the mate died of fever. Paul took command as the only qualified officer, brought her about, and returned the ship safely home. The owners, Currie, Beck, and Co. were so pleased that they appointed him master and ship's agent (in charge of buying and selling the cargo) for the *John's* next voyage to America.

John Paul had become a captain because of his own grit, determination, and courage at the age of 21. He was slight and wiry with a bright eye and willing heart. He was known as a "dandy skipper" and assumed the manner of a young gentleman. He was always neatly dressed and fond of the ladies. He had a violent and volatile temper that blessed and cursed him throughout his career. It was while captain of the *John* that he was accused in Tobago by Mungo Maxwell, the ship's carpenter, of having flogged him excessively with the cat o' nine tails (a standard punishment aboard ship for the time). Maxwell, the son of a prominent Scottish gentleman, was examined and his complaint was dismissed as "lacking merit." Later he died returning home on a different ship and his father complained that his son "*was most unmercifully, wounded on his back… and of which wounds he soon afterwards died.*"

Captain Paul was arrested and charged with murder when he returned to port in Scotland, but evidence was presented from Tobago and elsewhere that was sufficient to acquit him. The master of the ship that Maxwell had boarded for passage home declared that the man was in perfect health when he came on board. Soon after this ordeal, Paul was accepted as a mason, showing that few people in Kirkcudbright believed the charge. But the story dogged him for the rest of his life.

Captain John Paul next took command of the *Betsy*, a West Indies company ship and remained for some time in the Caribbean in commercial business. He seems to have put away a small fortune. But in 1773, he had to leave the West Indies after he killed the ringleader of a mutiny, "*a prodigious brute of thrice my strength,*" with the 'flat' of his sword in a dispute over wages (shattered the man's skull). Local feeling was against him, so he fled to Virginia, destitute but alive, and changed his name, first to John Jones and later to John Paul Jones, and the rest, as they say, is history!

> "*I wish to have no connection with any ship that does not sail fast, for I intend to go in harm's way.*"
> —Captain John Paul Jones

Events were working up to the American Revolution. From his letters, it can be seen that Jones was strongly on the colonists' side. When Congress formed a Continental Navy, Jones offered his services and was commissioned as first lieutenant on December 7, 1775. His first ship was the *Alfred*. The American Navy at this time consisted of the ships *Alfred* and *Columbus* (3 masts, 32 guns), the brigantines *Andrew Doria* and *Cabot* (2 masts, 22 and 18 guns respectively), and the sloop *Providence* (1 mast, 12 guns, but fast as a marlin!). Thirteen more frigates were on order (like "Old Ironsides" the *USS Constitution*, 3 masts, 32 guns, built for speed, and almost indestructible). Jones served as lieutenant of the *Alfred* and later a captain of the *Providence* where he gained practical experience in naval warfare. His reputation as a hard charger and effective captain went far and wide. He advised Congress on the drawing up of US Navy regulations, and in November 1777, he sailed as captain of the *Ranger* for a tour of duty based out of France where he struck up a close friendship with the American minister "plenipotentiary" (means has authority to do just about anything) in Paris, Benjamin Franklin. As lieutenant aboard the *Alfred,* Jones had raised the first United States "navy flag" (called an ensign) in history, now as captain of the *Ranger*, he received the first national gun salute to "the Stars and Stripes" from France at Quiberon Bay—the first time it had been hoisted in a foreign harbor.

On April 10, 1778, Jones sailed from France on a cruise to prowl the Irish Sea, where he captured or destroyed a number of small vessels. The trip through the Irish Sea would make the entire crew wealthy men. You see, taking enemy ships as "a prize" meant money for all, and Jones' crew acted more like "privateers" than navy men. Case in point: Just before midnight on April 21, Jones made his "unannounced" return to his home port of Whitehaven when he carried out a daring nighttime hit-and-run raid. A shore party of two boats (about 30 men) landed at midnight in calm weather but choppy seas. There were two batteries that guarded the harbor and the plan was for each boat to capture one. Jones' boat captured the garrison bloodlessly and spiked the fort's cannons on his side of the harbor, but when he went to the other fort, he discovered that the other crew had captured the garrison of guards of the battery and taken them to the local dockside pub and were freely enjoying the beer and spirits. Not good to regard orders in war as guidelines! After chewing out his drunk and near mutinous crew, Jones knocked out the other fort, spiked its cannons as well, set fires aboard several coal ships, and managed to get all the raiding party safely back to the ship by daybreak!

Four hours later (at 10am), Jones reached Kirkcudbright Bay, his home turf. His plan was to capture the Earl of Selkirk who lived on St Mary's Island and exchange him for captured American sailors. When they landed, they met the estate's head gardener and told him that they were a British press gang (men looking to "shanghai" unsuspecting able bodies for the British navy). The gardener went screaming into the night, spread the story, and caused the locals to flee! After learning that the Earl was not at home, Jones wanted to leave immediately, but his crew insisted on looting the mansion since they had returned empty-handed from Whitehaven (See? Privateers!). He agreed to let them take the family silver only. The Earl's wife had just finished breakfast when she saw some "*horrid looking wretches*" surrounding the house. Lady Selkirk took the opportunity to ask them "a thousand questions" about America and afterwards said that "*they behaved with great civility.*" When Jones heard that Lady Selkirk had acted with "such dignity in trying circumstances," he was filled with admiration for her. He purchased the silver himself and returned it after the war was over with a letter of apology.

After leaving Kirkcudbright, Jones spotted the *HMS Drake,* a 20-gun sloop, near Carrickfergus in Northern Ireland. Both ships were evenly matched and the battle lasted just over an hour. Captain Burden of the *Drake* was killed and his second in command, Lieutenant Dobbs, was mortally wounded. The *Drake* surrendered—another ship "taken a prize"… things were looking up!

"I Have Not Yet Begun to Fight!"

When the cruise was over, Jones' name became a household word across the Atlantic. In America, he was a hero; in Britain, he was seen as a scoundrel, a pirate, and a nautical "boogie man!" A full squadron of HMS ships (royal navy…no foolin' around now) was ordered to seek him out and put him "on the bottom." Militia units were called up and stationed along the coast in case of Jones' future raids.

On his triumphant return to France, Jones was given command of the *Duc de Duras*, a large and formidable French merchant ship that Benjamin Franklin had had converted into a warship. He renamed her *Bonhomme Richard* in honor of Dr. Franklin, whose book *Poor Richard's Almanac* had been translated into French with the title *Les Maximes du Bonhomme Richard*. On August 14, 1779, he set sail on another cruise of Britain as commodore of a squadron of seven ships (Aargghh! Lock up yer daughters and wives,

Jones and his gang are going back to sea!). The plan was to destroy British commerce in the North Sea and Jones sailed round Ireland and Scotland entering The Firth of Forth (the Forth Fjord) and terrorizing Leith Harbor on September 16. He intended to capture the harbor and "Edinboro town" if possible and extract a ransom of £50,000 (that's almost $8 million in today's money, a hefty ransom for the day!), but he was thwarted when a gale sprang up and blew him back out to sea.

Eight days later, on the night of September 23, 1779, he fought the most famous battle of his career and one of the most famous engagements in US Naval history when he attacked the *HMS Serapis* and the *Countess of Scarborough* off Flamborough Head on the English coastline of the North Sea. The *Serapis* had superior firepower, but Jones had the wind! After a furious exchange of broadsides where *Bonhomme Richard* took the worst of it, Jones boldly and skillfully brought his ship alongside *Serapis*, ramming the British frigate and lashing his ship to her starboard (right) side. It was at this early point in the battle that Captain Richard Pearson, commanding *Serapis*, asked if Jones wished to surrender by calling out, *"Sir, do you strike?"* (meaning will you strike your colors?—take down your flag). The defiant Jones gave his famous reply, *"Sir, I have not yet begun to fight!"* Then the battle began in earnest. Boarding parties on both ships

prepared to go "over the side" with pistols, pikes, swords, and axes. Marines of both navies went to the "fighting tops" (platforms on the lower masts) to rake the enemy decks with swivel guns and musket fire. The carnage was some of the worst ever in naval warfare. Both ships were burning, *Bonhomme Richard* was "taking water" and shot to pieces, over half of the crews of both ships were either killed or wounded, and many men had been horribly burned. Near the end of the four-hour fight, *Alliance*, part of Jones' squadron, fired at the *Serapis,* but hit *Bonhomme Richard,* as well, and shot away its flag. Seeing that Jones' flag was gone, Pearson again called out to Jones, *"Sir, now do you strike?"* To which Jones gave the less famous, but more fitting reply, *"I may sink, but I'll be damned if I strike!"*—saucy language for the day if you were an officer and a gentleman. Finally, Jones' Marines were able to clear the "tops" and decks of *Serapis,* board her, and force Pearson to surrender. Jones' audacity and the courage of his men had won the day. It was the greatest sea victory for the US of the entire war! And Jones' place in American history was forever assured.

While attempting repairs to *Bonhomme Richard,* it became evident she wasn't going to make it back to port. On September 25, the proud flagship of the American Atlantic squadron "went under." Jones had to "transfer his flag" (means take command of) and his crew to the *Serapis,* and together with his consort ship, the *Pallas,* which had captured the *Scarborough,* he sailed to neutral (but American-leaning) Holland with over 500 prisoners.

For his great victory (and even greater embarrassment of the British navy in English waters), Jones was given a gold sword, the title of chevalier (knight), and made a member of the Order of Military Merit by the King of France, Louis XVI. He became the toast of Paris and Philadelphia. A bust of him was commissioned. Jones had another 20 made to send to his friends (no vanity there). In 1781, he returned to America and Congress passed a vote of thanks to him for the way *"he had sustained the honour of the American fleet,"* and in 1787, awarded him a gold medal. He was to be given command of the new flagship, *America,* still under "fitting" (being built). She was to be the largest ship in the American navy, but politics intervened and Jones never had another combat command during the Revolution. He spent the remaining years of the war commanding a desk and advising on the training of naval officers.

Have Sword, Will Travel

When peace "broke out," Jones returned to Paris to collect prize money for the officers and men of the *Bonhomme Richard*. Thomas Jefferson, the new American Ambassador, knew that Jones was still anxious to go to sea and see some action, so he recommended Jones for service with Russia (the conflict between Russia and the Ottoman Empire was the only war available). In 1788, he was made a Rear Admiral in the Russian Navy by the Empress Catherine II, a higher rank than he had held in the US Navy. As Kontradmiral "Pavel Ivanovich" Jones, he served with distinction under Prince Potemkin against the Turks in the Black Sea campaign. At the Battle of Liman, he scouted the Turkish Fleet in a rowboat during the night (one intrepid old salt!) and broke the Turkish attack, killing about 3,000 Turks, destroying 15 ships, and taking over 1,600 prisoners. In 1789, his temper and disaffection for other officers got in the way and after a brief audience with Catherine, Jones left Russia, never to return.

After a brief trip to England, he returned to Paris in May 1790, taking an apartment at 52 Rue de Tournon. His health was failing and he spent his final years writing letters to Catherine of Russia, to his two married sisters in Scotland, who were not on speaking terms, begging them to make up, and to the French Minister of Marines to pay arrears of salaries due to the men of the *Bonhomme Richard.*

On July 18,1792, sitting in an easy chair, he dictated his will to Gouverneur Morris, the new American ambassador to France. Morris then left for an important dinner engagement and when he returned later that evening, Jones had passed away. He had nephritis and jaundice, but pneumonia had quickened his passing. He was 45 years old.

Pride of the Navy

Jones' body lay in an alcohol-filled coffin in an unmarked grave in a cemetery for foreign Protestants in France for over a century. The turn of the 20th century was a time of great American naval expansion, encouraged by President Theodore Roosevelt. An intensive search was made to find Jones' grave and bring him home. In 1905, it was rediscovered. Surrounded with great ceremony, he was brought back to the United States in the *USS Brooklyn,* accompanied by three other cruisers. A seven-battleship honor guard met them off the American coast and as a single column, they sailed into Chesapeake Bay. There, the first four battleships peeled off and fired 15-gun salutes to welcome the hero home. The *Brooklyn* steamed on to the United States Naval Academy at Annapolis, Maryland. The initial interment was presided over by President Roosevelt himself.

In 1913, the body of John Paul Jones was finally laid to rest in a magnificent marble and bronze sarcophagus in the chapel crypt of the Naval Academy at Annapolis. A United States Marine Corps honor guard stands watch daily from dusk 'til dawn to honor the Fighting Spirit of the Father of the American Navy, Captain John Paul Jones!

Loved fireworks, loved artillery, loved Liberty.
Washington's bulldog: Henry Knox!

CHAPTER 15

Henry Knox

Things that Go Boom!

He had a presence. He was large: 6'2" and close to 300 pounds. He was robust, burly, and surprisingly athletic. He was larger than life: gregarious, affable, and able to command a room with his ample humor and thunderous voice. He was a Son of Liberty who understood sacrifice and was willing to risk everything for the victory of Liberty and Independence. He was loyal: he stood by Washington through thick and thin for eight and a half bloody years. And he was smart. In fact, there may have been no one in the Continental Army who was his equal in knowledge of "all things military." He was Henry Knox, Washington's chief of artillery and closest friend in the service. He was the first Secretary of War and the true father of the American Navy. He was a prodigious personality and to his dying day, a Patriot and true Son of the Republic!

A Self-Made Soldier

July 25, 1750, that was the day Henry Knox was born to William and Mary Knox of Boston, Massachusetts. Because William's shipbuilding business had tanked, he abandoned his family for the West Indies, never to return. Knox, seventh of 10 children, but the oldest son still at home, dropped out of the Boston Latin School at twelve years old to find work in a bookshop and be the principal support for his family. He was a diligent and faithful employee. In fact, the owner of the store gave him the run of the place—he could take books home at will and he always returned them. He read voraciously on the subject of war, focusing mainly on artillery. Knox even taught himself French so he could read books on the subject that had not yet been translated. Though self-taught, Henry was well-educated. He was proficient at mathematics and sciences, philosophy and rhetoric, and was well read to say the least. Knox went on to open a bookshop of his own, the London Book Store, when he was 21.

As he grew up, it seemed he just kept growing. As a youth, he was over six feet tall, "stout and muscular." He was involved in Boston's youth gangs and was a renowned "street fighter" (what do you know, Brains and Brawn!). Eventually, his interest in the "manly art" of brawling and his love of military science led him to volunteer for the Boston Grenadier company of militia in 1772. Grenadiers were special troops who used explosive devices like grenades and satchel charges. Seemed "Harry" always loved things that went BOOM! He was given the rank of first lieutenant, or second in command. He had been a witness to the Boston Massacre and may have participated in the Boston Tea Party. It's not certain if he did or not, but he was on guard duty shortly before it happened, making sure no one unloaded the tea ships. Knox was an avid supporter of the Sons of Liberty. Hey, where there's smoke…there's fire.

One bright sunny afternoon, as the proud grenadiers were drilling on the Common (Boston Common, that is), Miss Lucy Flucker, age seventeen, saw "her hero" (yes, our "large and in charge" Henry Knox) and was instantly smitten. Lucy began visiting "Harry's" bookshop often. While

Knox had been born into poverty, Lucy was born into aristocracy. Despite her Loyalist parents' insistence that she marry a man born into wealth like herself, Lucy had her heart set on Knox. Shortly before her 18th birthday, Lucy married the 23-year-old Henry Knox on June 16, 1774. They were a formidable pair. Not only in size (they both weighed over 250), but they both had personalities that would fill any room. The couple had a happy marriage with 13 children, though only three of them, Henry Jackson, Lucy Flucker, and Caroline Flucker Knox, survived to adulthood. Shortly after the war broke out in 1775, the two quickly fled the city as their Patriot point of view was no longer welcome in British-occupied Boston. During the war, Lucy seemed always to be moving around and staying with friends or family, but more often than not, she was "in camp" with her husband.

Knox joined the militia army when the siege of Boston began. He served under General Artemas Ward, who asked Knox to develop fortifications around the city and direct rebel cannon fire during the Battle of Bunker Hill. Upon his arrival in Boston that July, General George Washington took an immediate shine to Knox, impressed by all he had done at Bunker Hill, his fortifications, and the recommendation of John Adams (who knew that Knox was a military genius).

After Fort Ticonderoga had been captured, Knox suggested that the cannons at the fort could have a tremendous impact on the situation around Boston. Knox received a commission from Washington as a colonel and led the expedition to retrieve the artillery. Ox-drawn sleds hauled 60 tons of cannons over ice-covered rivers and snowy mountains all the way back to Boston, amounting to be about 300 miles. It is known today as the "noble train of artillery" or the Knox Expedition. Knox had originally estimated the journey would take two weeks, but it ended up lasting 56 days, from December 5, 1775, to January 24, 1776. On that day, Washington welcomed his "artillery chief" home with open arms. Knox had accomplished the difficult task in spite of freezing cold and heavy snows.

Washington gave Knox "permission to place the ordnance" (set up the guns) on Dorchester Heights as soon as possible. The artillery was "locked and cocked" (in position and ready to fire) on the morning of March 4, 1776. When the fortifications and artillery were observed by British commanding officer General William Howe, he remarked, "*The rebels have done more in one night than my whole army could do in months.*" It was evident that the Redcoats were in deep "kim chi": those guns could rain hell right down on the British positions and navy ships at Washington's whim. After planning an attack for March 5, but being defeated by the

weather, Howe reasoned that discretion was the better idea and departed Boston on March 17, 1776. The British finally quit Boston for Halifax because of those "*damnable cannon!*"

With the Siege of Boston over after more than ten months, Lucy moved back home while Henry got to work on improving the defenses of Connecticut, Rhode Island, and New York. While in New York, Knox met and befriended Alexander Hamilton and Benjamin Lincoln. Knox would stay close with Hamilton until the latter's "death by dueling" in 1804.

Building an Army

During the New York and New Jersey Campaign, Knox stayed with Washington's Army and was present for every devastating loss and the few small victories. Knox was nearly captured in the confusion of the British invasion of Manhattan, but was able to barely escape with the assistance of Aaron Burr. In the crossing of the Delaware River, Knox was put in charge of the logistics. He was able to get all the men, horses, and artillery across the river safely, as well as managing the return trip that included hundreds of prisoners of war and tons of supplies. At the Battle of Trenton on December 26, 1776, Knox placed the artillery in position to command the town. He took the "high ground" just as at Dorchester and it proved to be decisive! After the Christmas raid, Knox was promoted to the rank of brigadier general for all he had done during and before the battle. Knox fought and served with distinction in the Battle of Assunpink Creek and the Battle of Princeton that January.

Washington sent Knox back to Massachusetts while the army was stationed at Morristown, New Jersey, in the winter of 1777. While there, Knox worked to improve the army's artillery manufacturing capability. Not only that, but he raised a battalion of fresh artillerymen, as well. Knox also established armories in Springfield, Massachusetts, and York, Pennsylvania. He returned to Morristown with the spring thaw. His armories proved to be critically important for the rest of the war.

When French soldier Philippe Charles Tronson du Coudray was appointed to command the artillery (upon the recommendation of American Minister to France Silas Deane and the "will" of Congress), Knox was furious, and threatened that he would resign. The appointment of Coudray upset many others, George Washington and Nathanael Greene included, who both wrote letters of protest. Instead, du Coudray was given the billet of inspector general, but it didn't make much difference; du Coudray and his horse both drowned while crossing a river that September.

Knox was present at the Battle of Brandywine that took place during the Philadelphia Campaign in 1777. Before the Battle of Germantown, Knox had suggested to Washington that they capture the Chew House instead of bypassing it like they had planned. The long assault of the Chew mansion and a terrible friendly fire incident hurt the Continental efforts that day. While the Army wintered at Valley Forge, Knox again returned to New England to rustle up supplies and "motivate" the several governors to do more for the cause of liberty. Again, he returned with the spring and was helpful in the new training led by General von Steuben because of his ability to speak French. At the Battle of Monmouth, Knox commanded the artillery with "exceptional brilliance" as it was said in his commendation for the artillery's performance.

In the winter of 1778, Knox established the first school for artillery and officer training under the Continental Army (precursor to the US Military Academy at West Point). The Northern Army was largely on garrison duty when the war moved south. So Knox spent the summer of 1779 training over 1,000 soldiers. Previously, Knox had also established the Continental Artillery Cantonment Site in New Jersey in 1778.

When Major John André was convicted for assisting Benedict Arnold in spying on the Continental Army, Knox served as a court martial. He continued to help "the cause" by traveling north to get more men and supplies. Knox then fought during the Siege of Yorktown that had begun on September 25, 1781, and lasted until October 19. He was "decisively active" yet again on the field and Washington recommended to Congress that they promote Knox to major general after the victory there.

On March 22, 1782, Knox was officially promoted to the rank of major general, becoming the youngest major general in the Continental Army. Knox was part of the delegation that attempted to negotiate prisoner exchanges with British officers. The negotiations failed and Knox returned to join the army in Newburgh, New York. He then worked to inspect West Point's conditions and was appointed by Washington as the commander of the academy in August of 1782. Knox soon fell into a state of depression when his nine-month-old son passed away. Still, he went forward, attempting to negotiate with the Continental Congress on soldiers' compensation, but Congress was not willing to further negotiations. Knox wrote a warning letter, which led to Washington holding a meeting the following March. From then on, Knox was a firm believer that the United States must have a stronger federal government.

Building a Nation

Major General Henry Knox took over the reins of command after George Washington's resignation, becoming Senior Officer of the United States Army. Not long after, Knox established the "Society of the Cincinnati" to honor Washington and the brotherhood of arms that had been forged by the ordeal of the war. In 1784, Knox resigned from the army.

Now that the war was over, Knox and his family returned to Massachusetts and established a home in Dorchester. Lucy's parents had land in Maine that had been confiscated from them (remember they were Loyalists) and Knox went to work to reassemble the land. He put together a multi-million-acre piece of property in Maine.

Knox became Secretary of War on March 8, 1785, after Congress had dilly dallied for a long time deciding on a candidate. By then, the army was much smaller than it had been before. Congress had established a standing army of only 700 men. Knox proposed that a military academy be established, but many opposed the idea of having one when the country was not at war. He also proposed an army that could be rapidly "called up" that would consist of state militia. Under the Articles of Confederation, there wasn't much of a chance of that happening—weak congress, weak nation.

When the Constitution was awaiting state ratification, Knox became an avid supporter of the new document and government. Many even saw him as a good candidate for vice-president, but Knox stayed in the War Department, becoming the first United States Secretary of War under the Constitution on September 12, 1789. He was happy to again serve under his beloved friend, *President* George Washington (Knox still publicly referred to him as General).

Now that he was the Secretary of War, Knox was responsible for creating the Militia Act of 1792 and worked hard to evaluate arms and the readiness of the militia. He soon learned that only 20 percent of the militia's 450,000 men were capable of arming themselves when called. Upon realizing this, Knox recommended to Congress that they should buy more weapons and ban the exportation of weapons made in the USA. Knox also recommended they establish armories to make and stockpile weapons. During his time as Secretary of War, Knox was also responsible for the recreation of an American Navy and the Naval Act of 1794, which provided for a "new" fast navy. We built six frigates, very fast ships, 2 with 44 guns each and 4 with 36 guns a piece. Knox was also responsible for relations with Native Americans and that situation went sideways fast. The First Nations saw no need to leave what had traditionally been their land, even though they had fought for King George III in the last war and would again in the upcoming, they were not "open for negotiations" and decided to take the war path. It all ended up with the Battle of Fallen Timbers and General "Mad Anthony" Wayne, but that is someone else's story.

On January 2, 1795, Knox resigned from his post and joined his growing family in Thomaston, Massachusetts (now in Maine). When he arrived home, Knox had a three-story mansion built that they called Montpelier in Thomaston. For years he was engaged in business at his home and entertained guests "in splendid fashion" with Lucy. In 1805, Knox was elected a Fellow of the American Academy of Arts and Sciences and attempted to make even more money and grow his fortune. Knox was visiting one of his close friends in the fall of 1806 when he swallowed a chicken bone. The bone got lodged in his throat which led to a bad infection. Three days later, Henry Knox died on October 25, 1806, at his Montpelier estate, once again reunited with his General and friend, George Washington. Lucy followed 18 years later. They lay side by side on their estate in Maine, never separated in life and now for all eternity.

This tall, broad, and brawling frontiersman led the capture of Fort Ticonderoga and set the stage for American victory in Boston!

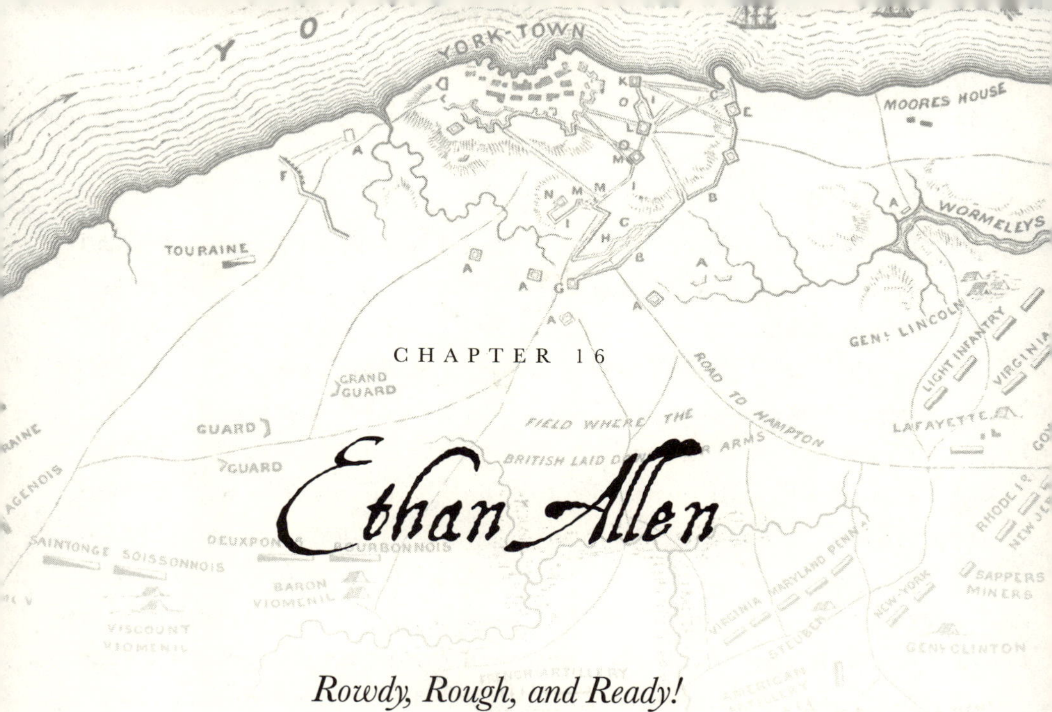

CHAPTER 16

Ethan Allen

Rowdy, Rough, and Ready!

Throughout history, there have been those who have been gathered to achieve certain ends who have been labeled "impetuous" and "unrestrained," hell, even rebellious, wild, and unruly! The Green Mountain Boys of Vermont were just such a group. In their day they were seen by most as we would see a biker gang in buckskins! (No such thing as gangs, just a bunch of guys who love ridin' together!) People called them "wild, hard-drinking mountain men" and "obnoxious braggarts." Their leader, Ethan Allen, was (without a doubt) the most wild, hard-drinking, and "braggadocious" of the bunch.

Now, why are y'all saying "wild, hard-drinking mountain men," and "obnoxious braggarts" like those are bad things? From time to time, that's just what the doctor ordered. The tale and accomplishments of Ethan Allen and the Green Mountain Boys is a rough and rip roarin' slice of Americana! These men exemplify many of the basic themes and struggles of the Revolution. But you have to put it all in context to get the real picture.

Back to the Beginning

In the 1750s and 60s, the New York and New Hampshire colonies had been issuing competing land grants to settlers in the northwest frontier region that later became Vermont. In 1764, King George III ruled that the area was part of New York, and the New York government was going to evict the "New Hampshire Grants" settlers who would not swear loyalty to New York. But the New Hampshire Grant settlers felt that even if New York owned the area, they had no right to evict the land holders. To them, the New Yorkers intended to destroy their livelihoods and deny their personal liberty by evicting them from the farms they had carved from the wilderness. They saw this as giving them every right to defend themselves. In 1771, they resolved to resist the New York "take over" bid with a loosely styled militia called "the Green Mountain Boys." Land speculator, farmer, entrepreneur, philosopher, and bar-room brawler, Ethan Allen was elected their colonel and commander.

Allen was born on January 21, 1738, in Litchfield, Connecticut. He was the first child of Joseph and Mary Baker Allen. Joseph and Mary went on to have five more sons and two daughters. Ethan, who grew up tough and mean, developed a reputation as a firebrand and rabble-rouser. He married Mary Brownson in 1762 and they had five children before Mary died in 1783. Allen married again in 1784. He and his second wife, Fanny (actually Frances), had three children. Fanny had a calming effect on Ethan. She was well-educated and the Allens enjoyed a very happy and fulfilling marriage.

Now, back to business. Though his Green Mountain Boys had only the most basic of educations, most of them were also responsible heads of farming households in their 20's and 30's (as well as rowdy, rough, and ready). Allen, who was just as diligent in his home life, was still thirsty for fame, but considering them *all* wild, drunken mountain men would be over reaching.

Allen and the Green Mountain Boys were certainly tough frontiersmen, and if you define the concept of "self-defense" to mean "scaring the knee-breeches off the New Yorkers," then they were great at their job. Beginning in 1771, they launched a campaign of terror tactics such as threats, humiliation, and intimidation to scare away any who attempted to exert New York control over the area, including land surveyors, law officials, and settlers...and especially politicians.

For example, in July 1771, New York sheriff Henry Ten Eyck took a 150-man posse to evict the New Hampshire settler James Breckinridge. An equal force of armed Green Mountain Boys gathered at the Breckinridge homestead in opposition. Ten Eyck went as far as trying to break down Breckinridge's door but the Green Mountain Boys leveled their muskets at him. Ten Eyck backed off and his posse melted away, leaving only a yellow stain on the lawn. In November '73, many settlers in the town of Durham sided with New York. Allen threatened to "*Lay all Durham in Ashes and leave every person in it a Corpse.*" Got to give the man props for directness. Then Allen and a company of Green Mountain Boys kidnapped a Durham justice of the peace named Benjamin Spencer in the middle of the night. Allen convened a frontier court that found Spencer guilty of cozying up to the New Yorkers. Spencer's sentence was the torching of his house (though only the roof burned). After that, most of Durham's residents purchased land titles from New Hampshire. Then there was the time the Green Mountain Boys drove off the New York settler Charles Hutcheson, who received his land grant for service in the French and Indian War. While his soldiers set fire to Hutcheson's house, Allen held the man by the collar and shouted, "*Go your way now and complain to that Damned Scoundrel your Governor. God Damn your Governor, Laws, King, Council and Assembly.*" Through many acts like these, but never to the point of bloodshed, Allen and the Green Mountain Boys foiled almost every attempt by New York officials to exert their influence in the "New Hampshire Grants" from 1771 to 1775.

The concepts of self-defense and personal liberty mattered little to the officials of New York, who expected the settlers to address their grievances through proper authorities. New York Governor William Tryon thought of the Green Mountain Boys as the *"Bennington Mob,"* and initially issued warrants for the arrest of Allen and crew, with a £20 (about $3,000 today) reward for their capture. With Allen still "at large" and gaining control in late 1773, Tryon requested British soldiers to end the resistance. The Royal commander of the region, General Frederick Haldimand, declined to send troops to quiet *"a few lawless vagabonds."* Tryon's response was to issue a proclamation against the Green Mountain Boys for *"atrocities"* and he upped the reward for the arrest of Allen and other leaders to the sky-high sum of £100 (about $15,000 today and a sum normally associated with high treason). His decree only gained him further anger from the Hampshire Grant settlers, since it came at the same time that Britain outraged all Americans with the "Intolerable Acts." Allen tied his local fight to the overall cause of American liberty, and the Green Mountain Boys solidified their control of the area. Big picture, little picture: If the Grants equaled America, then New York equaled Britain.

Allen and his "merry band" had been at it for almost four years by the time the Revolutionary War began, so how about the capture of Fort Ticonderoga? What's the story there? Well, when all the shootin' started in April 1775, Allen knew that the British forts on Lake Champlain—Fort Ticonderoga and Fort Crown Point—were the keys to controlling the area, and that the forts made easy targets after their years of neglect by the British. To secure the region for the Americans, and to hitch his wagon to the larger war, Allen planned to seize the Lake Champlain defenses with his Green Mountain Boys and make himself a hero!

Patriot, War Hero, etc., etc.

In early May 1775, in cooperation with and seemingly (wink, wink) at the direction of the Connecticut Committee of Safety, Allen gathered about 130 Green Mountain Boys and about 60 Connecticut and Massachusetts militiamen on Lake Champlain to attack Fort Ticonderoga. They planned a waterborne assault, but had no boats (would have been a long swim), so they had to search for them along the lake. While they searched, Col.

Benedict Arnold arrived at their camp with a huge ego and "orders" from Massachusetts to seize the fort. He demanded command of the attack. As if. There was no way the unknown and arrogant Arnold was going to win over the Green Mountain Boys. Besides, Arnold brought nothing to the fight except himself. Allen's soldiers said that they would return home before they followed Arnold. Allen could easily have sent Arnold packing back to Massachusetts, but to soothe his bruised honor, Allen offered Arnold a "joint command."

On the night of May 10, with Allen and Arnold leading them, about 85 Green Mountain Boys and Massachusetts men (that was all that could fit into the two boats they found) rowed quietly up to the base of Fort Ticonderoga. The isolated British garrison of about 50 men was not even aware that a war had started with the American colonies. Allen and Arnold strode into the fort's main gate side by side. A sentry blocked their way and Allen knocked aside the soldier's musket while the Green Mountain Boys clambered over the fort's walls shouting, *"No quarter!"* Allen pointed his sword at a British soldier and demanded the location of the fort's commander. The location revealed, he and Arnold bounded up the

stairs to the commander's quarters as Allen shouted, *"Come out of there you damned British rat!"* The dazed officer surrendered the fort after Allen threatened to kill him. Officially, Allen was reported to have said, "*By the*

Great Jehovah and the Continental Congress." He ordered the surrender. When asked by the stunned British officer by what authority he acted, Allen probably said something like "the authority of cold steel!" Ticonderoga was known to have two valuable possessions: 60 cannons (to be relocated to Boston), and some of his majesty's finest rum. Now that Allen commanded the fort, the first orders issued were "Bottoms up!"—much to the dismay of the tea totaling Benedict Arnold. The party lasted for two days. The members of the Green Mountain Boys who weren't present for the assault on Ticonderoga seized Fort Crown Point the next day. On May 17th, Arnold did take a more active role when more Massachusetts troops arrived and they raided the British garrison at Fort St. Jean on the Richelieu River. But the only thing Arnold did at Fort Ticonderoga was tag along for the story and the glory.

Allen had gained prominence in the fight with New York by thrusting himself forward and being decisive when indecision existed. He used "threats, bluff, and outrageous self-exaggeration" as leadership techniques and weapons of war. His brand of bravado was successfully driving the train until the summer of 1775. That's when Allen decided to seize Montreal, Canada, in a joint attack with about 200 Massachusetts militia under Major John Brown without orders or authority from anyone. It may have been that the relatively easy capture of Ticonderoga and Crown Pointe had fueled his ego, but reality was about to hit him like the proverbial "freight train comin' his way." When Allen did move against the city on September 25, Brown's force did not show up because they couldn't get across the St. Lawrence River. Allen had once boasted, "*with fifteen hundred men and a proper artillery, I will take Montreal.*" But when he attacked the city with only 100 men and no artillery against a force twice his size, it's no surprise that the attack failed and Allen was captured.

"I've Seen Better Days"

Allen's reputation for bizarre (if not lunatic) behavior grew during his time as a prisoner of war. The British held him in several places including on board British ships off the coasts of England, Ireland, and Long Island. And the British couldn't stand him. He constantly fought with his captors, called himself a "conjuror," shouted profane insults, and lectured them about the British mistakes in America. And he was always trying to escape. He was given his parole on Long Island. He became ill from his harsh treatment and depressed because of his separation from his family and the death of his son Joseph from smallpox. Allen wandered around the parole area drinking heavily and engaging in a favorite pastime—fighting in local taverns to "chase away the demons." While drunk, Allen would relive his glory days, regaling anyone who would listen. The British thought that "the cheese had slid off his cracker" and figured the man was mad as a march hare.

Allen was released in a prisoner exchange in 1778 to the great relief of the British. He returned to a hero's welcome in Vermont and recalled, *"I was to them as one rose from the dead."* He settled near present-day Burlington and in '79, published his exploits in his memoirs, *A Narrative of Colonel Ethan Allen's Captivity, written by Himself.* He recounted his adventures in a heroic, thrilling, and swashbuckling style. The book was an instant best-seller. Ethan Allen well understood that if you don't blow your own horn, who will? His *Narrative* established the Allen mythology and legacy as both a gallant, dedicated Revolutionary leader *and* an untamed product of the Green Mountains—which is exactly what he wished (Hey, if you can't take his word for it . . .). But it seems there were many who agreed with his "self-assessment." Even the Green Mountain Boys felt that their leader was, at least, a loose cannon, and after the Ticonderoga campaign, elected Seth Warner, a steady and experienced warrior, to be the official Colonel of the Vermont regiment, now part of the Continental Army.

While Allen was "away," Vermont had claimed the status of an independent Republic in 1777, and Allen unsuccessfully petitioned the Continental Congress for its recognition. Between 1780 and 1783, he negotiated with Britain for Vermont to become a Crown province, which was probably unwise. Congress charged Allen with treason but never pursued prosecution. In 1785, he published a second book, *Reason: The Only Oracle of Man*, which attacked Christianity. Probably a bit *too* radical for its time, it was a complete failure. Allen focused on farming, continued writing pamphlets, and sold off some of his own land, but was rarely flush with money. He died in 1789, possibly from a stroke or from falling drunk out of a sleigh, depending on the story. Either way, it was unfortunately only two years before Vermont became the 14th state. Despite his setbacks, many Americans still regarded Allen as a hero of the Revolution and his death was national news.

Allen and the Green Mountain Boys deserve their place in American history for their role in the founding of Vermont and the capture of Fort Ticonderoga, which gained invaluable artillery for the Continental Army. Sure, they burned some houses, but that's the trouble with rebellions—one person's freedom fighter is often another's dangerous criminal. Overall, Allen lived the concepts of local and individual liberties, which were two important Revolutionary themes.

By the way, the Green Mountain Boys also fought in the Saratoga campaign, and today's Vermont Army National Guard and Air National Guard still carries the moniker "Green Mountain Boys."

Are you sure you want to pick a fight with these boys?

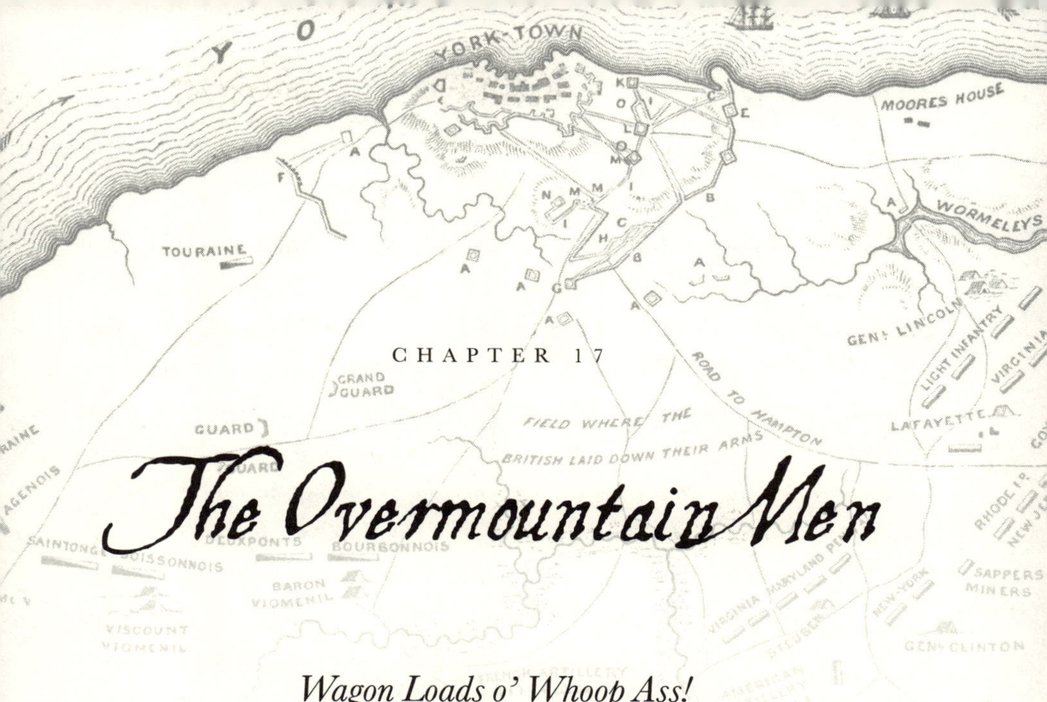

CHAPTER 17

The Overmountain Men

Wagon Loads o' Whoop Ass!

To the folks living on the far side of the Appalachian Mountains, the American Revolution was a distant war that had commenced in the villages of New England and was more about seafaring men and the moneyed elite than the hardy settlers of the backwoods. Most of the "overmountain people," as they were known, came from immigrants who had been deported (for one reason or another) from Ireland and Scotland after the many wars of English succession. The sons and daughters of these Scot-Irish "outlaws" had defied King George III's 1763 proclamation that forbid settlements west of the mountains. They claimed the "unauthorized" wilderness for their own, cutting down trees and clearing the land for farming, building solid but simple log cabins, growing what they needed, and living as they pleased. You know, real American stuff, self-reliant and absolutely independent (crank up the bluegrass and Hank Jr. hoss!).

"Country Folks Can Survive!"

They had a lifestyle all their own. One shocked and disgusted Anglican missionary who had been sent over the mountains in 1766 to convert them from their evil ways said they had a *"low, lazy, sluttish, heathenish, hellish life."* He seemed unable to remove his eyes from the "young women," who had *"a most uncommon practice, which I cannot break them of. They draw their shift as tight as possible to the body and pin it close to show the roundness of their breasts and slender waists (for they are generally finely shaped) and draw their petticoat close to their hips to shew the fineness of their limbs"* (this guy's a missionary?! I don't think so!).

The young men were equally well-made: strong, tall, and rawboned, these boys were dead shots with their "kentucky rifles" and wondrous in the wilderness. They had a straightforward way about them and an uncomplicated humor. They were plainspoken and fair-minded. Their "backwoods" manner wasn't uneducated, just unsophisticated. And to be clear, most of these families had close relations who had fought and died at Culloden Field (the latest Scots rebellion against the British in 1746).

Many of these folks were people who hadn't come from England and to whom Scotland and/or Ireland were now folk memories that few had even seen. They were a new and different breed of American. They had NO love or kind feelings for the British monarchy, and as Presbyterians, they had renounced the highly-structured mysticism of the Anglican Church in favor of the democracy of the "meetin' house." As a North Carolina minister and Patriot explained "his people's" simple beliefs: *"The Creator had long ago implanted into man's nature a capacity for civic responsibility. God had taught men to consider themselves His stewards, had given them talents and opportunities and expected them to make the most of those endowments."* This was the heart of the Overmountain Folk.

By the spring of 1780, the Revolution was no longer far, far away. The British Army had invaded the South in a campaign aimed at splitting the colonies and forcing an end to the war. The Southern strategy was based on the assumption that local Tories would fight alongside British troops and help restore British rule. Never in the history of colonial North

America had so much blood been shed as was spilled in the "civil war" that raged within the Revolution. Continental Army Maj. Gen. Nathanael Greene, commander of the Patriot Army in the South, wrote a fellow officer that *"the Whigs and Tories pursue each other with the most relent[less] fury, killing and destroying each other wherever they meet…plundering one another and committing private murders."* A better description of the "hillbilly" blood feud may never be found.

Charleston and large chunks of the Carolinas had fallen to the Redcoats. By September 1780, the Continental Army was a damn sight scarce everywhere in the South. The king's troops and their Tory pals were snug in the southland, their flanks covered by the sea to the east and the Appalachian Mountains to the west. Timid members of Congress suggested the time had come to "cut and run." They proposed that all three of those states (Georgia, South Carolina, and North Carolina) be allowed to revert to colony status under the British occupation. Well, we'll jus' see about that.

In late September, General Lord Charles Cornwallis decided to expand Britain's control of the South by leading his army through North Carolina and into Virginia. He gave the job of protecting the British left flank to Major Patrick Ferguson and the American Volunteers, Ferguson's well-trained Tory militia. Cornwallis placed enormous confidence in Ferguson, who was in charge of recruiting and training the thousands of Southern Tories signing up to fight for "king and country."

A hard-driving infantry tactician, Ferguson produced well-trained militiamen, teaching recruits to follow signals from his silver whistle so they could understand his orders even when the landscape or the "fog of war" (romantic name for the literal clouds of burnt powder smoke blowing across the battlefield) obscured him from view. This British officer was the inventor of the Ferguson breechloading rifle; capable of firing five shots a minute (that's a lot of lead down range for the day). He had been born in Scotland in 1744, and had served as a soldier since age 17. At the September 11, 1777, Battle of Brandywine, he led a rifle company whose men used his rifle. A Patriot musket ball shattered Ferguson's right elbow that day and he was never again able to bend that arm. He returned to duty in May 1778 and taught himself to shoot and wield a saber with his left arm.

Following the Cornwallis custom, Ferguson had been pressuring Carolina Patriots to sign "loyalty oaths" and receive pardons, as about 1,400 men had done in Augusta, GA. But so many Overmountain Men had refused to sign the oaths that an angry Ferguson sent a paroled Patriot prisoner into the mountains carrying a warning from the Major: *"If the rebels did not desist from their opposition to the British arms,"* he would *"march his army over the mountains, hang their leaders and lay their country waste with fire and sword."* Not the language to use with Southern boys, 'specially *armed* Southern boys.

The prisoner brought the warning to Patriot militia Colonel Isaac Shelby in a part of North Carolina that is now Tennessee. Enraged by the threat, Shelby immediately rode 40 miles to meet with neighboring Patriot leader, John Sevier. They agreed there was only one way to respond to the British threat: muster as many men as possible and strike first, fast, and hard. Messages were sent throughout the Overmountain districts. And it wasn't long before Colonel William Campbell, militia leader from the Virginia backwoods, heard the news and brought 400 of Virginia's "Blue Ridge and Kentucky riflemen" to the party.

On September 25, the militia leaders assembled over 700 men on the Watauga River at an outpost called Sycamore Shoals (near present-day Elizabethton, Tenn.). Samuel Doak, a Presbyterian minister, addressed the rifle-totin' irregulars from Virginia, Georgia, and the Carolinas, saying, *"The enemy is marching hither to destroy your homes... Go forth, then, in the strength of your manhood to the aid of your brethren, the defense of your liberty and the protection of your homes."* (I think he just said "tap the keg o' whoop ass!")

As the backwoods warriors left Sycamore Shoals, more men joined in. The hillbilly host had no supply train, no orders from the Continental Army, and no military structure, with the exception of the militia colonels and a handful of officers elected en route. The men, most of them mounted, carried what they needed and prodded cattle along the trail for food on the hoof. They were more hunters than soldiers and they didn't carry muskets as they were "proficient at killin'" with the more accurate and longer-barreled American rifles. For these fellas, it wasn't so much about defending the nation or their cabins and farms—it was a question of honor. They rode out to answer a challenge. Ferguson wanted a fight and by Thunder, he was entitled to a good ol' fashioned country ass whoopin'. As the challenged party, the Overmountain Men had their choice of when and where. The Boys headed south in search of Ferguson and his Tory troop. We would soon see who was gonna kick the $#*! outta whom.

The militiamen rode a wilderness road that led across mountains to the eastern slopes of the Blue Ridge in North Carolina. At one point on the 330-mile journey, the army split into two groups, again joining forces near the North Carolina–South Carolina border. Volunteers kept coming. As the army closed to within a few days of their prey, the men numbered more than 900.

For his part, Ferguson was heading north, covering Cornwallis' western flank. He had expected to be supplied by Loyalist plantations. More often than not he found *"those damnable Rebels"* instead. At one settlement, a surprised Tory officer found *"the most violent Rebels I ever saw, particularly the young ladies."*

Ferguson was aware that a *"ragtag army"* (Freeman's Militia, probably the first) was pursuing him. He played on the fears of the local Loyalists by issuing a proclamation warning of the imminent arrival of *"the backwater men"* (a rude and disparaging British term for colonists who lived on the other side of the proclamation line of 1763). Wrote Ferguson to the Loyalists:

> *I say, if you wish to be pinioned, robbed and murdered and see your wives and daughters, in four days, abused by the dregs of mankind; in short, if you wish or deserve to live and bear the name of men, grasp your arms in a moment and run to camp. . . . If you choose to be degraded forever and ever*

> *by a set of mongrels, say so at once and let your women turn their backs upon you and look out for real men to protect them.*

Few of the intended showed up. They knew who was coming, and they knew just as well that Hell was coming with them.

On October 1, Ferguson's spies informed him that the "jig" was up, his pursuers were on his trail. He sent a courier to Cornwallis with an urgent request for reinforcements: *"I am on my march towards you by a road leading from Cherokee Ford, north of Kings Mountain. Three or four hundred good soldiers, part dragoons, would finish this business. Something must be done soon."*

Near the border of the Carolinas, Ferguson made camp with his 1,100 men (Tories all) along a rocky ridge called Kings Mountain, which rose 150 feet above the valley floor. Local hunters had cleared the ridge of trees to create a "kill zone" when hunting deer. The hunters could drop a deer at over 200 yards.

After settling in at the mountain crest, Ferguson wrote a letter to a Tory officer and friend who had been a schoolteacher in New Jersey: *"Between you and I, there has been an inundation of barbarians, rather larger than expected."* If Ferguson was worried, he did not show it. He had two women with him. One left before the shooting began, taking the letter with her.

On October 7, a fast-riding detachment of about 900 Overmountain Men, joined by local Patriots who didn't want to miss the shootin', pinpointed Ferguson's mountaintop retreat. They dismounted, silently surrounded the ridge, and started climbing. Rainfall from the night before had soaked the leaf-carpeted forest floor, muffling the militiamen's footsteps and keeping down any telltale dust. Knowing that, like them, the Tory troops would not be wearing uniforms, the Rebel soldiers put bits of white paper in their hats to distinguish friend from foe (Ferguson's men used pine sprigs). Charging with a Rebel yell, the Overmountain boys took Ferguson's command by complete surprise! They formed a circle of fire as they climbed, pumping accurate rifle fire into the Tories, falling back briefly before the enemy's desperate bayonet charges, then moving in again as Ferguson's men retreated upslope.

During the hour-long battle, Ferguson chirped on his silver whistle and tried to rally his men, riding his white horse from one strong point to another. He wore a red-checkered hunting shirt over his uniform, making him an irresistible target. Catching sight of him silhouetted against the sky, some Patriot rifles barked out angrily, and Ferguson fell with at least seven bullets in him, including two head shots. Captain Abraham DePeyster, a New York Tory, took command and quickly raised a white flag. But the furious riflemen kept right on firing until one of their officers shouted, *"Don't kill any more! It's murder!"* Finally, the firing died out, and Patriot officers advanced to accept the soundly defeated Loyalists' surrender.

The next day, local Tories came to seek their loved ones. *"Their husbands, fathers, and brothers lay dead in heaps, while others lay wounded or dying,"* one Patriot wrote. The Battle of Kings Mountain had lasted a mere 65 minutes. Ferguson's command was no more. Almost 300 Tories had died outright, and no one knows how many of the 163 wounded survived.

The Overmountain militia had lost 29 men and led off nearly 670 prisoners. At "drumhead courts-martial" (make-shift military trials), 36 of those hapless Tories were condemned to death. They had been charged with treason, desertion from patriot militias, and inciting the Indian tribes. Nine were hanged by torchlight, three at a time, from the limb of a great oak. As three more awaited the noose, Colonel Isaac Shelby managed to stop the executions. Many of the prisoners did escape, however. Yet the back of the Loyalist militias had not only been broken, it had been torn out and shattered. The Loyalist would rise no more in support of the British military. It was the beginning of the end for the Redcoats.

General Sir Henry Clinton, commander in chief of British forces in North America, later referred to the Battle of Kings Mountain as *"the first link of a chain of evils"* that ended in *"the total loss of America."* After Ferguson's defeat, Cornwallis retreated into South Carolina. The Continental Congress called for Nathanael Greene to lead the new Southern Army, which ultimately bested Cornwallis in several more battles, and chased him out of the Carolinas and into Virginia, where, at Yorktown, George Washington forged the last link in the chain of American Victory.

In *The Winning of the West,* Theodore Roosevelt wrote of Kings Mountain, *"This brilliant victory marked the turning point of the American Revolution."* Thomas Jefferson called it, *"The turn of the tide of success."* President Herbert Hoover at Kings Mountain said:

> *This is a place of inspiring memories. Here less than a thousand men, inspired by the urge of freedom, defeated a superior force entrenched in this strategic position. This small band of Patriots turned back a dangerous invasion well designed to separate and dismember the united Colonies. It was a little army and a little battle, but it was of mighty portent. History has done scant justice to its significance, which rightly should place it beside Lexington, Bunker Hill, Trenton, and Yorktown.*

Prescott and his men mauled the British
and could have won the day—
if only the powder would last!

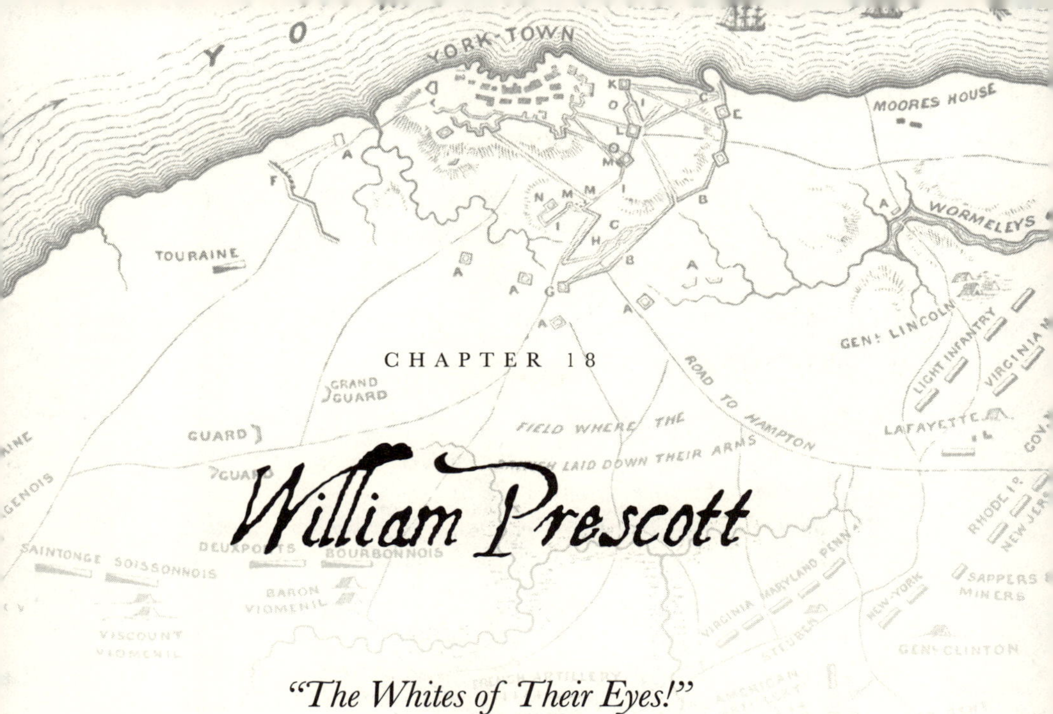

CHAPTER 18

William Prescott

"The Whites of Their Eyes!"

William Prescott was a tough, no-nonsense soldier, born in Groton, Massachusetts, on February 20, 1726. His father, Judge Benjamin Prescott, owned a large estate in Pepperell. William was well-educated and joined the Provincial militia during the French and Indian war. In 1755, he served as lieutenant and captain under General John Winslow during the expedition against Nova Scotia. His actions and professionalism throughout that campaign attracted the attention of the British general, who offered him a commission in the regular army, which he declined. After the war, he retired to his estate at Pepperell.

As the years passed, Prescott became a devout Son of Liberty. He supported in every way he could those in Boston, who he felt bore the brunt of British tyranny. So passed the Intolerable Acts, the Townshend Acts, the Massacre, and the Tea Party. After the Tea "incident," King George ordered the Port of Boston closed and the people of Boston starved into submission (more tyranny). The Committee of Correspondence sent word to the other Colonies, which responded by calling for a Day of Fasting and Prayer on June 1, 1774, *"to seek divine direction and aid."*

In August of 1774, William Prescott was the "angel" God sent. He led the men of Pepperell, Massachusetts, who delivered loads of rye to Boston, telling the inhabitants:

> *We heartily sympathize with you, and are always ready to do all in our power for your support, comfort and relief; knowing that Providence has placed you where you must stand the first shock. We consider we are all embarked in (the same ship) and must sink or swim together…If we submit to these regulations, all is gone. Our forefathers passed the vast Atlantic, spent their blood and treasure, that they might enjoy their liberties, both civil and religious, and transmit them to their posterity…Now if we should give them up, can our children rise up and call us blessed? Let us all be of one heart, and STAND FAST in the liberty wherewith Christ has made us free; and may he, of his infinite mercy grant us deliverance out of all our troubles.*

I'd call that damn fine preachin' for a layman!

In 1774, Prescott was also appointed to command a regiment of minutemen, who marched to Lexington on April 19, 1775, to oppose the expedition that was sent out by General Thomas Gage. Before Prescott and his men arrived, the British had already been shot to pieces on their long retreat from Concord back to Boston. Prescott's command went on to Cambridge where they entered the growing army, most of his officers and men volunteering to serve with him during his first campaign. The militias that had gathered for the battles of April 19 now formed the "Provincial" Army. And the Siege of Boston had begun.

General Gage still hoped to find a "peaceful" resolution to the troubles, but the king was furious and insistent and Parliament was bent on "flexing their authority," with General Gage stuck between the "rock and a hard place." His orders were to put fear of the king's wrath in the hearts of the people…oh, yea, and win those same hearts *and* minds (sound familiar?).

It wasn't long before the Americans got word that the British were planning to take Dorchester Heights and Bunker Hill to force an end to the siege and restore English rule. Bunker Hill is in Charlestown, overlooking the town of Boston, and strategically located between the Mystic and Charles Rivers, while Dorchester Heights commands Boston Harbor. Control the high ground and you "have the advantage." The British were hard-pressed to put an end to the rebellion—it was literally "do or die." The Redcoats had been shot to bits by the minutemen on their retreat from Concord and a second humiliation was unthinkable.

On June 16, 1775, Colonel Prescott was given command of the forces at Charlestown by the Committee of Safety in Massachusetts. His orders were to fortify Bunker Hill and defend it until relieved (no Redcoats allowed). After marching from Cambridge, he gathered his officers at the top of Bunker Hill. They decided to build the fortification on Breed's Hill (un-named at that time, but part of it was known as Breed's Pasture). Breed's Hill is not as high as Bunker Hill and is closer to Boston, much better to bring the harbor under fire and to defend *Bunker Hill.* They worked feverishly all night to fortify the position. A redoubt (earthen fort), breastworks (trench), and rail fence were quickly constructed.

Early in the morning of June 17, 1775, lookouts on British warships and sentries in Boston saw the Patriot positions being strengthened above Charlestown and opened fire from nearby warships and from artillery batteries on Copp's Hill in Boston to soften the "rebel" line. The Americans had received few reinforcements and were woefully undersupplied. Just before the battle, Prescott gave the famous command: *"Don't fire until I tell you! Don't fire till you see the whites of their eyes!"* It was a standard order of the time period for two reasons: first, muskets aren't accurate beyond 50 yards or so and second, Prescott desperately wanted to conserve gunpowder—he meant to make every shot count. So without a doubt, he gave the order to "hold fire" until the Redcoats were well within "effective range."

Musket and cannon balls were flying fast and furious before the battle began in earnest, and early in the day, a young soldier was killed when a cannon ball removed his head, causing confusion in the American lines. A few men left the field. Seeing the need to inject confidence and heart, Colonel Prescott climbed up onto the wall of the redoubt and nonchalantly walked around inspecting the works as if no enemy was firing at all. British General Gage, who was on Copp's Hill and using a glass to observe, saw Prescott standing defiantly upon on the wall. Gage asked his aid if Prescott would fight, to which he replied, "*[Prescott] is an old soldier, he will fight for as long as a drop of blood is in his veins.*" Gage's response was, "*The works must be carried.*"

Early cannon fire aimed at the fortifications quickly awoke the town and countryside. By mid-morning, General Gage had decided to assemble troops and mount an attack to clear this threat. While a cannonade from both British ships and Copp's Hill began to bombard the area surrounding Prescott's redoubt, Prescott ordered his men to continue to expand the fort and "dig in" for the assault he knew was coming. As the day continued, militia units received conflicting orders whether to stay put or reinforce Prescott. Because Charlestown was a peninsula, it was risky to send too many men to a place that could easily be cut off by a successful British attack. 2,400 British soldiers and Marines assembled in Boston for the attack on Charlestown while Prescott's numbers were dwindling as men fled the scene under the cannonade.

By midday, the first wave of boats landed British soldiers. They assembled out of musket range and awaited the second wave of troops. General William Howe was given command of the field by Gage and it seems that his strategy was to send his forces in two thrusts: One battalion would advance on the redoubt as a feint, a second would march to the right through an open pasture and flank, surround, and crush the "rebels" inside the redoubt. The tall grass in the area, however, covered up many of the hazards and obstacles that faced Howe's men in the flanking attack. Fortunately for Prescott, desperately needed Colonial reinforcements were soon arriving under the command of New Hampshire Colonel John Stark. Rather than send his men into the redoubt with Prescott, Stark led his command of roughly 800 men to a fence that ran along a downhill pasture to Prescott's left. This put Stark's men at the opposite end of the very same pasture Howe hoped to "blitz" in his flanking attack.

Into the Jaws of Hell

By early afternoon, Howe felt he had enough men to launch his assault. As the British forces began their advance, the cannonade from Copp's Hill and British warships ceased. In line formation, the two wings had to negotiate fences and other obstacles as they slowly neared the Provincial line. The men from Massachusetts, Connecticut, and New Hampshire were ordered to hold their fire until the enemy drew so close that their musket fire would have its most devastating effect.

British Marines, light infantry, and grenadiers (the best Howe had to send) advanced through what was thought to be a "clear" pasture. The massed regiments of foot soldiers, 4 deep and over 100 wide, feinted an assault on the redoubt. American musket fire was horrifically effective when the British came into range. The flanking attack ran right into a wall of lead, the dead and dying littering the once peaceful and serene field. On the hill, fire from both the redoubt and snipers hidden in buildings at the edge of the abandoned town of Charlestown harassed the feint attack, as well. At one point, Prescott ordered his men to cease fire. Howe was forced to retreat.

Near the landing beaches, the Redcoats regrouped. A second assault was ordered with the same outcome. Again Howe was forced to retreat. After Concord, the results of the day so far were absolutely unacceptable. General Gage made that clear. He sent Howe more reinforcements for a final and merciless assault to be focused solely on the American redoubt. Meanwhile, British naval gunners trained their cannon on the abandoned town and set the buildings ablaze with red-hot cannonballs to drive out skirmishers at the edge of town. Howe's final assault marched to the left of the redoubt rather than the right. As the British forces increased pressure upon the redoubt, men inside were exhausted and running desperately low on ammunition. As British soldiers and Marines mounted the walls, they engaged with bayonets in bloody hand-to-hand combat. The American retreat was orderly and done with "*military precision,*" as one British officer wrote. Colonel Prescott was one of the last to leave the redoubt, parrying Redcoat bayonets with his (up till then) ceremonial saber. The British forces gave chase as far as the next hill—today's Bunker Hill. Survivors and whole units that had never engaged regrouped on the mainland on hills opposite Bunker Hill. Both sides awaited a counter-assault or follow-up attack. Neither came.

Aftermath

The battle lasted no more than two hours. But the costs were staggering. Of the nearly 2,400 British troops engaged, over 1,000 soldiers and Marines were killed or wounded—a high number of them officers. Many of the wounded would die over the next days, weeks, and months from their injuries. Of the roughly 1,800 Colonial militia soldiers directly engaged at Breed's Hill, 115 were killed in action, among them Dr. Joseph Warren, a great voice of early Independence. Almost 300 were wounded in action, but were successfully evacuated because of the courage of the men of New Hampshire and Connecticut who stood as rear guard for Prescott's withdrawal. Only 30 Americans were captured that day, 20 of whom were mortally wounded and died within hours. The Battle of Bunker Hill should have taught the British not to underestimate the American cause or military ability. Instead, it made their high command question the ability of their commanders "on the ground." Gage would be replaced by Howe, who would plead for a "bigger hammer." More British troops would be sent to crush the rebellion.

His participation in Boston over, Prescott stayed on for the New York campaign and Washington's winter victories at Trenton and Princeton. But in early1777, he resigned and returned home. In autumn of that year, he joined the Northern Army under General Horatio Gates as a volunteer and was present at Saratoga. After this battle, he returned home and was elected to the legislature of Massachusetts for several years. Before the Revolution, he was successively major, lieutenant colonel, and colonel in the militia, and early in 1776, he was appointed a brigadier general of militia for the county of Middlesex and became a member of the Board of War. In 1777, he was elected a member of the supreme executive council of the state, in 1778 he was appointed third major general of militia in the commonwealth, and in 1781 he became second major general, but soon afterward resigned. William Prescott was a man who loved liberty, freedom, and peace. He lived a life of duty and honor. Prescott passed away in 1795 at his home in Pepperell.

Proud, brave, and belligerent, John Stark led from the front in two of the most important battles of the war!

CHAPTER 19

John Stark

Fortune Favors the Brave!

"*Live free or Die: Death is not the worst of Evils!*" This is the wisdom of General John Stark, Revolutionary war leader and hero of the Battle of Bennington. He wrote this line to the men who served with him during the war and more than a century after his death, it became the New Hampshire state motto.

Warrior of the North Woods

John Stark was born on August 28, 1728, in Nutfield (now Londonderry) New Hampshire, the son of Archibald Stark and Eleanor Nichols. John was the second of four sons and when he was eight, the family took up residence in Manchester, NH. In 1752, Stark, his brother William, and neighbors David Stinson and Amos Eastman went on a hunting trip and were ambushed by Indians. Stark warned his brother and Stinson, who tried to make their escape. Stinson was killed, but William managed to escape. The Indians made John run "the gauntlet" where the prisoner must pass through two rows of young warriors (each one with a "coup stick") and be beaten while running. Stark punched the first warrior, took his stick, and beat the others into submission. The clever maneuver made him a tribe favorite and he was adopted into the band. Six weeks later, William and a group of colonists from the Connecticut River area rescued Stark by paying a ransom of $103.00.

Two years later, Stark led an expedition on behalf of New Hampshire's Governor Benning Wentworth to explore the western part of the Colony. There were reasons for concern (if not alarm) regarding French activity along the frontier. The territorial designs of both the French and British empires had dramatically increased in a short time. The famous outfit "Roger's Rangers" was established to patrol the border and keep the peace. John Stark was commissioned a first lieutenant in January 1757, the beginning of his military career. Not long after, the French and Indian War came calling.

Aside from "sneak and peek" patrols to the Lake Champlain area to watch and monitor French activities, the Rangers saw no real action until March of '57 when the French attacked Fort William Henry. The regiment of Regulars stationed there had been raised in Ireland, and the French knew they would have heavily celebrated on St. Patrick's Day. The French were right—the regulars were in no condition to fight. But Stark had denied his Rangers any "celebratory beverages," and as a result, the Rangers drove off the French. This was the first known example of Stark's uncanny ability to anticipate the moves of his enemies.

Stark saw action throughout the War. At the siege of Fort Ticonderoga, the Rangers reconnoitered the Fort's defenses and reported to General Sir James Abercrombie that it was virtually impregnable. Abercrombie attacked anyway and the losses were horrendous. The American provincial troops (including Roger's Rangers) had 350 killed or wounded. The British suffered 1,600 casualties. Stark was smart enough to realize that the loss was due to the incompetence of the General Officers—an opinion he would hold till the end of his days.

After the war, Stark returned to his home and married Elizabeth (Molly) Page, the daughter of Caleb and Elizabeth Page, on August 20, 1758. The couple eventually had eleven children, including eldest son Caleb, who fought alongside his daddy during the Revolution. Ten of their children lived to adulthood, an extremely rare occurrence for the time.

A Practical Tactician

It is said that when word of the battles at Lexington and Concord reached Manchester, John Stark put on his uniform, saddled his horse, and was on his way to Boston within ten minutes, leaving instructions for his neighbors to meet him at Medford, Massachusetts. 1,200 New Hampshire men joined him for the muster call, the Massachusetts Provincial Congress unanimously appointed John Stark Colonel, and the 1st New Hampshire Regiment was born!

As the siege of Boston continued, the Americans learned that General Thomas Gage was planning a break-out from the city. To keep the Redcoats "penned in," the besiegers decided to fortify Bunker Hill on the Charlestown peninsula. The American defenders lined up on top of Breed's Hill, closer to the harbor and the British positions. Hey, if you're gonna challenge somebody…challenge 'em! The Yankee line included the New Hampshire Regiments. Colonel Stark's Regiment would be responsible for the northern flank of the American defenses. Here again, Stark showed his exceptional ability to foresee the coming action. He realized that the British attacking forces would be led by General William Howe, known for his aggressive use of light infantry, and would almost certainly attempt a flanking action along the beach of the Mystic River, the northern flank of the line. Stark ordered 200 of his best men to break up some stone walls and build a barricade along the pasture down to the beach. Stark then walked down the beach and placed a stake in the sand at about 30 paces, clearly indicating when the "whites of their eyes" could be seen. Just as Stark had predicted, the British sent 350 light infantry to move down the beach and flank the American defenses. Facing them was an unimpressive stone wall, only about three feet tall with few colonials visible to defend it.

The Redcoat light infantry advanced, fifteen across and deep as a forest, lowered their bayonets, and charged. As the British wave reached the stake Stark had planted, the stone wall exploded with musket fire. The first two ranks of light infantry, the Royal Welsh Fusiliers, dropped instantly. Still the light infantry pressed the attack. In the 18th century, it took at least 20 seconds to reload. In that short period of time, the attackers would cover the distance between them and use their bayonets. But this was not the case. A second rank of New Hampshire men stood up and devastated the next wave of light infantry and the Royal Welsh Fusiliers were no more. But the day had to be won! Charging forward, the King's Own Regiment took the lead, when a third rank of Colonials stood and fired point blank into their ranks with ruinous effect. Bam! The King's Own were out of the fight. The light infantry of the 10th Regiment surged forward, only to be met by a volley from the first rank of colonists, who had reloaded. Bang! 10th Light Infantry out! Next the 52nd Regiment's light infantry charged over the bodies of the dead, dying, and wounded of the first three waves. They met the same horrific fate. The surviving troops retreated in disorder, leaving 96 men dead, one third of their number, and twice that many wounded. The flanking action had failed. All the British could do now was launch risky frontal attacks. They were finally successful, but the cost was horrendous. They lost 1,150 men, 40 percent of their forces in Boston.

Although the defenses on top of Breed's Hill were finally captured, the Americans were not routed. They retreated with a rear-guard action being fought by John Stark and his New Hampshire men. British Major General John Burgoyne wrote of the retreat, *"This was no flight, it was even covered with bravery and military skill."* General Sir Henry Clinton, who would replace General Howe, wrote, *"A dear bought victory, another such would ruin us."* Colonel Stark wrote to the President of the New Hampshire Provincial

Congress, *"We remain in good spirits as yet, being well satisfied that where we have lost one, they lost three."*

Stark went with his regiment to New York, fought bravely during the disastrous campaign, and then retreated with General Washington across New Jersey. On December 25, 1776, he commanded the New Hampshire Regiment in the successful attack on Trenton and at the Battle of Princeton. Of all the general officers, he obviously respected Washington the most and was respected by him, as well. Congress was another matter. Following the winter campaign, Stark returned to New Hampshire to recruit replacements for his regiment. While there, he learned that he had been passed over for promotion to Brigadier General. He felt that he had earned the promotion and that the officers selected for promotion could not match his service record. Stark was right. On March 23, 1777, he resigned his commission and stayed home. Generals John Sullivan and Enoch Poor tried to talk him out of his resignation, but Stark pointed out that he felt the next threat would come from Canada and he would make himself available if that came about—right again, as usual.

In mid-June, Washington learned that British General John Burgoyne and some 10,000 troops were coming down the Hudson River toward Fort Ticonderoga. American Major General Philip Schuyler, commander of the Northern Department, started to gather his forces to drive out the invasion. He appointed General St. Clair to command the Fort. Stark, true to his word, started organizing a force to defend Vermont and New Hampshire, but was reporting solely to the New Hampshire Provincial Congress. They had selected Stark to lead their militia and granted him a commission as Brigadier General. He raised almost 1,500 men and officers and started west. Major General Benjamin Lincoln, one of the officers promoted over Stark, had been dispatched by General Schuyler to gather reinforcements from the New England colonies. Stark informed him that he served New Hampshire and not Congress and refused to submit to Continental command. To Lincoln's credit, he did not contest

Stark's insubordinate position, but enlisted Stark's support as an "independent ally."

Meanwhile, back at the fort…St. Clair realized that he could not defend Fort Ticonderoga with the force he had with him and abandoned the post. This action saved the ten Continental and two militia regiments under his command. The retreat was well organized and executed. Burgoyne dispatched General Simon Fraser to pursue the retreating Americans. He caught up with the rear guard at Hubbardton. The "rear guard" were the Green Mountain Boys now commanded by Colonel Seth Warner. After a fierce fight, the Americans were forced to retreat. Warner gave a very unmilitary order: "*Scatter and meet me in Manchester.*" For his part, St. Clair ordered the destruction of as much of the road south as possible to delay the British advance. This they did by chopping down trees and burning the many bridges on the southern roads, leaving Burgoyne to rebuild a road through the wilderness. The action slowed the British down to a snail's pace and allowed the American forces to gather and prepare defenses north of Albany near Saratoga Springs.

The delay not only ate up valuable time, but "burned up" the supplies needed to feed such a large army, as well. Burgoyne got "intel" that there were abundant supplies in the Connecticut River Valley and more importantly, lots of horses, which could be used to mount his dismounted Hessian dragoons. He was also told there was no organized defenders in the area. Burgoyne sent Lt. Col. Friedrich Baum of the Brunswick Dragoons with about 800 men to take the "undefended" stores and livestock. Remember what we've said about messin' with a dog in his own back yard? Never goes well, and this time the Redcoats came out on the wrong end again.

Goin' "All In"

On August 13, General Stark took action to halt the Hessian threat. He mustered all the men he could at Bennington. First contact was made at 0900 hours on the 14th at a mill known by several names, Sancoick's, Saint

Coick's, or Van Schaick's—you choose. American skirmishers led by Lt. Colonel William Gregg fired a single volley and then fell back to the main line. Baum followed, but at a "slow crawl." Having run into "unexpected resistance," Baum sent a message to Burgoyne asking for reinforcements. He then ordered his men to "dig in and make ready" and await reinforcements. When he got the request from Baum, General Burgoyne sent Lt. Colonel Heinrich Breymann of the Light Grenadiers with a force of 642 Hessians, joined by local Tories and native Loyalists, marching off to support Baum. Like Baum, Breymann moved agonizingly slowly (must have been a Hessian thing, you know these are the guys who build BMWs and Porsches…caution and safety first!). As both forces faced each other, a heavy rain precluded any action. Stark had sent a message to Seth Warner asking for reinforcements. Warner and the Green Mountain Boys hurried to Bennington, but both they and Breymann's troops were slowed by rain and muddy roads. Neither arrived in time for the first action of the battle.

On the morning of the 16th, Stark reportedly roused his troops with fiery words ending with, *"There are your enemies, the Redcoats and the Tories! This day, they are ours or tonight Molly Stark sleeps a widow!"* Stark's emotional commitment to the fight was contagious and his words had the desired effect—Stark's men fought with fury and overwhelmed all in their path. Stark had sent Colonel Moses Nichols with 200 New Hampshire troops to attack the left flank, and Colonel Samuel Herrick with 300 Vermont Rangers and the Bennington militia to attack the right, enveloping the embattled Hessians. A direct assault of Baum's redoubt was carried out by men under the command of Colonels David Hobart and Thomas Stickney, but General Stark knew what he was asking of his men and led the frontal assault personally. The fighting was brutal, but Stark's men crushed the Hessian positions. The Hessians lost their will to fight when their commander, Baum, was mortally wounded by a musket ball in the abdomen during a last-ditch saber charge hoping to rally his men. The Hessians quickly surrendered.

While Stark's troops were taking the Hessians prisoner and looting the enemy's supply train, Breymann showed up with his 600, but so did Warner and his 400. Turned out Warner's boys were enough to do the Redcoats serious loss. Stark attacked this new threat with the same ferocity and it wasn't long before Breymann realized his peril and ordered a retreat. He personally commanded his rear guard, who bought enough time for about two-thirds of his command to escape into the darkness. Shortly after, Breymann was forced to surrender. As darkness fell, the Americans held the field.

General Stark reported that he had lost 30 men killed and 42 wounded. The two Hessian/British brigades had lost 207 men dead, 700 men captured (or wounded and captured), and lost all of the Canadian, Tory, and Native American support for the British invasion of 1777. The loss at Bennington sank Burgoyne's entire operation. He had lost 1,000 of his fighting men, almost all of his provincial and native support (these guys had been his eyes and ears in the wilderness), and any possibility of foraging desperately-needed supplies from the countryside. It also had a devastating effect on the morale of his remaining men. The last battles of the Saratoga campaign were played out against the debacle caused by General John Stark and the militia men of Vermont and New Hampshire at the Battle of Bennington. In the final act of the British defeat, General Stark delivered the death stroke; he moved his command to block any attempt of the British to retreat to Fort Ticonderoga and safety. As a result, Burgoyne was forced to surrender on October 17, 1777. And the dominoes began to fall. The days of British rule in America were numbered.

General Stark remained active for the rest of the war. Congress had finally recognized his services and promoted him to major general on September 30, 1783. He resigned on November 3, 1783, when the war was officially over. After the war, he retired to his Manchester home and private life, living to age 94. *"Live Free or Die! Death is not the worst of evils!"* Great mojo, great motto, great man! General John Stark.

LIVE FREE OR DIE
DEATH IS NOT
THE WORST OF EVILS

They rode on the very winds of war!

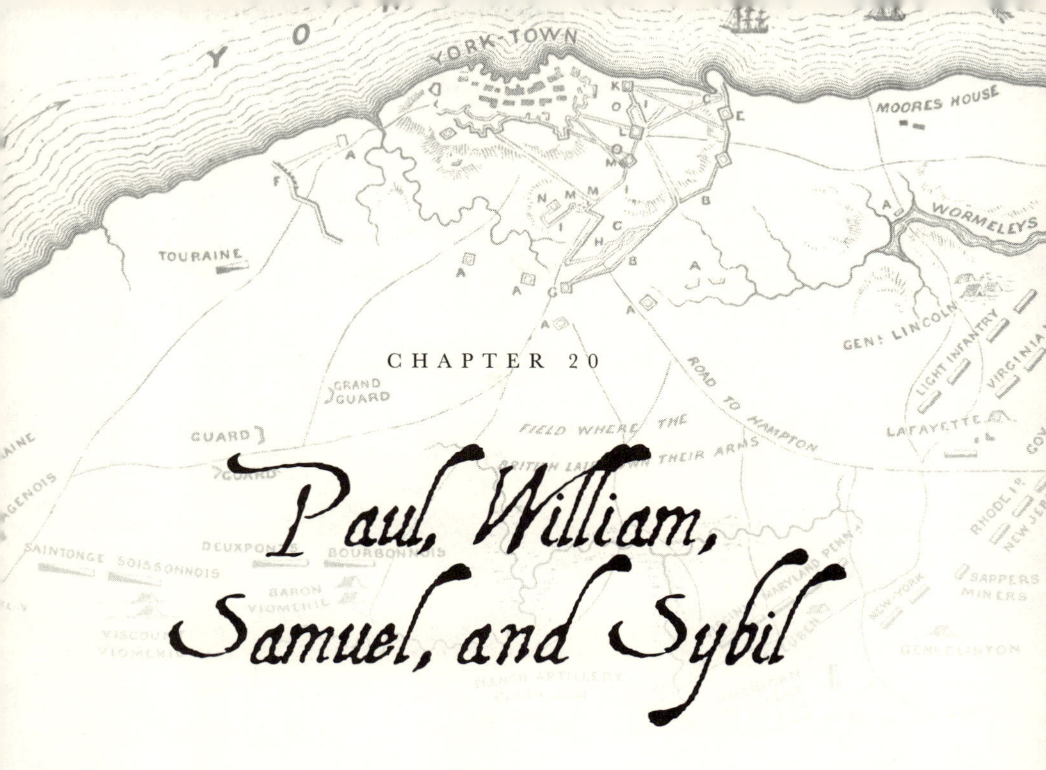

CHAPTER 20

Paul, William, Samuel, and Sybil

Horsemen of the Apocalypse

Poets, historians, and schoolbooks have retold the story of the legendary ride of Paul Revere for better than two centuries now. The best remembered re-telling is the poem entitled "Paul Revere's Ride" by Henry Wadsworth Longfellow. It begins:

> *Listen my children and you shall hear*
> *Of the midnight ride of Paul Revere,*
> *On the eighteenth of April, in Seventy-five;*
> *Hardly a man is now alive*
> *Who remembers that famous day and year.*

You'd think that for all the revisionist history going around right now (revisionism being the desperate attempt to "re-interpret" history according to the "new vision" that America is just the same as everywhere else… revisionists are descended from apes by the way), they could at least get right the couriers of doom of April 18, 1775. Sorry, nope…that doesn't fit their narrative. But let's remember that Longfellow was writing in an age when he saw the important values of American heritage and union being threatened by the specter of a bloody civil war. His poem wasn't meant to be historically accurate, but an inspiring and emotional call to remember the union and have courage for the coming fight.

Paul Revere

Thanks to Longfellow, hardly a man or woman alive doesn't know the name of Paul Revere and the important role he played that night. In fact, his part in the whole "midnight ride" may have been a bit gussied up and gilded by Longfellow, but Revere was still a pivotal player in the events that led to the battles of Lexington and Concord. Revere had gone on many rides at the direction of Joseph Warren and the Committee of Safety—some as far away as Connecticut. He was an ardent Son of Liberty, Boston Chapter, and rode often to warn the colonists of General Gage's "powder runs" (Redcoat attempts to seize the colonists' weapons stores and gunpowder). But April 18 was special and things changed forever on that date.

Paul Revere was born in Boston in 1734 to a French Huguenot father and Bostonian mother. He started out apprenticed to be a silversmith. After the death of his father in 1754, Paul enlisted in the Provincial Army to fight in the French and Indian War for the simple fact that it was the best job around. When the war was over, he returned to Boston to take over the family silversmith business, only to fall into financial difficulties due to the Stamp Act of 1765. Angered and embittered, this gave Revere cause to join the Sons of Liberty. He was a most zealous member and helped organize early revolutionary efforts while also developing a close association with Dr. Joseph Warren.

After learning of the British plan to raid Concord and seize Colonial weapons and powder (and probably arrest Patriot leaders John Hancock and Samuel Adams), Joseph Warren, leader of the Boston spy ring "the

Mechanics" and president of the "outlaw" provincial congress, would send Revere to bring the message that "the regulars were out." The "regular" troops were comin' to Charlestown and were on the move into the countryside. Revere rode through northern Boston, through what is now Medford, Somerville, and Arlington, warning the American Patriots about the enemy's planned sweep of the area.

His journey ended in Lexington where he met the other leaders of the Sons of Liberty, Hancock and Adams, and got them on their way safely to Philadelphia and the Second Continental Congress. Afterwards, meeting up with William Dawes and Samuel Prescott, the three men went their separate ways to continue sounding the alarm and improving their chances of escape from British patrols stationed along the road. Revere would be captured, but his compatriots would be more successful in their journeys.

Revere would remain outside of Boston for the entire siege. He fought at Bunker Hill and was part of a failed expedition to capture British strongholds in Maine. He identified the remains of Dr. Warren, killed at Bunker Hill and buried in a mass grave following the siege of Boston, by recognizing dental work he had done—maybe the first case of forensic practice in history. Following the war, he built a prosperous silversmith business and foundry, as well as America's first rolled copper mill. It was Paul Revere's company that "modernized" America's Navy by copper bottoming all of our ships, making them faster and less prone to barnacles and rot. His company also roofed the first Massachusetts state capitol building with copper. He passed away on May 10, 1818, loved and respected by the people of Massachusetts, but he was not a household name until HW Longfellow made him so in 1861.

William Dawes

Dr. Warren didn't just send out Paul Revere that night, but would entrust William Dawes to make the ride to warn the minutemen, as well.

In 1896, American poet Helen Moore would be among the first to correct this minor oversight of history when she composed a parody of Longfellow's poem with her own version:

> *Tis all very well for the children to hear*
> *Of the midnight ride of Paul Revere;*
> *But why should my name be quite forgot*
>
> *Who rode as boldly and well, God wot? (God Knows)*
> *Why should I ask? The reason is clear—*
> *My name was Dawes and his Revere.*

Dawes was born in Boston in 1745 and became a successful tanner and eventually a member of the Boston militia. He was a larger man and many think he was a big part of the theft of four cannons from the Boston Commons magazine in late 1774. The recovery of the cannons was one reason that the "regulars were out" on the night of April 18. Warren assigned Dawes, along with Revere, the mission of riding north to Lexington to warn Samuel Adams and John Hancock of their impending arrest, and to alert the minutemen that the British were on the move. Dawes arrived in Lexington about half an hour after Revere because the latter's horse had supposedly been faster. Though Dawes had begun his ride before Revere, the reason for his late arrival was more likely due to the longer route that Dawes had taken.

From the Hancock-Clark house in Lexington, the two men chose to ride on to Concord and warn the local militia that they were the target of the "powder run." Along the road, they meet up with Dr. Samuel Prescott (another Son of Liberty). Unfortunately, they were also met along the road by British soldiers. The three men split up, Dawes riding into the yard of a country inn, where his horse threw him and then ran away. Unable to locate his horse, Dawes was forced to walk back to Lexington.

Samuel Prescott

Samuel Prescott was a young and promising doctor the night of April 18, 1775. He was "the intended" of the lovely Lydia Milliken, a beautiful and accomplished young lady who had been courted by "the best and brightest" of Middlesex county. Her choice was Dr. Prescott. He was also a devout Son of Liberty, Concord Chapter, and as "fate" (Providence) would have it, was a post rider for the Massachusetts Committee of Safety. After a wonderful evening with Lydia, Samuel felt prompted to return home just in time to run into Dawes and Revere on the Lexington to Concord road. A born and raised native of Concord, Massachusetts, Prescott was familiar with the territory and would be able to serve as a guide for the two men on their nighttime journey.

When the three were met along the road to Concord by British patrols and were forced to split up, Prescott would be the only one of the three to reach Concord, carrying Warren's news to that part of the state. His knowledge of the terrain and his daring horsemanship allowed him to reach his destination safely. He warned Colonel Barrett, leader of the Concord militia, of the coming storm around 0130 hours.

Prescott would go on to warn other minuteman units "farther afield," at least in Acton and probably Stow, as well. Prescott's ride also triggered other riders as part of a well-coordinated alarm system that had been put in place by the ever-prudent Dr. Warren. By the time the first British column reached Lexington, the entire countryside had been raised against them. All that was needed was for some Redcoat to "light the fuse" and BOOM!—Revolution!

Dr. Prescott served with the Militia during the Siege of Boston and then went with a Privateer expedition as ship's doctor. He was captured, made a POW, and held on the prison ships in Wallabout Bay. Mistreated and malnourished, Dr. Samuel Prescott died while still trying to save his fellow prisoners in 1777. His grave is unmarked. Samuel Prescott gave his life and his future for the Liberty and Independence of the United States of America. He was 24 years old.

Sybil Ludington

The last of the famous "night riders" was, surprisingly, a young lady. We're talking real girl empowerment. None of that phony Hollywood crap like a Disney movie or The Hunger Games. This kid had straight-up courage and was willing to sacrifice. Although she didn't make her journey until April 26, 1777, her service to the American cause was no less remarkable, if not more so. The daughter of Colonel Henry Ludington, 16-year-old Sybil would make a ride double to that of Revere to warn the militia of the Danbury, Connecticut, area of the approach of the British.

When an exhausted rider came into the Ludington's farm to tell of the Redcoat's attack on Danbury, Colonel Ludington was faced with a problem—the rider and his horse were both "played out" and most likely wouldn't make the next hamlet, much less the next town. He had to stay to order and direct the gathering militia. Who to send? As a father, Ludington couldn't bear to send his eldest child when she volunteered to go, but then as Sybil protested her patriotism, he relented. She was off like a shot! Her father knew that Sybil was familiar with the roads and lands "round about" and hoped it would be enough to keep his girl out of harm's way. Sybil set out at 9pm the night of April 26, riding through Kent to Farmers Mills at a full gallop, summoning the militiamen to assemble. Then she raced back home again just before dawn, damp from the rain and exhausted, a round trip of better than 40 miles!

The men she recruited were too late to save the town of Danbury, which had been set aflame by the British, but they were able to drive the British troops from the area. Sybil was later commended by George Washington for her heroism. A statue of her was erected along her route in Carmel, New York, along with many other markers of her historic ride. Sybil Ludington was an American Heroine, a true Patriot and Daughter of Liberty. I don't think she cared if she was equal to a man, she just knew there was a job that had to be done, and she could do it—the real language of heroes.

Philadelphia born and bred;
maybe it's something in the water?

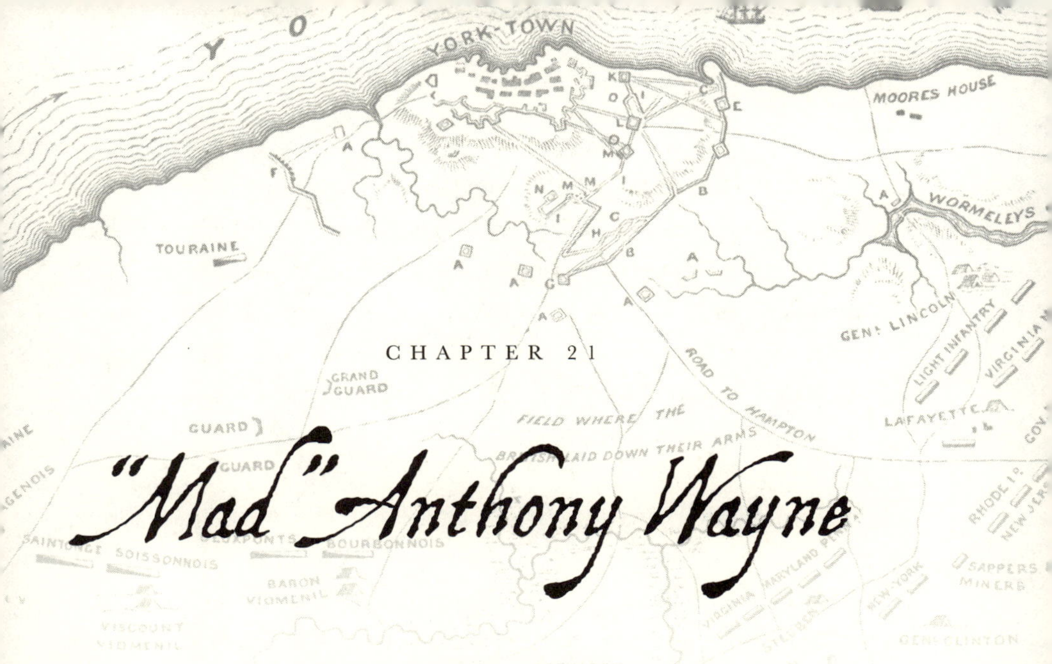

CHAPTER 21

"Mad" Anthony Wayne

Not Mad, Just a Little Crazy

General Anthony Wayne knew the Philadelphia area like his own back yard, pretty much 'cause it was his backyard… Wayne had grown up just outside "America's largest city." His granddaddy had been a highly decorated and distinguished British officer. When he retired, he purchased a large land grant in the rich farmlands west of the largest city in the Colonies, yeah, that was Philadelphia. Anthony was born in the "ancestral home," Waynesborough, in 1745, right close to many of the battlefields of the Revolution where he would earn a rough and rugged reputation for fierceness and courage.

Wayne had many similarities to his commander-in-chief, George Washington. Both were large men. Both were from wealthy families, but not educated at a college. Both preferred more active lives and became proficient surveyors. Both were keen students of military skills. Both were known for their personal bravery and strong sense of discipline. Both were extremely loyal to their junior officers and soldiers. Both cared far more for the ideals of liberty and "the republic" than for personal gain or glory. Both had fiery tempers, although the older Washington had learned to control his rage. And both would much rather be on the attack than having to avoid the enemy. Washington knew that "this dog could hunt!" He knew he could always count on Wayne to get after the British and to carry out orders. It's always good to have Generals who need to be reined in rather than prodded forward. And Anthony Wayne was a *pit bull*.

Aggressive, Daring, and Slightly "Touched"

Wayne commanded the Pennsylvania Continental line or military forces from PA assigned to Washington throughout the war. He commanded Fort Ticonderoga during the harsh winter after the failed Canadian campaign. His valor, shrewd leadership, and the respect he had earned from many of the Founding Fathers allowed him to rise rapidly to a brigadier general (one star) rank by 1777. However, throughout the rest of the war, Wayne stayed at that rank while commanding a force of men that called for at least a major general (2 star). While this was vexing, Wayne didn't get involved in all the "politics" of rank advancement and still used his connections to ensure that proper recognition and credit was given to his officers and troops. Many of his letters to the Pennsylvania state assembly were for pay and supplies, which he rarely got. It is sad to say, but the early state structure consistently short-changed our "Citizen Soldiers."

After the Battle of Brandywine, General Washington prepared to move the army into position for the Attack at Germantown. As he did, he left behind Brigadier General Anthony Wayne and a regiment of troops to either harass the rear of the main body of British troops or stand as a rear guard if attacked.

The British were camped at Tredyffrin in preparation for crossing the Schuylkill River and attacking Philadelphia. General Howe got word that Wayne was lurking in the area waiting to ambush his columns. Howe changed his plans. He would instead try to ambush Wayne at his camp in Paoli.

Just after midnight on September 21, the British led by Lord Grey launched a devastating strike into Wayne's unprepared American camp. Grey had ordered his men to remove the flints from their rifles before the attack began. Bayonets and stealth would be the weapons of choice. 53 Americans were killed and over 100 wounded in Grey's lightning raid. The use of the bayonet, coupled with the notion that the British stabbed or burned the Americans who tried to surrender, made martyrs of those maimed and killed at Paoli. For the rest of the war, the British lived in fear that Wayne's troops would try to avenge the affair that came to be known as the Paoli Massacre.

The British surprise attack at Paoli was a dark time for Wayne. He was accused by some of his officers of handling the matter poorly. Wayne's now legendary temper "went off" and he demanded (first) an official inquiry and (then) a full Court Martial—in no uncertain (and very colorful) terms. The Court Martial unanimously exonerated his actions and Wayne still had the trust and support of George Washington.

For Washington, they were never in question. He relied heavily on Wayne throughout the war. Before making strategic decisions, it was Washington's habit to have his top generals write out their suggestions. He knew he could always count on Wayne to propose aggressive, thorough, and well-organized plans. Wayne, like Washington, led from the front. His aggressive leadership was demonstrated at Brandywine, where his troops were opposite what Washington thought was the main British front and then at Monmouth, Wayne's rallying and counter-charge was pivotal in Washington's first major victory.

A year later, Washington and Wayne devised a daring raid that captured the supposedly impregnable British stronghold at Stony Point, NY. Washington had asked Wayne to form and command an elite "American Light Corps," the equivalent of today's Special Forces. Wayne used all his painfully learned lessons from Paoli, Germantown, and Monmouth. Borrowing from "No Flint" Grey's attack at Paoli, Wayne led his troops in a nighttime, surprise attack starting with a silent, bayonets only assault.

Wayne's attack was much more audacious since Stony Point was a heavily fortified stronghold on the top of steep Hudson River rock cliffs, protected by artillery in the fort and across the Hudson. Despite the many physical obstacles, Wayne's assault was successful and in just a few hours had captured the fort and its garrison. It was widely recognized as one of the most brilliant tactical operations of the Revolutionary War.

Just before the battle of Yorktown, Wayne saved Lafayette from a trap set by Cornwallis near Williamsburg, VA. Wayne's small contingent of 800 Pennsylvanians was the vanguard of the Continental Army. After passing over a swamp by a narrow causeway, he was ambushed by over 4,000 British. Instead of retreating, Wayne charged. This unexpected maneuver so surprised the enemy that they fell back confused, allowing the rest of Lafayette's command to avoid the trap.

After Yorktown, Wayne and his men conducted successful campaigns to dislodge large English and hostile Indian forces in Georgia and South Carolina. He remained in the South until the war officially ended with the treaty of Paris in 1783. Throughout the war, because of the way Congress set up promotions, Anthony Wayne had the duties and responsibilities of a major general but not the rank. Finally, he was awarded the rank of Brevet-Major General as the war ended (brevet means for bravery).

When George Washington became our first president, his respect for Wayne's military skills and judgment was demonstrated when in 1792, he appointed Wayne as the commander-in-chief of the American armies. Indian wars in the Northwest Territory had decimated frontier settlements and defeated two military campaigns. Wayne had to recruit, train, and lead a new army to restore order and defeat the Indian confederacy that was secretly supported by the British Empire. In three years, Wayne had created a disciplined army, defeated the Indians at Fallen Timber, and negotiated a treaty that gained all the lands from the Ohio River to the Mississippi for the United States.

In 1796, Wayne visited an outpost on the great lakes, Presque Isle (later Erie), PA. Wayne had suffered for many years with a serious case of gout and he had a severe attack at the fort. He passed from complications of the disease and was initially buried at the fort. Later, his son had his remains moved to St. David's church in Radnor, PA.

General "Mad" Anthony Wayne, Washington's war horse, had been a doer, even a doer of impossible deeds. He was the Revolution's "tough guy," a true son of Philadelphia.

First Commandant of the U.S. Marine Corps!

CHAPTER 22

Maj. Samuel Nicholas

When it positively, absolutely has to be destroyed overnight…

Major Samuel Nicholas was born into a wealthy family of Quakers in 1744. At age 7, sponsored by his uncle, he was enrolled at the newly-established Philadelphia Academy (now the University of Pennsylvania). His classmates came from prominent Philadelphia families, many of whom played important roles in the Revolution 15-20 years later. Young Samuel completed his studies in 1759. The next year, at age 16, Nicholas was admitted to the exclusive "gentlemen's club," the Schuylkill Fishing Company, whose *"associates assembled frequently on the banks of the river for fishing, fowling and feasting."* In 1766, at age 22, he was one of the organizers of America's first hunt club, the Gloucester Fox Hunting Club, some of whose members—*"generally of conspicuous prominence in the affairs of the day"*—formed the Light Horse of the City of Philadelphia in 1774.

At the same time, Nicholas had become joint proprietor of the popular tavern The Conestoga Wagon, a business owned by the family of Mary

Jenkins, the young lady he married in 1778. "The Wagon" was a popular retreat and watering hole near the docks on the Delaware River. There, the patrons could hear news from all around the world as told by the sailors and "old salts" who worked the many ships calling at the port of Philadelphia. Most of the Founding Fathers "found" their way down to "the Wagon" and "Old Tun Tavern" regularly. Tun Tavern was run by Nicholas' good friend Robert Mullen. Together, the two men knew all the folks of the waterfront…"the good, the bad, and the ugly."

Most "UN-Quakerly"

In 1775, the Second Continental Congress began looking for a means of resolving a chronic shortage of seamen for its fledgling navy. On November 5, it commissioned Samuel Nicholas Captain of the Continental Marines. On November 10, the date that the United States Marine Corps celebrates as its birthday, Congress authorized the enlistment of two battalions of Marines:

> *Resolved, That two battalions of Marines be raised consisting of one colonel, two lieutenant-colonels, two majors, and other officers, as usual in other regiments; that they consist of an equal number of privates with*

> *other battalions; that particular care be taken that no persons be appointed to office, or enlisted into said battalions but such as are good seamen, or so acquainted with maritime affairs as to be able to serve with advantage by sea when required; that they be enlisted and commissioned to serve for and during the present War with Great Britain and the colonies, unless dismissed by order of Congress; that they be distinguished by names of First and Second Battalions of American Marines, and that they be considered as part of the number which the Continental Army before Boston is ordered to consist of.*

And just like that, the USMC was born!

Recruiting for duty aboard the 24-gun frigate *Black Prince* (later renamed *Alfred*) began at Tun Tavern. On November 28, Congress confirmed Capt. Nicholas' commission in writing and set his pay at $32 per month. This document was a big deal. It was signed by John Hancock and was the first one issued for the Continental Naval Service, *predating* those of other early officers including Commodore Esek Hopkins and Captain John Paul Jones, both of whom were shipmates on *Alfred*'s first tour of duty.

Capt. Nicholas had a friendly way and inspiring presence. He was authorized to recruit two battalions and he would choose the roughest and toughest that the sea and the docks of Philadelphia could provide. For serving a "hitch" in the Marines, a man was promised many advantages and opportunities. Just see for yourself, here's Nicholas' recruiting poster:

> **GREAT ENCOURAGEMENT!**
>
> **AMERICAN REVOLUTION**
>
> **What a Brilliant Prospect does this Event Present to every Lad of Spirit who is inclined to try his Fortune in this highly renowned Corps.**
>
> **The Continental Marines**
>
> **When everything that swims the Seas must be a PRIZE!**

Thousands are at this moment endeavoring to get on Board Privateers where they will serve without pay or reward of any kind whatsoever, so certain does their chance appear of enriching themselves by PRIZE MONEY! What an enviable Station then must the CONTINENTAL MARINE hold—who with far superior advantages to these, has the additional benefit of liberal Pay, and plenty of the best Provisions, with a good and well-appointed Ship under him, the Pride and Glory of the Continental Navy; surely every Man of Spirit must blush to remain at Home in Inactivity and Indolence when his Country needs his Assistance. Where then can he have such a fair opportunity, reaping Glory and Riches in the Continental Marines, a Corps daily acquiring new Honors, and here, once embarked in American Fleet, he finds himself in the midst of Honor and Glory, surrounded by a set of fine fellows, Strangers to Fear, and who strike Terror through the Hearts of their Enemies wherever they go! He has likewise the inspiring idea to know, that while he sails the Ocean to protect the Liberty of these states, that the Thanks and good Wishes of the whole American people shall send him forth on his mission and participate in his Glory. Lose no Time, then, my Fine Fellows, in embracing the glorious Opportunity that awaits you: YOU WILL RECEIVE

Seventeen Dollars Bounty.

And on your Arrival at Head Quarters be comfortably and genteely CLOTHED. And spirited young BOYS, of a promissing Appearance, who are Five Feet Six Inches High, will receive TEN DOLLARS, and equal Advantage of PROVISIONS and CLOTHING with the Men. And those who wish only to enlist for a limited Service, shall receive a Bounty of SEVEN DOLLARS, and Boys FIVE. In fact, the Advantages which the MARINE receives are too numerous to mention here, but among the many, it may not be amiss to state—that if he has a WIFE or aged PARENT, he can make them an Allotment of half his PAY which will be regularly paid without any Trouble to them, or to whomever he may direct, that being well Fed and Clothed on Board Ship, the remainder of his PAY and PRIZE MONEY will be placed in Reserve for the Relief of his Family or his own private Purposes. The Single Young Man, on his Return to Port, finds himself compelled to cut a Dash on Shore, with his GIRL and his GLASS, that might be envied by a Nobleman. Take

> *Courage then, seize the Fortune that awaits you, repair to the MARINE RENDEVOUS, where on a FLOWING BOWL of PUNCH, on Three Times Three, you shall drink.*

> **Long Live the United States and Success to the Marines**

> *The Daily Allowance of a Marine when embarked is One Pound of BEEF or PORK. One Pound of BREAD. Flour, Raisins, Butter, Cheese, Oatmeal, Molasses, Tea, Sugar, &c. &c. And a Pint of the best WINE, or half a Pint of the Best RUM or BRANDY, together with a Pint of LEMONADE. They make Liberty in warm countries, a plentiful Allowance of the choicest FRUIT. And what can be more handsome than the Marines' Proportion of PRIZE MONEY, when a Sergeant shares equal with the Fleet Class of Petty Officers, such as Midshipmen, Petty Officers, &c. which is five shares each; a Corporal with the Second Class, which Is Three Shares each; and the Private with the Able Seaman, one Share and a Half each. Desiring Greater Particulars, and a more full account of the many Advantages of this Invaluable Corps, apply to CAPTAIN MULLEN at TUN TAVERN, where the bringer of a Recruit will receive THREE DOLLARS.*
> —January, 1776

You get the picture. The man had style and a boundless "entrepreneurial" spirit. By the end of the year, he had raised five companies of Marines and then sailed with them under Commodore Hopkins to the Bahamas. There, in March 1776, he led his 284 Marines in a lightning fast, nearly-bloodless raid on Nassau, catching the British entirely by surprise and capturing two forts, 88 cannon, 15 mortars, and a huge quantity of military stores. It was the Marines' first-ever amphibious landing and the most successful naval operation of the Revolutionary War.

Capt. Nicholas was still aboard *Alfred* during her pursuit of the British ship *Glasgow* off the Rhode Island coast on April 6. He saw his second lieutenant killed while at his side on the quarterdeck during the three-hour battle. He had become no stranger to the dangers and costs of the war.

Returning to Philadelphia, Nicholas resumed recruiting and training and on June 25, was promoted to major. He led three companies, 131 Marines (later reduced to 80) in the Trenton-Princeton campaign. He led his Marines as they were transferred to the artillery on February 1, 1777, remaining in the field with General Washington until the following spring when their terms of enlistment expired. Then, as a senior officer without a field command, Major Nicholas continued supervising recruiting, logistics, and training in support of ships' detachments of Marines.

By the time of the British surrender at Yorktown, the Marines' role had been firmly established as an invaluable asset of the naval service. In 1783, however, Congress "mothballed" the American Navy and the Marines were out of a job (they were recalled to service in 1798 to go back to sea and terrorize the French). The then-39-year-old Nicholas returned to his business and social life in Philadelphia. He died there during a yellow fever epidemic on August 27, 1790, and is buried in the Friends Burial Ground. He is respected as the Father and First Commandant of the United States Marine Corps.

SEMPER FI!

Now this boy had an axe to grind!

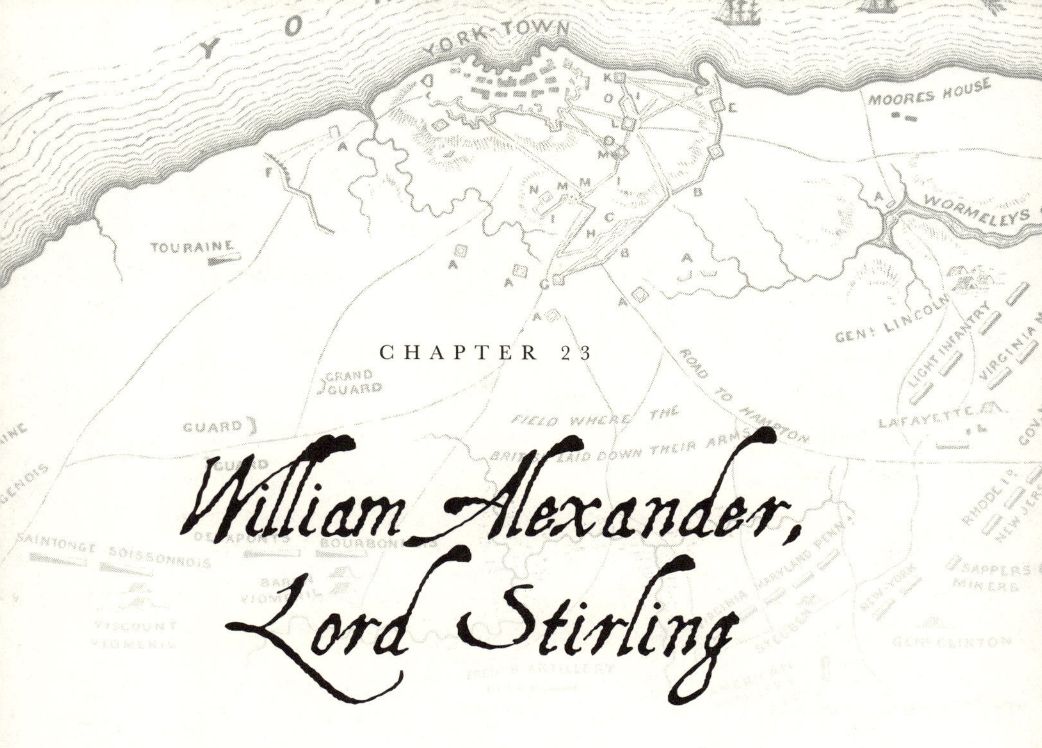

CHAPTER 23

William Alexander, Lord Stirling

If you can't join 'em, beat 'em—beat 'em bad.

William Alexander, aka Lord Stirling, was a living paradox. As one of Washington's men, he was one of the most loyal of the loyal, yet he maintained a title of British (actually Scots) nobility to the end of his days. He served as a general in the Continental Army, commanded troops "in the field," yet still was a member of "the peerage"—you know…House of Lords, friend of the King, that sort of thing. But when it came to fighting, he was all Patriot and all business.

Alexander was born in 1726 in New York City. His schooling was fairly normal for the time and he showed a remarkable talent for math and astronomy. Had the times turned differently, he may have been a world class physicist. But times were what they were and young William was brought into the family business. His parents operated a profitable "adventure outfitting" and dry goods concern—think of the Alexanders as a colonial Abercrombie and Fitch…the outfitters of President Theodore Roosevelt's adventures. Their business was so well regarded that it was chosen as "provisioning agent" to the British Army during the French and Indian War, with William being the Quartermaster (you know, beans, bullets, and dry socks). He worked as an assistant to royal governor William Shirley of New York and "rubbed shoulders" with many "colonial elites," including one up-and-coming hard charger from Virginia, none other than George Washington himself (you remember, the man who started the whole shootin' match in the first place). Alexander took an immediate liking to the young Virginian.

In 1756, while travelling with Governor Shirley to England, he learned of his family's "vacant" seat of Stirling in Scotland and put forward his claim to the title as last living male heir of the paternal side. The Scottish peers and courts found his claim to be "good and valid" and granted him title, William Alexander, Lord Stirling. Didn't sit at all well with the English peerage who claimed their "supremacy" and overruled the Scots, denying Alexander the "rights of lairdship and lands" belonging to the seat, but allowing him the title Lord Stirling (and technically a seat in the Scots Parliament). The English decision rubbed Alexander the wrong way and he began his journey to the Patriot perspective right then and there.

After the war, Alexander became increasingly critical of British policy *toward* and British military presence *in* the colonies. By 1774, he was active in most of the militant Patriot causes and by '75, was part of the open rebellion against the crown. In '76, he received a commission as brigadier general and became one of Washington's favorites.

His greatest military contribution came during the Battle of Long Island in August of 1776. General Alexander led the rearguard that allowed Washington's miraculous escape across the East River to take place. His division included the fabled Maryland Line, which charged the attacking British troops and gave the Continentals time to assemble and escape. Most of Alexander's boys were killed or captured that day. General Alexander himself fought through to the Hessians, refusing to surrender himself to the English (Aye! Now there's a proud son of Scotland. William Wallace would be pleased!). He was held as a prisoner on parole for several months in New York City, being exchanged later in the year and rejoining the army for the attacks on Trenton and Princeton. During the encampment that winter, he was promoted to major general in February 1777.

During the spring and summer of '77, Alexander saw service in the Hudson highlands, but returned to Philadelphia to fight alongside Washington at Brandywine and Germantown. He spent the hardest winter yet at Valley Forge and did much to strengthen the spirit of the troops. He exposed a plot by disloyal officers to remove Washington from command of the army in favor of the bumbling and inept Horatio Gates. It became known as the Conway Cabal, named for the officer General Thomas Conway (an Irishman who had come from service with the French) who led the disloyal and disaffected. General William Alexander, Lord Stirling, was one of several officers who challenged Conway to a duel—Conway never showed.

In 1778, Alexander fought at the Battle of Monmouth Courthouse where he directed the artillery with great skill and inflicted devastating casualties at the most important moment. He presided over the Court Martial of general Charles Lee who led the initial assault, yet inexplicably ordered a retreat when all wisdom (and his orders) said attack! Alexander and the court returned a verdict of guilty and Lee was dismissed from service. Many years later, it was revealed that this Lee was in cahoots with the British…he was a *"damnable traitor,"* to use Washington's description.

Alexander's men supported the successful attack on Paulus Hook and played a large role in the Staten Island campaign of 1780. Alexander also sat on the Board of Inquiry into the accusations of espionage against Major John André, Benedict Arnold's British accomplice and "handler."

At the end of the war, Alexander was in command of the Northern Department, headquartered in Albany, NY, keeping the U.S. safe from an invasion from Canada (not a possibility today, but during the Revolution, *always* a threat). He would remain "on duty" until his dying day. William Alexander lived life "large," like a man "to the manor born." His table was always open and in his presence, it "snowed food and rained drink!" His over-zealous feasting undoubtedly contributed to his death from gout on January 15, 1783. And so passed General William Alexander, Lord Stirling, Son of Liberty, son of Scotland, and Champion of Freedom.

Gentle Giant of the American Revolution.

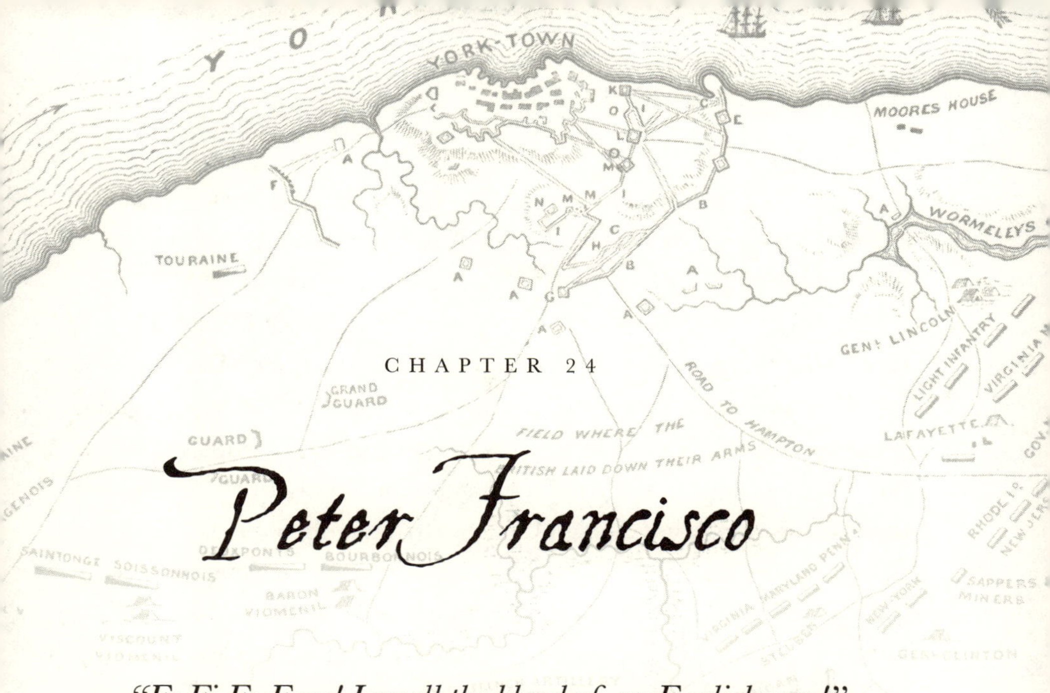

CHAPTER 24

Peter Francisco

"Fe Fi Fo Fum! I smell the blood of an Englishman!"

The story of Peter (Pedro) Francisco reads like something out of a Robert Louis Stevenson novel: Treasure Island, the Black Arrow, or Kidnapped! That may be giving away the plotline here. There is action, adventure, and intrigue! Here be treachery and skullduggery!

Is is believed that Pedro was kidnapped from his wealthy parents' estate on the Azore Islands for ransom or revenge. However, things were meant to work out. Pedro never made it home. At the tender age of five, he was dumped on the docks at City Point (now a part of Hopewell), Virginia, on June 23, 1765. He spoke no English, he just repeated again and again, "Pedro, Pedro Francisco." The gentlepeople of City Point took the boy to the authorities and he was later made a "ward of the crown"—an orphan—and sent to the county poor house. Pedro grew to become the largest man in America and the most remarkable warrior of the American Revolution, a true giant of a soldier who earned the respect of all. Not least of these being General George Washington, who said of him, *"Without Peter we would have lost two crucial battles, perhaps the War, and with it our freedom,"* or so legend says. And truth be told, this guy was a revolutionary "Johnny Rambo," a real One-Man Army.

Not long after young Pedro was taken to the Prince George County Poorhouse, his tale came to the attention of Anthony Winston, a local judge and uncle of Virginia's famed firebrand, Patrick Henry. Judge Winston took the boy in and taught him to speak the "King's English." Once Pedro could talk with his new guardian, he told what he remembered of his past. Sadly, it wasn't much. He remembered living in a mansion near the ocean. He believed that his mother spoke what he thought was French, and his father spoke something else—what it was, he couldn't say. As Pedro and his younger sister were playing in the garden, they were grabbed by rough men. The girl fought and got away, but Pedro was bound, gagged, blindfolded, and taken to a ship. After a long voyage, he was "dumped" ashore at the City Point dock.

The Judge never learned more of Pedro's past, nor did he put much effort into it. Whether the sailors intended to sell the boy into indentured servitude or not, that pretty much became his fate. Judge Winston called him Peter and the boy received very little formal schooling. Winston chose instead to put him to work doing chores around "Hunting Tower," his 3,600-acre estate in Buckingham County, Virginia.

When he "came of age," Francisco had grown like a weed: he stood six-feet-six-inches tall, towering almost a full foot over average men of the day and weighing in at better than 280 pounds. He was King Kong in a three-cornered hat! Even as a teenager, Francisco was already a giant—tall and broad and immensely powerful, it was a "no-brainer" that he would learn the trade of the blacksmith. And it was his incredible strength, rather than his remarkable size, that won him fame.

The Giant Awakens

March 1775 is when Francisco's story really gets going. He went with Judge Winston to Richmond for a meeting of the Virginia Convention.

Tempers were hot as the delegates debated Virginia's relationship with Great Britain. Young Peter jumped right onto center stage when he broke up a tavern fight by hoisting the belligerents high into the air and bashing them together until they "lost their desire for further argument."

It was during this time that the young man stood in the crowd outside St. John's Church and heard through the window the fiery speech of Patrick Henry that ended with this bold call to action: *"I know not what course others may take, but as for me, give me liberty or give me death!"* Francisco was ready right then and there to take up arms against the Redcoats and fight for liberty or die in the attempt! Judge Winston convinced him to wait. Even though Francisco was large enough to go to war (he was large enough to be a platoon!), he was not quite old enough. In 1776, Winston agreed that at the age of sixteen, Peter could enlist. And enlist he did, as a private with the 10th Virginia Regiment.

Although he did not fight at Bunker Hill or Saratoga, his military career, at almost every turn, followed the course of the War of Independence. After the most basic training in New Jersey following his enlistment, Francisco got his "baptism of fire" in September 1777 at Brandywine Creek in Pennsylvania. There General Washington's Continental Army attempted to halt the advance toward Philadelphia of better than 12,500 British troops commanded by General William Howe. Outmaneuvered and outflanked by Howe's army, we suffered defeat at Brandywine and Washington's army was forced to retreat. Francisco's regiment held the line at a narrow defile called Sandy Hollow Gap for a grueling 45 minutes, allowing the rest of the force to withdraw and preventing an all-out rout. Young private Francisco was WIA (wounded in action)—a gunshot wound to his leg during the heroic stand of the 10th Virginia. It would be the first of five injuries. While hospitalized in Bethlehem, Pennsylvania, he met the Marquis de Lafayette, the 20-year-old major general in Washington's Army who had been wounded during the battle, as well. These boys came from different sides of the tracks, yet they "healed up" together and became friends.

By October, Francisco was well enough to rejoin his regiment for the Battle of Germantown, five miles north of Philadelphia. Even though the British eventually forced our retreat, this fight restored the Continental soldier's morale and spirit. They would have held the day but for an unfortunate friendly fire incident, and now they knew that they could best the British.

He was with the Continentals at Fort Mifflin on Port Island in the Delaware River until mid-November when the post was abandoned because of a furious British barrage. So Francisco went with the army to Valley Forge, where he was hospitalized for two of those hellish months. For the remainder of his enlistment, he and his regiment fought through a series of critical battles. Along the way, he performed feats of such an incredible strength and courage that by war's end, he was regarded as the most famous private of the Revolutionary War. He fought at Monmouth Courthouse against the best the British had on June 28, 1778, where a musket ball tore into his right thigh (same leg as before), leaving a wound that troubled him for the rest of his life.

On the night of July 15, 1779, Francisco was part of the daring sneak attack led by General "Mad" Anthony Wayne on Stony Point, the British Army's fort on the Hudson River north of New York City. The assault columns were spearheaded by two 20-man commando teams known as "forlorn hopes" (meaning not a snow ball's chance in hell of surviving the attack). Francisco was in the northern team, led by Lieutenant Gibbon. Gibbon's group sustained so many casualties that only he, Francisco, and one other man reached their objective. Fortunately, the main force was right behind them. Wayne's men were victorious and seized the fort. During the attack, Francisco got his third wound of the war, a nine-inch gash in the stomach, but that didn't even slow him down! He still killed three enemy grenadiers (elite soldiers) and captured the enemy's flag. After healing in Fishkill, New York, the wounded warrior "kicked his heels" with the rest of the troops until December 1779 when his three-year "hitch" was up, and he returned to Virginia.

Francisco's journey back down south followed a turn in the same direction of the conflict itself. In early 1778, the British decided to move their heaviest activities to the South, partly because they expected to have the backing of the many Loyalists they assumed resided in the region. When Peter heard of the enemy's plans, he re-enlisted as part of the Virginia militia.

Goliath Goes South

The British idea was to capture Savannah and secure all of coastal Georgia, then attack Charleston, South Carolina. Congress chose General Horatio Gates, an unpleasant and unable man whose political connections and victory at Saratoga in 1777 (due to the heroics of others, especially Daniel Morgan and Benedict Arnold) had falsely inflated his reputation, as the man to check the Redcoats' advance in the South. The following battle at Camden, South Carolina, was an unparalleled debacle. And Francisco was there to experience the disaster first-hand.

The Battle of Camden was fought on August 16, 1780. It was an utter rout and ranked by 19th-century historian John Fiske as *"the most disastrous defeat ever inflicted on an American army."* In the jaws of defeat and disaster, Francisco performed two of his most shining acts of heroism. Overrun and surrounded by British soldiers during the frenzied skedaddle, he impaled a British cavalryman with a musket and bayonet, threw him from his horse, and then "saddled up" himself and escaped through the advancing enemy by pretending to be a Tory. When he caught up with his buddies, he gave the horse to his colonel, saving the exhausted officer's life (not to mention the life of the exhausted horse). Next, seeing that one of two Continental cannon was being left behind, Francisco squatted beneath the half-ton gun, lifted it from its carriage and onto his shoulder, and carried it off the field, allowing the weapon to fight another day. No wonder Francisco was regarded as the strongest man in America!

Francisco again returned to Virginia after the disaster at Camden. When he heard that Captain Thomas Watkins was raising a cavalry troop, he got himself a horse and returned to action. Watkins' boys served under the command of Colonel William Washington (George Washington's cousin) and were soon back in the thick of things, making sure to be part of the critical confrontation at Guilford Courthouse, North Carolina, on March 15, 1781.

The Continentals were now led by Gen. Nathanael Greene, who, unlike Gates, was an able commander and one of Gen. Washington's most trusted lieutenants. Greene's tactical and strategic actions in the Southern campaign were decisive in bringing the war to a victorious end. Technically, the Battle of Guilford Courthouse was a British victory—Greene's army "quit the field" after a hard-fought contest (means they left the English holding the ground). By rules of the day, the enemy won. But if it was a victory, the British could ill afford another like it. The losses suffered by the Redcoats were so heavy (upwards of 27 percent) that the British army was effectively ruined. English commander Lord Cornwallis later wrote of his opponent, *"the Americans fought like demons in what was surely one of the bloodiest battles of the war."*

At Guilford Courthouse, Francisco was wounded twice more for American Independence and earned the nickname "Ol' Magnet Ass"—seemed he could attract metal from anywhere on a battlefield. In his book *1850 Pictorial Field Book of the Revolution*, historian Benson Lossing reported:

> *Francisco, a brave Virginian, cut down eleven men in succession with his broadsword. One of the guards pinned Francisco's leg to his horse with a bayonet. Forbearing to strike, he assisted the assailant to draw his bayonet forth, when, with terrible force, he brought down his broadsword and cleft the poor fellow's head to his shoulders!*

> *Despite his latest wound, Francisco did not leave the battle, and in one final assault against the British he killed two more of the enemy before receiving a bayonet thrust in his right thigh the whole length of the bayonet, entering above the knee and coming out at the socket of his hip. As his comrades retreated, the fallen cavalryman was left for dead on the field. A Quaker named Robinson is said to have taken Francisco to his home and cared for him until he rallied.*

Note that the broadsword mentioned above was a present from Gen. George Washington in recognition of Private Francisco's valor. After this exchange, Francisco once more limped home to Virginia. Having suffered five wounds for his country's cause, he could easily have "retired from further service," but his desire for action (let's say) lured him back to the front. He volunteered as a scout to keep watch on British Col. Banastre Tarleton and his horsemen, now running wild through Virginia. While on one such mission, Peter stopped off at an inn to quaff a mighty thirst with a pint or two. Nine of Tarleton's dragoons (horse soldiers) surrounded the tavern and demanded Peter's surrender. (Seemed he had them right where he wanted them!) One of the soldiers further demanded that Peter surrender his silver shoe buckles, as well. Francisco told him to take them himself, if he could—or words to that effect. As the cavalryman approached to take his trophy, Peter snatched his captor's saber and struck him hard on the head. The wounded man fired a pistol, grazing Francisco in the side for his sixth wound of the war (Ol' Magnet Ass!). At the same time, the Giant American cut the soldier's hand nearly off. Another cavalryman aimed a musket at the huge target, but when it misfired, Peter wrenched it from the poor fellow's grasp, knocked him to the ground, and escaped on the fallen man's horse.

With this last act of "military mayhem," Peter's career of terrorizing British soldiers was over. He was, however, allowed the final honor of being present when Cornwallis surrendered his army at Yorktown on October 19, 1781.

A Country Gentleman

After the war, Francisco returned to Richmond in the company of Lafayette. There is a local legend that says as the two were "reminiscing of days gone by" in front of St. John's Church, a young lady leaving the building tripped down the stairs and was caught by our strapping hero. And that was how Peter Francisco first met Susannah Anderson, the elegant young lady he would marry. Before the marriage, however, Peter got the education he had earlier been denied. The story of his determination to rise above his humble status and give his "bride to be" the best life he could offer is as inspiring as the tales of his battlefield bravery. He went to school, sat his huge carcass down next to the children, and within three years was "reading the classics."

While Peter pursued his "book learnin'," he worked as a blacksmith. During this time, a writer named Samuel Shepard saw him at work and recorded:

> *I never before saw muscles as great and developed in so young a man, or youth, he is still a youth, or at least, youthful…his great hands, long broad the fingers square, the thumbs heavy and larger in the nail than the usual great toe. His feet are as exceptional for length and thickness as is his whole body. His shoulders like some old statue, like a figure of Michelangelo's imagination like his Moses but not like David. His jaw is long, heavy, the nose powerful, the slant [of his] forehead partly concealed by uncombed black hair of a shaggy aspect. His voice was light, surprising me as if a bull should bellow in a whimper.*

Other men's accounts emphasize Francisco's gentle nature, his temperance, good temper, and charity. He truly was a gentle giant.

Peter and Susannah were married in December 1784. Peter became a member of the "landed gentry" and it suited him right down to the ground. He became locally famous for his hunting and fishing trips and his gracious house parties where he would sing like Pavarotti. One guest said of Francisco's voice, *"It has a power, depth, and sweetness of tone, with wonderful potency. His pathetic earnestness is irresistible."* Not bad for a big man!

With age came reward. Francisco became rich in renown and fame. In 1819, Congress granted him a monthly pension. In 1824, when the Marquis de Lafayette made his triumphal return to the United States, he made a point of visiting his old hospital buddy. And in 1825, Francisco was named sergeant-at-arms of the Virginia legislature.

The story of Peter Francisco is filled with the love of a patriot for the country that had given him a home. He was known as "the Virginia Giant" or "the Giant of the Revolution," but personally, he preferred Peter or "Pete" to his closest friends. He was generous and forthright and a true friend to the republic.

Peter Francisco passed away from what seemed to be appendicitis on January 16, 1831. He was buried with full military honors in the Shockoe Hill Cemetery in Richmond, one of Virginia's favorite adopted sons.

Alexander Hamilton earned his place in American History with this critical victory during the Battle of Yorktown.

CHAPTER 25

Alexander Hamilton

"Do You Feel Lucky?"

Of the many young rising stars of the Revolution, Alexander Hamilton overcame the greatest odds. He rose from almost insurmountable social challenges—impoverishment, illegitimacy, becoming orphaned, and coming from a Caribbean backwater—to become not only Washington's personal aide during the war, but his "right hand" for the next 20 years. Hamilton and Washington would work closely together during the Revolutionary War, the framing of the Constitution, and Washington's Presidency. The dark times of 1777-1778 were pivotal to the success of the Continental Army, the Congress, and ultimately that of the United States of America. It was also important for Alexander Hamilton. It was during this time that he proved his worth to the nation.

"Get Up, Stand Up! Stand Up for Your Rights!"

Alexander Hamilton was born in the West Indies on the island of Nevis on January 11, probably 1755. His daddy was a Scotsman, in fact the fourth son of a minor lord. He had tried his hand at the "get rich quick" scheme of the day, the sugar trade, and he was a terrible businessman. His mother had been married off at a very young age (less than 16) and was now trapped in a loveless marriage. She left her husband after he accused her of adultery and had her imprisoned (things were very different in those days, even in the morally bankrupt West Indies). When she "got out," she met and "shacked up" with James Hamilton, yep, he's the dad, and had two children together: James Jr. and Alexander. It wasn't too long before James abandoned the family (most likely due to debt), forcing the boys' mother to rely on friends and relatives for financial support. Around the age of ten, Hamilton's family had moved to the nearby island of St. Croix where his mother died soon after in 1768. Friends and relatives took an interest in the future of the young Alexander by getting him work as a stock clerk and teaching him to read and write.

Hamilton had a thirst for knowledge, and mastered "reading, writing, and 'rithmatic" despite his lack of proper schooling. Hamilton's formal education began after a visiting minister, Reverend Hugh Knox, a Presbyterian, gave a sermon that so inspired Hamilton that he wrote a description of it for the Royal-Danish American Gazette. When a group of readers found out that the words were those of an underprivileged 15-year-old, they decided to sponsor his way to the American Colonies and his first taste of formal education.

Hamilton attended King's College (now Columbia University) just outside of what was then 18th century New York City. In this prime location, Hamilton was surrounded by talk of rebellion, as well as arguments against it. Events and issues would shortly lead up to the Battles of Lexington and Concord and although outright rebellion and war against the mother country might have been unthinkable, a war of words was Hamilton's reality. The time had come to make a choice and Hamilton chose to side with the radicals. The popular politics of "the colonies," both pro and con, were expressed using printed and distributed pamphlets. One particular New York Loyalist, known as "the Farmer," favored royal British authority in the American colonies and denounced all actions of a colonial American congress. "The Farmer" got several hot responses from Hamilton and other rebellious and spirited Patriots. "Friend to America," a "nom de plume" of Hamilton, responded to "the Farmer" in his pamphlet. He defended the American congress, writing in reference to members of Parliament on December 15, 1774, *"That they are enemies to the rights of mankind is manifest, because they wish to see one part of their species enslaved by another. That they have an invincible aversion to common sense is apparent in many respects: They endeavor to persuade us, that the absolute sovereignty of parliament does not imply our absolute slavery."* Hamilton continued to write in defense of colonial-American rights throughout the war.

With a shooting war at the doorstep, Hamilton buried himself in the study of artillery, tactics, and military maneuvers. In March of 1776, he joined the New York Artillery and was recommended for an officer's commission by General Alexander McDougall. He was given the title "Captain of the Provincial Company of Artillery." One of his classmates wrote of him:

> *Hamilton's abilities as a conscientious and businesslike leader were evident from his earliest days of military service. He not only had to recruit and train his own men; he also had to see that they were fed, clothed, and paid. While many young New Yorkers may have fought the enemy as bravely as Hamilton did, few battled the local authorities so stubbornly to provide for their troops.*

In May of 1776, Hamilton wrote to the New York Provincial Congress regarding the condition of his men. He was concerned because the men in his company of artillery were not quite at full strength. Hamilton had an additional problem because his men were paid less than other artillery companies and their duties were the same. There was only so much the New York Provincial Congress could do, however. British and Hessian troops under General William Howe disembarked from Halifax for New York City during the summer of 1776. Meanwhile, General Washington marched his army from Boston and proceeded to strategically fortify the main waterway approaches to New York City.

A Blaze of Glory

Hamilton's New York Artillery Company was used in strategic areas in New York City. After losing successive battles for control of New York, he covered the Continental Army's retreat in a number of withdrawals. At first, Hamilton's company was placed at Fort George on the waterfront of Manhattan. During the Battle of White Plains, Hamilton placed his cannon right where they needed to be to turn back an extra-large sized Hessian advance. His quick thinking (and even quicker action) left a positive impression of Hamilton among the American commanders (especially General Washington) and played an important part in delaying the British offensive, giving the Continental Army the time needed to effect an orderly skedaddle. After the Continental Army evacuated New York City, Forts Washington and Lee fell to the victorious British like dominoes. With most of the army's enlistments expiring at the end of December, Washington led a desperate retreat through New Jersey and into Pennsylvania. Hamilton's company was specifically called up to cover the hasty retreat from New Brunswick, New Jersey.

The victory at the Battle of Trenton on December 26, 1776, made Hamilton a celebrity in a Continental Army that had gained new hope and confidence with the surprise winter attacks. General Howe would post troops throughout New Jersey to liberate Philadelphia and Pennsylvania in the coming spring of 1777. Washington recognized Howe's attempt to demoralize the cause and found it absolutely necessary to establish a "toughness" within his army. During the night of the surprise attack on Hessian soldiers at Trenton, Hamilton's skill and experience were crucial. Serving in Lord Stirling's brigade, Captain Hamilton and Captain Forrest's artillery companies were assigned to cover King Street and the parallel Queen Street. The batteries of Hamilton and Forrest were up to the task; each had two six-pound cannon, while Forrest also had a pair of Howitzers. With both streets covered by the artillery, Hessian commander Colonel Johann Rall decided to form up his infantry and artillery and march on the Americans from King Street.

As soon as the Hessians stepped forward, the round-shot from Hamilton's battery tore through their ranks. The Hessians retreated in the opposite direction of the incoming fire (makes sense), and many ended up surrendering because of the effective fire from Hamilton's artillery. General Hugh Mercer placed his American infantry between houses from the direction of Queen Street on the right flank of Colonel Rall's Hessians. The suppressive fire from Hamilton's guns, combined with the marksmanship of Mercer's troops, devastated the Hessian ranks. A general retreat among the Hessian troops was made impossible by Washington's strategy of surrounding Trenton before advancing. Many of the Hessians were enveloped and forced to surrender to the victorious Continentals.

After Hamilton's gallant and heroic actions at Trenton, he was appointed an aide to General Washington. In this position, his writing skills and keen sense of judgement proved essential to the highest command in the army. The 1777 winter encampment at Morristown, New Jersey, found Hamilton with an army of well under 10,000. The army, however, was reinforced steadily as the winter turned into spring. During this time, Hamilton recorded, *"the many deserters coming in from the enemy showed them to be in desperate straits…Since the possibility that the French might enter the war in Europe would disincline the British from sending reinforcements overseas."* General Howe's army made a halfhearted foray into northern New Jersey in the spring of 1777, attempting to draw the Continental Army out of the highlands of Morristown. It would be weeks before Washington learned for certain that Howe's intention was Philadelphia. During that time, Hamilton received valuable OTJ (on-the-job) training and became accustomed to the cramped living style as a part of General Washington's staff.

While the Continental Army waited for the approach of General Howe and the British Army from Wilmington, Delaware, Hamilton described the atmosphere before the Battle of Brandywine. On September 1, 1777, he wrote of General Howe's slow and ponderous movements, the Continental Army's morale, and of the surrounding landscape:

> *He still lies there [Greys Hill, Pennsylvania] in a state of inactivity; in a great measure I believe from the want of horses, to transport his baggage and stores. It seems he sailed with only about three weeks provender and was six at sea. This has occasioned the death of a great number of his horses, and has made skeletons of the rest. He will be obliged to collect a supply from the neighboring country before he can move… The enemy will have Philadelphia, if they dare make a bold push for it, unless we fight them a pretty general action. I opine we ought to do it, and that we shall beat them soundly if we do. The militia seem pretty generally stirring. Our army is in high health & spirits. We shall I hope have twice the enemy's numbers. I would not only fight them, but I would attack them; for I hold it an established maxim, that there is three to one in favour of the party attacking.*

Among the dispatches arriving at the Ring House (Continental Army HQ) were conflicting reports concerning the right flank of the British Army. The secretive movements made by Howe and Cornwallis had couriers bringing in reports all morning. One of Hamilton's duties at the home of Benjamin Ring was to establish the immediate importance of incoming dispatches. After deciding to reinforce the right flank of the Continental Army with Nathanael Greene's Brigades, General Washington and Lafayette, along with Washington's staff, rode along with Greene's troops. At the scene of the battle, they tried to rally the Continentals of rapidly crumbling Continental divisions. The American stand at Brandywine Creek almost proved fatal, but there was no other alternative for Washington. During the nine months that remained in the 1777-78 Philadelphia Campaign, Hamilton was sent on many missions (both confidential and important) at the request of General Washington.

When General Washington decided to keep his army between Howe and the Continental Army's supply line deeper in Pennsylvania, he sent Hamilton on a mission to destroy a supply of flour and prevent other supplies from falling into British hands as they marched toward Philadelphia. Hamilton led a group of eight cavalrymen which included Captain Henry Lee, and was about to burn the mill at the small village of Valley Forge when two sentries fired warning shots from their posts. The force of British Cavalry, largely outnumbering Hamilton's force, at first chased Captain Lee, who took flight across the millrace with a pair of mounted American cavalry. The British dragoons gave up the chase with Lee and went after Hamilton. While Hamilton attempted to cross the Schuylkill River in a small boat, the green-coated dragoons fired numerous volleys at him and the remainder of his party. The musket fire wounded one man, killed another, and crippled Hamilton's horse. Hamilton had no choice but to swim to the other side of the river whereafter he wrote to John Hancock, President of the Continental Congress, that the British could possibly be in Philadelphia as early as that evening. Upon returning to Washington's headquarters, Hamilton was embarrassed to hear that he had been given up for a casualty. Meanwhile, the Continental Congress and Philadelphia Patriots were in a panic, securing valuables, and fleeing from the city. But the British did not enter Philadelphia that night or even within the next week.

Hamilton's next mission was to go into Philadelphia and "scavenge" shoes, blankets, clothing, and other important supplies for the Continental Army. On September 26, the British under Howe finally marched into Philadelphia. Hamilton's missions were not completely over, and after the Battle of Germantown was fought in October 1777, he was sent north to New York. General Horatio Gates was the recent victor of Saratoga, where he defeated British General "Gentleman Johnny" Burgoyne. Gates was reluctant to send reinforcements to Washington, and when he would not acknowledge Washington's request through dispatch, Hamilton was hurried into negotiations. By the time reinforcements had arrived to beef up Washington's numbers, Fort Mifflin and Fort Mercer had fallen into British hands and the Royal Navy now had complete access to the Delaware River and could supply the occupying army at Philadelphia shipping ports. Hamilton would spend the remainder of the winter at Valley Forge in Washington's Headquarters at one of the homes of Isaac Potts, the famous Quaker farmer.

After the desperate winter at Valley Forge and the formal alliance with France, Hamilton watched as the Continental Army became a new animal nearly mauling the Redcoats at the Battle of Monmouth. Hamilton and Lafayette were close behind General Washington on the battle line as he rallied the Continentals to near victory. Hamilton was described during the battle as *"incessant in his endeavors during the day in reconnoitering the enemy, in rallying, and in charging."* During the remainder of his time, he served in the position of aide-de-camp. Washington would not allow Hamilton to independently command a force of troops because it would be unfair to other Continental Army officers who surpassed him in seniority. General Washington and Colonel Hamilton had a falling out in the spring of 1781 and Hamilton resigned as aide to the Commander-in-Chief. After several letters of apology and outright pleading, he was given an independent command during the Yorktown campaign. Hamilton led the daring night-time assault and the capture of the strategic fortification (redoubt #10), at the siege of Yorktown, that allowed the Allied (French and American) trench lines to move forward. Artillery of every kind was now close enough to Yorktown to completely compromise the British position. Cornwallis had no choice, and just like that…it was over.

Following the surrender of General Cornwallis and his army at Yorktown, Hamilton was appointed a member of Congress. He worked closely with fellow New Yorker, Gouveneur Morris, in financing the fledgling (and foundering) national government. Hamilton's steady work with the colonial assembly in congress sums up his wartime activity. His rapid advancement from the Caribbean Islands to college in New York, along with the experience he obtained and contributions he made while in the Continental Army (especially as an aide to Washington) continued with his tremendous influence during the framing of the Constitution and beyond. The extraordinary achievements he made during the War for American Independence impressed just about everyone (except Aaron Burr). Alexander Hamilton's contributions to the United States during this early period will not be forgotten any time soon, and, who knows, just might turn into a "pop" musical.

Fighting the Revolution in the Backyard!

CHAPTER 26

George Rogers Clark

The Original Monster of the Midway

George Rogers Clark was born near Charlottesville, Virginia, on November 19, 1752. He didn't get much in the way of formal schooling, but in his late teens, Clark's granddaddy taught him how to survey the land. And in 1772, Clark put his training to use. He set out from Fort Pitt (now Pittsburgh, PA, right at the three rivers) and rafted down the Ohio River. When he reached the Kanawha River, he surveyed land near the junction of the two rivers. He travelled farther into the Ohio Country the following year, as well, and surveyed land on the northern bank of the Ohio River.

In 1774, Clark was a soldier in Lord Dunmore's War. He served with the Virginia militia and fought at the Battle of Point Pleasant. Following the war, Clark worked for the Ohio Company, surveying land in the Kentucky territory. Some Kentuckians hoped to break away from Virginia and form their own state. Clark opposed this plan, believing that Kentucky would grow much more rapidly with Virginia's assistance. When the

American Revolution broke out, Clark went home and served once more in the Virginia militia.

Kentucky: the Bloody Ground

Clark was vital in protecting Kentucky from British and Native American attacks and the Virginia legislature rewarded him for his actions by promoting him to the rank of lieutenant colonel. In 1778 and early 1779, Clark led an army in the dead of winter against British outposts and Native American villages in Indiana and Illinois. In this campaign, Clark and his men faced many hard months in the wilderness and made many tough sacrifices. Their greatest success was capturing Vincennes, as well as the British commanding officer Henry Hamilton. In 1779, Clark led an army against Fort Detroit, but couldn't capture the British stronghold. He spent the remainder of the war fighting against the British and their Native American allies who were trying to throw out the American settlers west of the Appalachian Mountains. In the early 1780s, he defeated an army led by Henry Bird. In 1782, Clark destroyed several Shawnee villages and defeated the Shawnee Federation at the Battle of Piqua. On this campaign, Clark also destroyed an important English trading post, called Loramie's Store, that greatly reduced British influence along the Ohio.

Hard Times and Misery

Following the war, the Continental Congress appointed Clark as an Indian commissioner. In 1785, he was part of the committee that negotiated the Treaty of Fort McIntosh. This treaty was highly suspect because it was reported that "the committee" had gotten many of the Native American delegates drunk during the proceedings. The treaty confined Ohio's American Indians to a reservation in western Ohio and promised that the U.S. government would protect Ohio's American Indian people against continued white encroachment on these protected lands. The U.S. government, in practice, did very little to discourage white settlers from "homesteading" these lands. In 1786, Clark warred against the Ohio

Country tribes for purportedly violating the Treaty of Fort McIntosh. During this misadventure, Clark seized supplies from some Spanish merchants. This led to an embarrassing diplomatic situation for the U.S., and Clark fell out of favor.

No longer employed to assist the young United States in venturing out on the western frontier, Clark now became involved in some ventures of his own. In 1788, he asked the Spanish government to allow him to form a colony for them along the western bank of the Mississippi River near the Ohio River's junction. Spain refused because Clark intended to establish religious and political freedom in his colony (Spain was still devoutly catholic—you see where the problems began). In 1793, France recruited Clark to attack the Spanish in the Louisiana Territory, but President George Washington used his personal "veto." In 1803, Clark moved to Indiana, but came home to Kentucky after suffering a stroke in 1809 and losing a leg to amputation. He died at his sister's home in Louisville, Kentucky, on February 13, 1818.

They Gave
Their Lives
for Liberty

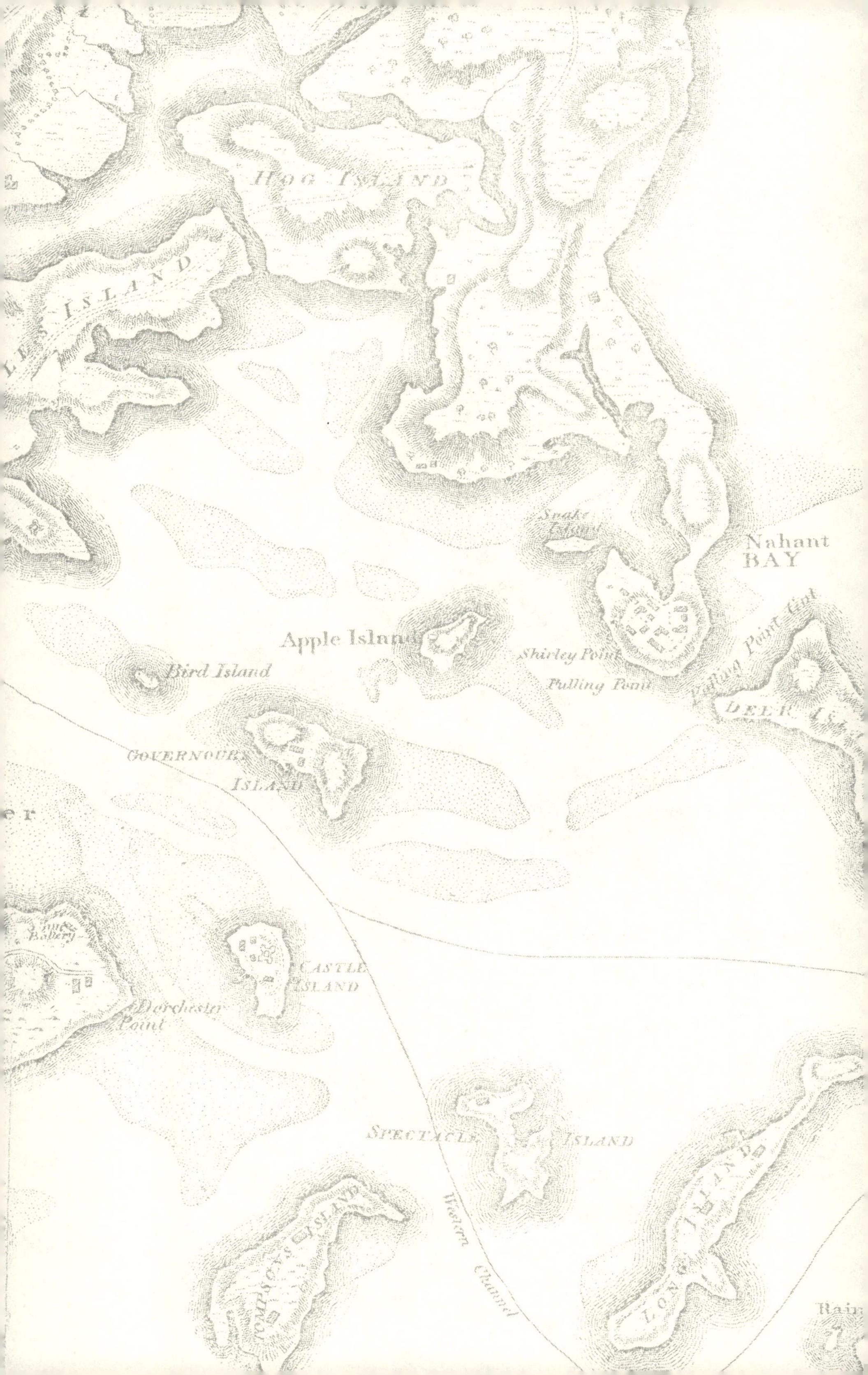

HOG ISLAND

Snake Island

Nahant
BAY

Apple Island

Bird Island

Shirley Point

Pulling Point

Pulling Point Gut

GOVERNOURS ISLAND

CASTLE ISLAND

Dorchester Point

SPECTACLE ISLAND

Western Channel

TOMPSONS ISLAND

LONG ISLAND

This man was everthing to the early Revolution.

CHAPTER 27

Dr. Joseph Warren

The Most Important Rebel You've Never Met

Joseph Warren might have been many things: a great general of the Revolution, a great voice at the Constitutional Convention, even a great President of the United States. But he gave his life at the battle of Bunker Hill just days after his 34th birthday. He left four small children orphaned at his death (their mother had passed in 1773). Ironically, it was Benedict Arnold, who had befriended Dr. Warren earlier, who came to their rescue. He gave $500.00 for the children's education and petitioned Congress in 1778 for the pension of Dr. Warren to be paid to his children until the youngest had "come of age."

Dr. Joseph Warren had lived great and he died well as a hero. He helped to light the lamp of liberty and independence, gave light to all around him, and for a brief moment, stood at the top of "the Mountain" and saw what America might be.

Radical, Rebel, Revolutionary

Joseph Warren was born in Roxbury, MA, on June 11, 1741, the eldest of four sons of Joseph Warren, a thrifty farmer much respected by his townsmen, by whom he was elected to several offices of trust. In October 1755, while gathering fruit in his orchard, Joseph Sr. fell from the ladder and was killed instantly. His son, Joseph, graduated from Harvard in 1759 (I know, I know! Another Harvard grad!), and in the following year was appointed master of the Roxbury grammar-school. He studied medicine with Dr. James Lloyd and began to practice medicine in 1764. He married Miss Elizabeth Hooton, a young lady who had inherited an ample fortune, on September 6, 1764.

The passage of the Stamp Act the next year compelled Dr. Warren to publish several articles in the Boston "Gazette" (a Patriot newspaper). About this same time, he took up with Samuel Adams, who had a warm and sincere admiration for the good "doc"' and soon came to see him as a staunch and clear-headed ally—someone he could count on under all circumstances. With the passage of the Townshend Acts, Dr. Warren published more articles criticizing English rule. These appeared under the signature of "A True Patriot," and they aroused the anger of Gov. Francis Bernard, who brought the matter before his council. The Governor wanted to prosecute the publishers of the Gazette, *"for giving currency* (printing and distribution) *to seditious libels,"* but the grand jury refused to find fault against these gentlemen. The affair created a lot of excitement in Boston and led Gov. Bernard to write to Lord Hillsborough, British secretary of state for the colonies, recommending the arrest of the publishers on a charge of treason. Never happened.

In the affair of the sloop *Liberty* in June, 1768, Dr. Warren was one of the first Sons of Liberty, Boston Chapter, and was appointed by them to a committee to *"wait upon the governor at his country-seat at Jamaica Plain, and protest against the impressments of seamen and the vexatious enforcement of the revenue laws"* (many of these complaints are part and parcel of the Declaration of Independence). He was present at every town meeting held in Boston from the arrival of the British troops in October 1768, to their removal in March 1770, and he was one of the committee of safety appointed after the "Boston Massacre" of March 5.

In July, he was appointed to a committee *"to consider the condition of the town, and send a report to England."* It was apparently of him that a Tory pamphleteer wrote: "*One of our most bawling demagogues and voluminous writers is a crazy doctor.*" You gotta love it! In March 1772, Dr. Warren delivered the anniversary oration on "Massacre Day." In November, his name was recorded immediately after those of James Otis and Samuel Adams on the list of the first committee of correspondence. During the next two years, he was deeply involved with Samuel Adams, and when, in August 1774, Adams went to attend the meeting of the Continental Congress at Philadelphia, the leadership of the party in Boston fell to Dr. Warren.

On September 9, 1774, the towns of Suffolk County met in a convention at Milton, and Dr. Warren read his opinions and points of view concerning the British treatment of American colonists (since known as the "Suffolk Resolves"). The resolutions—which were adopted unanimously, by the way—declared that a king who violates the chartered rights of his people forfeits their allegiance; they declared the Regulating Act null and void and ordered all the officers appointed under it to resign their offices at once; they directed the collectors of taxes to refuse to pay over money to Gen. Gage's treasurer; they advised the towns to choose their own militia officers; and they threatened Gage that, should he venture to arrest anybody for political reasons, they would retaliate by *"seizing upon the crown officers as hostages."* A copy of these resolutions, which pretty much put Massachusetts in a state of rebellion, was forwarded to the Continental Congress, which forthwith approved them and pledged the faith of all the other colonies that they would aid Massachusetts in case armed resistance should become inevitable.

After the meeting of the Provincial Congress at Concord in October, Dr. Warren acted as chairman of the committee of safety, charged with the duty of organizing the militia and collecting military stores. As the 5th of March 1775 drew near, several British officers were heard to declare that anyone who should dare to address the people in the Old South Church on this occasion would surely lose his life. As soon as he heard of these threats, Dr. Warren himself took up the dangerous honor, and at the usual hour delivered a stirring oration upon *"the baleful influence of standing armies in time of peace."*

The crowds in the church were so great that when Warren arrived, every approach to the pulpit was "blocked up" and rather than elbow his way through the crowd, which might lead to some disturbance, he procured a ladder and climbed in through a large window at the back of the pulpit. About 40 British officers were present, some of whom sat on the pulpit-steps and sought to annoy the speaker with groans and hisses, but everything went off quietly. On Tuesday evening, April 18, observing the movements of the British troops, Dr. Warren dispatched William Dawes, by way of Roxbury, and Paul Revere, by way of Charlestown, to give the alarm to the people of the countryside all the way out on the roads toward Concord. Next morning, on hearing the news of the firing at Lexington, he left his patients in charge of his assistant, William Eustis, and rode off to the scene of action. He seems to have attended a meeting of the committee of safety that morning at the Black Horse tavern in Menotomy (now Arlington), and there to have talked and planned with Gen. William Heath. By the time the Redcoats reached Menotomy on their retreat, Gen. Heath had assumed command of the militia and the fighting there was perhaps the severest of the day. Dr. Warren kept his place near Heath and a pin was shot off his hat by a musket-ball. During the next six weeks, he was tireless in making military preparations for the New England colonies. At the meeting of the Provincial Congress at Watertown on May 31, he was unanimously chosen its president, and thus became chief executive officer of Massachusetts under this provisional (and now completely outlaw) government.

BUNKER HILL

On June 14, Dr. Warren was chosen as major general of the Massachusetts militia. On the 16th, he presided over the Provincial Congress and passed the night in public (government) business. The next morning, he met the committee of safety at Gen. Ward's headquarters on Cambridge common. About noon, hearing that the British troops had landed at Charlestown, he rode over to Bunker Hill. It is said that both Israel Putnam and William Prescott stated their readiness to take orders from him, but he refused, saying that he had come as a volunteer to take a lesson in warfare under such well-tried officers.

At the final struggle near Prescott's redoubt, as he was endeavoring to rally the militia, Gen. Warren was struck in the head by a musket-ball and killed. After the battle, his remains, along with those of other fallen Americans, were dumped into a mass grave by the British grave detail. After the American victory at the Siege of Boston, Paul Revere identified Dr. Warren's body by recognizing the set of false teeth he had made for him. Dr. Warren was laid to rest, with honors, in the tomb of George R. Ninot in the Granary burial ground; he was removed in 1825 to the Warren tomb in St. Paul's church, Boston. In 1855, he was again removed to Forest Hills cemetery, where he now rests in honored peace.

Dr. Joseph Warren never asked any man to risk what he would not risk himself. He led from the front in peace, in politics, and in war. He never took a dime for his service to cause and country. He is a perfect example for those who would lead our nation today.

Courage, Honor, Sacrifice!

CHAPTER 28

Nathan Hale

Bravely and Boldly a Man Should Go…

Nathan Hale was a young man who had every prospect for a happy and fulfilling life. He was very well educated for his day—a Yale graduate in an era when very few went to college. There are many contemporary accounts regarding his appearance and personality and it seems nobody had anything negative say about Nathan even before he became "famous." In fact, he was vividly remembered and admired by his friends and acquaintances—longer than 60 years after his death.

Accounts from classmates, friends, relatives, fellow soldiers, teachers, and students all carry the same general theme: Hale was kind, gentle, religious, athletic, intelligent, good looking (apparently VERY good looking, at least according to the ladies), and as one friend wrote, *"the idol of all his acquaintances."*

Both women *and* men commented on his striking appearance. He had fair skin and hair, light blue eyes, and stood just under six feet tall. No wonder folks said that all the girls in New Haven were in love with him.

Nathan's love of sports included wrestling, football, and broad jumping (stakes marking one of his record-breaking broad jumps are said to have stood on the New Haven Green for many years). Those who knew him commented on his kindness and strong Christian ideals. He attended religious services while in the army and prayed with his men who were ill.

His friendliness, intelligence, and love of learning are best shown by his remarkable collection of friends, his outstanding career at Yale, and his growing success as a schoolmaster. Yet in spite of the above, this remarkable young man ended his life in the most ignominious manner known to his day and age: death by hanging—the ultimate degradation—reserved only for the most despicable of criminals.

Nathan Hale is representative of many young 18th century "upwardly mobile" professionals obsessed with being of service, and who, foreshadowing a 20th century brand of patriotism, asked not what their country could do for them, but rather what they could do for their country.

Captain Nathan Hale

Nathan Hale of Coventry, CT, was born in 1755 into two respectable New England families. His parents, Richard Hale and Elizabeth Strong Hale, were staunch Puritans who believed in religious devotion, a strong work ethic, and education. The Hale family boasted many Harvard graduates and the Strongs included numerous ministers and teachers with solid ties to Yale College. As a prosperous farmer and deacon of the church, Richard Hale was a pillar of the Coventry community.

The sixth of ten surviving siblings, Hale's early years were marred by sickness, but he eventually grew into a strong, healthy boy with a quick mind. Both his mother and grandmother favored education (lots of it, too) and he was tutored by the local minister, Rev. Dr. Joseph Huntington, who profoundly influenced young Hale's love of learning. Both Nathan and his older brother, Enoch, were sent to Yale College in 1769 at the ages of 14 and 16, respectively. They became part of the shining Class of '73, many of whom were destined to have honorable careers in the service of their state and country.

Yale, at the time, provided a "Spartan" life for its students: a thorough, disciplined education in religion, mathematics, science, and the classics (how things have changed!). Its main purpose was to prepare young men for the ministry; however, many of them chose to pursue other lines of work such as law, medicine, or business. During his college years, Hale was exposed to the "cosmopolitan atmosphere" of New Haven (for the time period, it was a happenin' town) and to many new, progressive ideas of the 18th century. It was a different world from the isolated farming community where he had grown up.

His college years were full of activity, friends, and varied interests. Hale was very involved in Linonia (a prestigious, if somewhat stuffy, literary society), participating in numerous debates, plays, parties, and speech-making. During his three-year membership (freshmen weren't admitted), he held every office in the fraternity, including chancellor, and also helped form the first secular library at Yale. Hale graduated from college *summa cum laude* (highest honors) at the age of 18, participating in the 1773 commencement debate: *"Whether the education of daughters be not without any just reason, more neglected than that of sons."*

After teaching school in the "boonies" of North Connecticut for a time, Hale was offered a position back in a big city and he jumped at the chance! New London—this berg fit the bill! It even had a newspaper that was liberal in character, published by Timothy Green, a proprietor of the Union School. Hale's classes consisted of about 30 young men who were taught Latin, writing, mathematics, and the classics. In 1774, he also conducted a summer school for young ladies from 5 to 7 AM. That the young ladies of New London were willing to attend a 5 AM class on the classics was perhaps more a tribute to the schoolmaster's good looks than any attraction to the subject matter.

Hale enjoyed teaching and his mild manner of imparting knowledge was greatly appreciated by both students and their parents. So, in late

1774, he was offered a permanent teaching position as the master of the Union School. It is interesting that his uncle, Major Samuel Hale, a veteran of the French and Indian War, was a famous educator and headmaster of the prestigious Latin School in Portsmouth, NH. Hale soon wrote to this uncle asking for some quick advice about accepting the permanent position and its proposed salary. His uncle most likely replied in the affirmative because Hale decided to take the offer and make teaching his profession.

During this same year, like many patriotic young men in New London, Hale joined a local militia and was soon elected 1st sergeant by his comrades—the highest rank of any new recruit. Apparently, his enthusiasm and military talent were also being recognized by his pals and peers.

When war broke out in April, many chapters of the Connecticut militia rushed to Massachusetts to help their neighbors during the Siege of Boston. Hale's militia marched immediately, but he remained behind, probably because his current teaching contract didn't expire until July 1775. Or maybe he was unsure. Contemporary letters tell of the conflict that went on in his friends' minds—whether to join the new army and fight in Boston or to keep quiet and wait—and the new master of a prestigious private school does not without considerable risk take on the label of rebel and traitor.

In early July 1775, Nathan received a heartfelt letter from a Yale classmate and one of his best friends, Benjamin Tallmadge, who would later become famous as a Revolutionary War soldier, Washington's friend and spymaster, a prosperous businessman, and a U.S. congressman from CT. Always pragmatic, Tallmadge (then teaching in Wethersfield, CT) had gone to see the war for himself. Upon his return, he poured out his heart in a letter to Hale dated July 4, 1775 (I smell somethin' cookin'). After analyzing the pros and cons of joining up, Tallmadge finally told Hale that, in spite of his friend's engagement in a noble public service (teaching school), *"Was I in your condition…I think the more extensive Service would be my choice. Our holy Religion, the honour of our God, a glorious country, & a happy constitution is what we have to defend.*"

The day after receiving Tallmadge's letter, Nathan Hale accepted a commission as 1st lieutenant in the 7th CT Regiment under Colonel Charles Webb of Stamford. He resigned his teaching job with great regret and it was said that his students were "most distressed" at his parting.

After a last visit to Yale and several weeks recruiting men, Hale was ready to join in the siege against Boston. Amid much fanfare—fifes and drums blaring—the 7th Connecticut Regiment paraded defiantly out of New London on September 23, 1775. 1st Lieutenant Nathan Hale marched proudly among them, strong and eager, ready for anything; his new officer's commission and his precious Yale diploma folded carefully in his camp bag. He had exactly one year to live.

During these early army days, Hale kept a diary which records the mostly mundane activities of a young officer on the siege line. Stationed at Winter Hill, he enjoyed military life and threw himself wholeheartedly into the duties of a company commander, trying to be the best officer he could, yet yielding to and clearly enjoying the new, macho experiences of camp life. Like most young soldiers, he complained about his superiors and worried about his subordinates, on one occasion offering his own salary to his men if they would stay in the army another month. Still (he told his friends), he was enthusiastic, happy to be there, and wouldn't accept leave even if he could get it (which he couldn't).

When George Washington reorganized the army in January 1776, Hale received a captain's commission in the new 19th CT Regiment and (to his credit) several men asked to be placed under his command. When spring arrived, Washington's Army moved to Manhattan to prevent the British from taking New York City. Hale spent six months camped at Bayard's Mount, building fortifications and preparing for the inevitable battle. During that time, it was commented that he cared very much about his men's welfare, even praying with them when they were ill. He was also a strict disciplinarian, once cutting up forbidden playing cards, but in a lighthearted way that caused more laughter than resentment.

When the British invaded Long Island in August 1776, Hale had still not seen combat. Later, during the disastrous Battle of Long Island on August 27th, his regiment manned the forts which were never attacked. He doubtless helped with Washington's brilliant retreat across the East River, but his military career was not living up to the exciting discussions of war that had marked his student days at Yale. After almost a year in the army, he had kept records, drawn supplies, written receipts, and supervised guard duty. These were not the exploits young men dreamed of when they went to war.

The Shadow War

At the beginning of September 1776, with the British in command of Western Long Island and the rebel army trying to defend Manhattan, Washington formed an elite special forces-type group of New England Rangers. They were placed under the command of Lt. Col. Thomas Knowlton of Ashford, Connecticut. Knowlton had distinguished himself at Bunker Hill and was rapidly becoming one of Washington's most favored officers. The rangers were assigned to patrol the Westchester and Manhattan shorelines and other points around Hell Gate. Hale was soon invited to command one of the four ranger companies whose mission was forward reconnaissance—difficult and dangerous work…at last!!

Since he could never defend all of Manhattan, Washington desperately needed to know the probable site of the upcoming British invasion. The best way to obtain this pivotal information was to send a spy behind enemy lines. Because paid civilian spies were often unreliable or "turncoats," Washington sought army volunteers for this critical mission. A memo written at this time outlines his desperation, pressuring his generals to find someone, *anyone*, and fast. Unfortunately, in honor-conscious 18th century minds, spying was considered to be a demeaning, dishonest, and indecent activity, unworthy of a gentleman.

Nevertheless, Knowlton was under enormous pressure to find such a volunteer and by whatever inducement, persuaded Hale to go behind enemy lines on Long Island. He may also have been sent into New York City (then at the lower tip of Manhattan Island) to "make discoveries." Before leaving, Hale asked his army buddy, Captain William Hull, for advice. Hull tried hard to dissuade him from the dangerous and controversial mission, but in the end, Hale justified it by saying that any task necessary for the public good became honorable by "being necessary." Most likely he also wanted to do something exciting and useful for a change (with a bit of adventure added in).

Accompanied by his sergeant, Steven Hempstead, Hale left Harlem Village in early September and headed north along the East River. Although armed with an order allowing him to commandeer any armed American vessel, Hale was prevented from crossing to Long Island by numerous British ships on patrol. He finally found passage at Norwalk, CT, and crossed the sound in a rebel longboat. Leaving his uniform, commission, silver shoe buckles, and other personal possessions with Hempstead, Hale slipped into the darkness at Huntington Bay and dropped out of sight.

Unfortunately, details of his spying activities are lost to history. He undoubtedly spent several days behind enemy lines in his contrived disguise as a schoolmaster looking for work. Before he could return with any useful information, however, the British invaded Manhattan at Kip's Bay (East River at 34th St.), taking most of the island on September 15 and 16. His mission now pointless, Hale probably decided to cross into British-occupied New York City, presumably to gain whatever intelligence he could for Washington, who was forced to regroup behind the fortified bluffs of Harlem Heights.

On September 20, New York City caught fire, causing confusion, rioting, and a heightened anxiety to seize rebel sympathizers. By this time, Hale is thought to have returned to Long Island, probably for the planned rendezvous with the longboat (and extraction). On the evening of September 21, 1776, he was somehow stopped, perhaps near Flushing

Bay, by a company of Queen's Rangers led by Lt. Col. Robert Rogers (of Northwest Passage fame).

The circumstances of his capture have never been completely explained, although many ideas have been put forward. Almost immediately after Hale's death, rumors flew that he had actually been recognized while undercover by his first cousin, Samuel Hale. A Harvard-educated lawyer, Samuel was a devout Loyalist then in New York working for the British to care for American prisoners. Back home in New England, Samuel was accused of heartlessly betraying Nathan and turning him over to the enemy. These allegations were denied by Samuel and what part, if any, he had in his cousin's fate has never been confirmed. Nonetheless, "Samuel the Tory" was vilified for the remainder of his life and forbidden to return to his native state of New Hampshire after the war (he had fled to England). Even his descendants were disgraced by Samuel's alleged betrayal of an American hero.

Nathan Hale was immediately brought for questioning before the British commander, General William Howe, who had just moved into the Beekman Mansion (near the present corner of 51st Street and 1st Avenue). Intelligence information was found on Hale's person and since this was not in code or invisible ink, he was irrevocably compromised. He therefore thought it best to identify himself, his rank, and the purpose of his mission. This may have been done to establish a record of his fate or perhaps to regain some semblance of an honest soldier (rather than a spy). Although Howe was moved by the young man's demeanor and patriotism, it could not be denied that he was out of uniform behind enemy lines. The customs of war were clear and Hale was sentenced to hang the next day.

Tradition says that Hale spent the night confined in a greenhouse on the Beekman estate and that he was denied a minister or even a bible by the provost marshal, an unsavory villain named William Cunningham. The next morning, Sunday, September 22, 1776, at 11:00 AM, Nathan Hale was marched north, about a mile up the post road to the Park of Artillery. It was located next to a public house called the Dove Tavern, about 5 1/2 miles from the city limits. This mileage along the Post Road corresponds closely with the traditional site of the Dove Tavern at the present NW corner of 66th Street and 3rd Avenue.

After making what a British officer called a *"sensible and spirited speech"* to those few in attendance, the former schoolteacher and Yale graduate was executed by hanging—an extremely ignominious and horrible fate to one of his time and class. A British engineer, John Montresor, kindly sheltered Hale in his marquee (tent) while they were making preparations for the hanging. Hale entered and appeared calm, asking Montresor for writing materials. He then wrote two letters: one to his favorite brother and classmate, Enoch Hale, and the other to his military commander. These letters have never been found and were probably destroyed by the provost marshal, Cunningham, who later gained possession of them.

Captain Montresor witnessed the hanging and was touched by the event, the patriot's composure, and his last words. As "fate" would have it, Montresor was ordered to deliver a message from General Howe to Washington (under a white flag) that very afternoon. While at American headquarters, he told Alexander Hamilton, then a captain of artillery, about Hale's fate. A few days later, Hale's friend, Captain Hull, went with the delegation returning Washington's answer to Howe and managed to speak with Montresor. The British engineer told Hull that Hale *"had impressed everyone with his sense of gentle dignity and his consciousness of rectitude and high intentions."* Montresor quoted Nathan's words on the gallows as, *"I only regret that I have but one life to lose for my country"*.

This elegant statement, paraphrased from Addison's popular play of the day, *Cato* (one of General Washington's favorites, by the way), is the quotation best remembered from the execution of Nathan Hale. He must have been telling the British that his cause still had great merit and that someone like himself—intelligent, educated, and decent—was willing to die for it without regret. Puttin' it in perspective, however, means that the "cause" was in bad shape in September 1776. The much-defeated and demoralized Continental Army had been chased into upper Manhattan, ripe for total destruction by the vastly superior British. American soldiers were deserting by the dozen now, sometimes whole companies at once, and the end seemed only a matter of time. But Hale told the British straight up, standing on the gallows, that *"his country"* was still worthwhile and worth dying for. The enemy was rightly impressed, especially since most of them saw "the rebels" as a dirty, rag-tag mob of contentious rabble.

Another dependable statement from Nathan Hale's execution is found in the diary of Lt. Robert MacKensie, a British officer stationed in New York at the time. The diary entry was made on the very day of Hale's execution, September 22, 1776: *"He behaved with great composure and resolution, saying he thought it the duty of every good Officer, to obey any orders given him by his Commander-in-Chief; and desired the Spectators to be at all times prepared to meet death in whatever shape it might appear."*

This witness supports the idea that Hale wanted to be remembered as a "soldier under orders" and not a spy. Other Nathan Hale's "last words" from "contemporary" sources are as follows:

"You are shedding the blood of the innocent; if I had ten thousand lives, I would lay them all down, if called to it, in defence of my injured, bleeding country." (Essex Journal, February 2, 1777)

"I am so satisfied with the cause in which I have engaged, that my only regret is that I have not more lives than one to offer in its service." (Independent Chronicle, May 17, 1781, Hull may have been the source)

"There is no death which would not be rendered noble in such a glorious cause." (Memoirs, 1837, Marquis de LaFayette. Note: LaFayette was not in America at the time and is probably reporting stories he heard at headquarters)

The best evidence of Nathan Hale's courage and dedication come from a Tory and a British officer. Only the most timid and jealous from the "ivory tower" of revisionism would doubt the honor and bravery of Nathan Hale; true patriot and martyr to the cause of Liberty and Independence.

And so it was that an insignificant schoolteacher who never wrote anything important, never owned any property, never had a permanent job, never married or had children, never fought in a battle, and failed in his final mission made history in the last few seconds of this life. He is to be admired because of his courage in accepting a difficult mission (both dishonorable and dangerous) that he did not have to do. Then he had the cool presence of mind to set the British straight about American patriotism, literally in the shadow of the gallows. Regardless of exactly what he said, it must have been impressive and powerful. Hale deserves to be remembered for his genuine dedication, courage, and willingness to pay the ultimate price for love of country with honor and dignity.

Nathan Hale's body was left hanging for several days near the site of his execution and was later buried in an unmarked grave. He was 21 years old.

He led a hero's life—
and met a hero's fate!

CHAPTER 29

Casimir Pulaski

Cavalier, Crusader, and Champion of Liberty

Casimir Pulaski is remembered in many ways. In Poland, he is remembered as a man who fought for freedom on two continents and is given the title "Soldier of Liberty." In the United States, numerous streets, bridges, counties, and towns are named for him in honor of his aid to American forces. In Savannah, Georgia, a large monument commemorates his sacrifice fighting for the city during the American Revolution. Above all, he is the man who provided the American Army with their first true horse soldiers, cementing his place as "The Father of the American Cavalry."

"L'AUDACE, L'AUDACE, TOUJOURS L'AUDACE!" FREDERICK II OF PRUSSIA (BOLDNESS, BOLDNESS, AND EVER MORE BOLDNESS!)

Born on March 6, 1745, in Warka, Poland, Casimir Pulaski was the middle of the three sons of Josef Pulaski. He came from a family of chivalrous and knightly traditions. The Pulaski family took part in the victorious wars of King John III Sobieski against the Turks in the 17th century.

By age 21, Pulaski proved to be a real military prodigy, fighting in battles across the European continent. By 1776, Pulaski heard of America's struggle for independence. The call of liberty and the romance of the "rebel" was too much for the daring young officer. He gallantly offered his services to the American cause. Pulaski arrived in Boston in July 1777. He served next to George Washington, who appreciated Pulaski's vast military experience. On September 15, 1777, the American Congress promoted Pulaski to the rank of brigadier general in command of cavalry. Pulaski quickly distinguished himself at Brandywine, where he covered the retreat of Washington's troops, preventing a total rout. He gained more success at Germantown by effectively screening the Continental withdrawal.

Pulaski stayed with the army in the harsh conditions of Valley Forge and in May 1778, began to form an independent cavalry unit that would be known as the Pulaski Legion. Pulaski's group had an "international" flavor, being made up of Americans, Germans, Frenchmen, Irishmen, and Poles, and they would see immediate action in October along the New Jersey coast. The Pulaski Legion would later guard the northeast border of Pennsylvania before heading south.

In May 1779, the Pulaski Legion helped defend Charleston, South Carolina, against the British. The following months, the legion engaged in reconnaissance and guerrilla warfare in South Carolina.

By that fall, the Pulaski Legion headed toward Savannah, Georgia, to join other French and American troops to retake Savannah from the British. In the attack on October 9, 1779, American and French forces fell short of retaking the city. Pulaski was mortally wounded by grapeshot in a courageous charge attempting to break the British lines. He would die two days later aboard the American ship *Wasp* en route to Charleston. Pulaski was buried at sea near the place where the Savannah River flows into the Atlantic.

In 1833, the new fort being constructed on Cockspur Island outside of Savannah was christened Fort Pulaski in honor of General Casimir Pulaski, father of the U.S. Cavalry and hero of the American Revolution.

Foreign
Friends of
Freedom
Powder Magazine
Winter Hill Fort
Plowed Hill
Redoubt
Cobble Hill
Little Cove
CHARLESTOWN
Hudsons P.
Mill Pond
BOS
Rowes Wharf
Windmill
3 Gun Batt.
Brookline Fort
Cedar Swamp
4 Gun Batt.
Redoubt
Block Ho & Battery
Muddy River
3 Gun Batt.
George Tavern
BOSTON NECK
Brookline
ROXBURY
Roxbury Fort
DORCHESTER NECK
CHARLESTOWN

HOG ISLAND

LES ISLAND

Snake Island

Nahant
BAY

Apple Island

Bird Island

Shirley Point

Pulling Point

Pulling Point Gut

DEER IS

GOVERNOURS ISLAND

er

Battery

CASTLE ISLAND

Dorchester Point

SPECTACLE ISLAND

Western Channel

TOMPSONS ISLAND

LONG ISLAND

Rain

A French noble who shouldered the burdens of a common soldier and was a true friend of liberty!

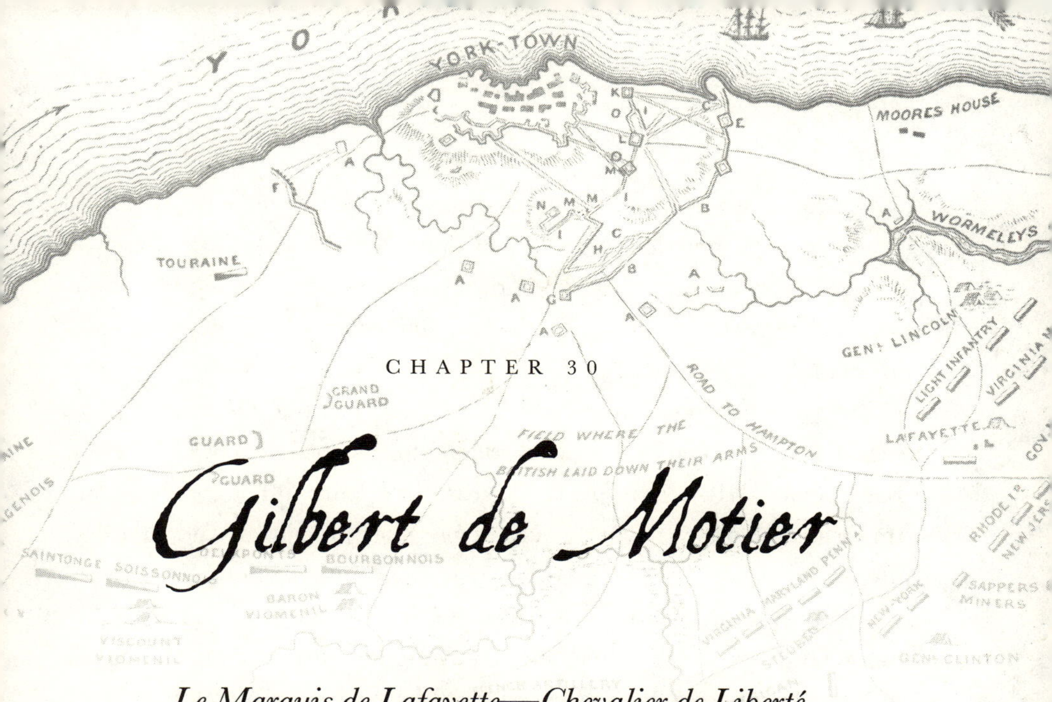

CHAPTER 30

Gilbert de Motier

Le Marquis de Lafayette—Chevalier de Liberté

Marie Joseph Paul Yves Roch Gilbert du Motier, Marquis de Lafayette, was born on September 6, 1757, at the chateau de Chavaniac in Auvergne, France (and you were wondering why he liked to be called plain ol' Lafayette!). His father, Gilbert, Marquis de Lafayette, and his mother, Marie Louise Julie de Riviere, were both descendants of ancient French nobility. Lafayette's father was a colonel in the French Grenadiers and was killed during the Seven Years' War at the Battle of Minden on August 1, 1759. Lafayette's mother died on April 3, 1770, and his grandfather died several weeks later. When Lafayette inherited his grandfather's estate, it swelled his already considerable fortune to an income of 120,000 livres per year. That's about 30 million dollars annually in interest on his wealth today! Wealthy doesn't begin to describe this guy.

Lafayette greatly desired to follow his father's footsteps and have a military career. At the age of 13, he entered the King's Musketeers on April 9, 1771. He was transferred to Colonel Noailles's regiment in

1773, where he was made a second lieutenant. A year later, on April 11, 1774, Lafayette married the colonel's daughter, Adrienne Frangoise de Noailles. The marriage, which had previously been arranged by their parents, sealed Lafayette's political connections to one of the most powerful families of the realm.

Lafayette first heard about the American Revolution at a dinner on August 8, 1775, given by the Comte de Broglie for the Duke of Gloucester (King George III's brother). The Duke spoke openly and favorably of the American revolutionaries and Lafayette became immediately and intensely interested. He saw in the American struggle for independence the opportunity for avenging France's defeat in the Seven Years' War (1756-1763) and for the loss of his father's life. Lafayette had also read the works of the French philosophers and the idea of the American Revolution fired his mind and his passion. As a young man, he found the opportunity for glory intoxicating and resolved to help in the cause of independence.

"Allons-Y!"

At first, Lafayette didn't tell his family of his desire to fight for the Americans. Then, on June 11, 1776, he resigned from the French Army and began actively conspiring with Silas Deane and Arthur Lee, two of the Continental Congress agents in France. They were thick as thieves, and soon everyone knew the young Marquis was a devout revolutionary! Agreements drawn up in December 1776 and February 1777 gave Lafayette a commission in the Continental Army, but reserved his right to return to France if called by his king or family. He set sail for America on April 20, 1777, and arrived in Georgetown, South Carolina, on June 13. When he came to Philadelphia, Congress gave him a commission as a major general on July 31, 1777. Not long after, a dinner was given by several members of Congress where George Washington met the 19-year-old general. This began a lifelong friendship between the two men. In Washington, Lafayette found his hero, his mentor, and his model of republican virtue and a worthy "father figure." Lafayette even named his son

George Washington du Motier and his youngest daughter Virginie, after Washington's home state. The American commander-in-chief greatly admired and enjoyed the patriotic enthusiasm of the young French aristocrat and placed Lafayette on his private staff.

Lafayette received his "trial by fire" at the Battle of Brandywine in September 1777. Wounded in the leg, the young Frenchman immediately became "one of us," a true patriot in the eyes of the American revolutionaries. He was sent to "heal up" at a Moravian hospital in Bethlehem, Pennsylvania (where he met and became friends with Peter Francisco) and rejoined Washington in October 1777. Congress finally gave Lafayette his own command on December 1, appointing him major general of a division of Virginia infantry. Lafayette spent the winter of 1777 with Washington's Army at Valley Forge, which further bonded the young general to the Americans. The enlisted men began referring to Lafayette as "the soldier's friend."

The campaigns of 1778, however, proved frustrating to the French adventurer. In January, the Board of War placed Lafayette in charge of a ridiculous scheme to invade Canada. Lafayette accepted the position with great enthusiasm, but upon reaching Albany, he discovered that no preparations had been made and no attack was possible. Enraged, Lafayette returned in April to Valley Forge. He served well but without distinction at the Battle of Monmouth, New Jersey, in June 1778, and acted as liaison officer to French Admiral d'Estaing in the disastrous joint French-American attack on Newport, Rhode Island, in August. Disappointed, Lafayette asked for and received a furlough from Congress. He returned to France on January 11, 1779.

While in France, Lafayette's fortunes turned around. He became the toast of Paris and was received by King Louis XVI and Queen Marie Antoinette as a returning hero. Using his new-found prestige, Lafayette consulted with Louis XVI's ministers and floated plans for various kinds of expeditions against Great Britain. He proposed hiring the Swedish navy to fight against the British, securing a loan from Holland for the

United States, as well as plans for an invasion of Ireland, an invasion of Canada, an invasion of England, and sending a French army to America. The French government adopted the last two proposals. The invasion of England, a joint operation with Spain planned for August 1779, was finally dropped due to common sense, but the second idea met with more success. Lafayette was disappointed not to be given command of the army sent to America, which was instead led by the Comte de Rochambeau, a man of unsurpassed military experience. In March 1780, Lafayette again sailed for America, this time to prepare for the arrival of the "French expeditionary force."

Upon reaching the United States, Lafayette hurried to Morristown, New Jersey, to meet with Washington about coordinating an attack with the French Army and fleet. In July 1780, he met with the Comte de Rochambeau, who had arrived with a French army at Newport, Rhode Island. Lafayette proposed an offensive campaign, but Rochambeau rejected the plan. In September 1780, when Washington met Rochambeau for the first time, Lafayette served as an intermediary. Soon after, Lafayette returned with Washington to West Point, New York, where they learned of Benedict Arnold's treason. At the court martial of Major Andre, the British spy who conspired with Arnold, Lafayette voted for the death penalty. Major Andre was subsequently hanged.

In early 1781, Benedict Arnold, now a British general, invaded Virginia with a British army. Washington gave Lafayette command of 1,200 New Englanders and charged him with the responsibility of defending Virginia and capturing Arnold. Although Arnold dodged and escaped him, Lafayette successfully defended Richmond, the new capital of Virginia, against an attack by British General Phillips.

British General Lord Cornwallis' army was the next major threat to Virginia. After a costly victory over American General Nathanael Greene at Guilford Courthouse in North Carolina, Cornwallis hoped to rally Loyalist support in the Old Dominion. Cornwallis entered Virginia in May 1781. Lafayette had been reinforced with General "Mad Anthony" Wayne's

Pennsylvania troops and the combined force shadowed Cornwallis' army as it eventually moved back east toward Portsmouth, Virginia. Cornwallis subsequently retreated his army to Yorktown. Generals Washington and Rochambeau had already begun marching their armies south to trap Cornwallis and Lafayette joined the main French-American force for the siege of Yorktown. The allied victory at Yorktown proved the decisive battle of the Revolution, a fact which Lafayette grasped immediately. In a letter to the Comte de Haurepas following the battle, Lafayette proclaimed that *"the play is over, the fifth act is just ended."*

Liberte, Egalite, Fraternite

Lafayette left for France in December 1781. He was once again received by crowd and court alike as a conquering hero. After his return, Lafayette espoused a new vision for France. He wished to have a charter of liberties established, called for the abolition of slavery and civil rights for Protestants, and attacked the tobacco monopoly of the French Farmers-General. During the early years of the French Revolution, Lafayette was one of the most popular figures in France. He became an outcast, however, when extremists gained control of the French government and started the "Reign of Terror." Forced to leave France, he was captured by the Austrians and held in prison. Despite the efforts of the U.S. Congress and President Washington to gain his release, Lafayette was finally set free partly through the intervention of the recently victorious (and to the Austrians, *very* scary) General Napoleon Bonaparte.

Lafayette at first saluted the rise of Napoleon, but later disagreed with the French Emperor over matters of "rights and the people." Throughout his later life, he upheld the United States as a model for the rest of the world. In 1824, President James Monroe invited him to visit America. Lafayette, now in his mid-60s, arrived at Staten Island on August 15. He toured all over the United States and was greeted with unprecedented festival and ceremony.

In France's July Revolution of 1830, Lafayette hoped to finally establish the French Republic. Unfortunately, his actions ultimately helped restore the monarchy, and Louis-Phillip assumed the French throne. In his last public speech, Lafayette attacked the backward and archaic politics of the new king. Lafayette, the hero of two revolutions, died on May 20, 1834, at the age of 78. His grave at Picpus Cemetery in Paris is covered in American soil taken from the site of the Battle of Bunker Hill.

The Drill Instructor's Drill Instructor!

CHAPTER 31

General Baron Friedrich Wilhelm von Steuben

"What is your Major Malfunction??!"

Aside from George Washington, nobody was more important in the development of the professional United States Army than Major General Friedrich von Steuben. His very name was powerful: *von Steuben*. "Often imitated, never duplicated!" von Steuben was one of a kind, and without him there never would have been DIs (drill instructors) as they are known today; no "Gunny" Hartman from "Full Metal Jacket," no "Gunny" Highway from "Heartbreak Ridge," not even Sergeant Stryker from "Sands of Iwo Jima." But because of von Steuben, there are many DIs who have effectively turned teenage civilian recruits into the best soldiers and Marines in the world.

The Principle Problem

Many historians would have you believe that the Continental Army was a bumbling, undrilled mob before von Steuben got hold of them. But it was no mob that earned the American victories "in the field" (means facing the enemy in battle line, "goin' toe to toe" in an 18th century manner of speaking) at Harlem Heights, Trenton, and Princeton. Was it an undrilled mob that fell back before the British attack on Long Island? Yeah, it kinda was, and this was the problem Washington faced when his troops went into camp at Valley Forge in December 1777. For every time the Continental regiments and battalions maneuvered as well as their Redcoat and Hessian opponents, there was an equally embarrassing occasion where Continental formations just flat came unglued, sometimes on the same battlefield. What was the problem?

Part of the problem was that battle in the 18th century was, well… complicated and complex. Commanders had to successfully combine maneuver and fire to win. The battle of Germantown is a good for instance. Gen. Washington had a good plan for his army of 11,000 soldiers to move at night in four separate columns and converge like a vise on Gen. Howe's British camp of 9,000 men at Germantown. As in any action, for any brigade of four regiments to "deploy" from their marching column to the firing line requires the brigade commander to analyze the field and issue clear orders to form the line of battle. Then all 8 platoons in each regiment had to wheel twice in the correct sequence, for a total of 64 movements, to form the line. Yeah…it's a lot of math, as well. Captains, lieutenants, and sergeants kept the ranks in alignment and ensured that the soldiers moved in unison. And deploying from column to line was only step one—regiments also had to march at angles, countermarch, change front, and many other movements with multiple moving parts. Now imagine that occurring uncounted times throughout Washington's Germantown force of 15 brigades with over 50 regiments across a battlefield that was nearly 15 square miles in size, filled with obstacles like woods, fences, and farms. This only starts to describe the chaos. Nobody's even fired a bullet yet! Once the soldiers were lined up for battle, it took 15 or more separate actions to prime and load a flintlock musket and at least two more to fire on command. All this commotion was difficult to master on the drill field. Imagine how it was to pull it all off wrapped up in the smoke, noise, and confusion of battle. Then, when enemy musket balls whizzed through the air, it tended to break a man's concentration. That's what is called "the Fog of War." Repetitive drill was the method that gave soldiers the ability to perform these maneuvers the same way, every time, without thinking…especially under fire.

The other and possibly larger part of the problem was that few regiments did any of this the same way—even from the same states! Drill was the jealously-guarded right and privilege of the regimental commander, and these guys guarded and regarded their "special" mix of everything from the British Army manual *Regulations* and colonial militia hocus pocus with the same paranoid zeal as a rookie coach with a new playbook. Drill was not uniform, in practice or enforcement, so every unit had different levels of ability and execution. Von Steuben would later complain, *"Each colonel exercised his regiment according to his own ideas, or those of any military author that might have fallen into his hands,"* and, *"march and maneuvering step was as varied as the color of our uniforms."*

In large part, the American attack at Germantown broke down because of this disparity in drill and battle skill. Parts of Washington's plan worked well at first and many Continental units fought with great skill, but others…not so much. Platoons, companies, even entire battalions got lost on the march, some didn't press the attack, seams and gaps opened in the lines, and heavy fog and battle smoke drifted across the battlefield, adding to the confusion. Brigades literally collided with and fired at each other. Howe's Redcoats, however, recovered quickly under fire and launched a coordinated counterattack. The Americans GAVE the day to the British.

Two months after Germantown, the Continental Army marched into Valley Forge. By that time, Congress, Gen. Washington, and most of the senior officers had figured out that the army needed some fixin' or the problems with training and discipline would be their undoing. Congress had recently appointed Maj. Gen. Thomas Conway as the army's Inspector General to oversee the solutions to the problems, but Conway was a conniving and scheming hustler and ultimately a deadbeat phony. His famous cabal, attempting to oust Washington from command, caused him to rapidly fall from the favor not only of Washington and the officer cadre, but Congress, as well. For his Inspector General, at a time when the army desperately needed the best training, Washington needed an all-star.

Enter the Dragon!

In February 1778, just as Conway had fallen onto the trash heap of history and the army needed to begin training for the next campaign, Friedrich Wilhelm Gerhard Augustin the Baron von Steuben arrived at Valley Forge as a new volunteer from Prussia. His titles gained him no wealth, and von Steuben came to America as a cash-strapped, but proud former captain of the general staff of Frederick the Great. Von Steuben began without official rank or position in Washington's Army and spent his first few weeks at Valley Forge going all over the camp and "taking the temperature" of the army. He talked with common soldiers and their officers through interpreters (the man hardly spoke English) and quickly sensed that the Continental Army relied more on initiative and flexibility than the British and saw that American soldiers followed leaders out of respect, not blind obedience. He understood that British methods for drill and discipline, with their roots in European class structure, would be almost useless in training the more democratic and independent American soldier. Vton Steuben saw another problem with the Continentals: most officers left drill and discipline to sergeants, keeping themselves aloof and above the "common" soldiers, just like in the British Army. Luckily, von Steuben had a keen understanding of how to train soldiers, given his intense drill experience in the Prussian Army, and he had an uncanny ability to understand and relate to the American "citizen soldier." With the need for training at an all-time high, von Steuben was truly the right man in the right place at the right time. In early March 1778, Washington designated him as *acting* Inspector General, filling the billet in an unofficial capacity, while that loser Conway was DXed (read fired!) from the service.

Von Steuben began his unique brand of intense "specialized" training immediately with a "model company" composed of men hand-picked from each brigade in the army. He created a standard method of drill by combining, streamlining, and simplifying the most effective aspects of European tactics. He realized he had an opportunity available nowhere else—teaching an entire army standard drill from the ground up! Von Steuben taught his drill techniques to the soldiers of the model company, beginning with the basics of standing and facing, then marching with uniform speed and step, then combining all the skills while in ranks. He took great care to not only explain how and why the tasks were important, which helped his students learn "the Prussian exercise," as they called it, but he would get right down in the dirt with the men and demonstrate the techniques, as well.

Although the instruction included the "Manual Exercise," the "how to" of musket handling, and bayonet use, von Steuben's primary emphasis was on maneuvering. A natural-born showman, the barrel-chested Baron exuded confidence as he instructed the troops with the aid of a silver-tipped swagger stick and was an immediate "hit" with the Americans. The training methods made the most of von Steuben's theatrical drill master skills and perfectly suited the independent, common sense character of the American soldier.

Von Steuben trained the troops at an aggressive pace—faster than that of European armies. After the entire model company mastered the techniques, he expanded the program to the army's brigades with the help of newly-appointed sub-inspectors—recent graduates of the "model company" training. In early April, barely a month after beginning the program, entire regiments were successfully drilling as whole units. The program so impressed Washington that he banned all other drill until von Steuben's methods could proliferate throughout the army. Morale soared as the soldiers gained confidence. *"Discipline flourishes and daily improves under the indefatigable efforts of Baron Steuben—who is much esteemed by us,"* wrote one of Washington's veteran commanders. Some believed that any of the European officer volunteers could have done the same thing as von Steuben, but that assumption failed to consider the love and care the Baron had for every man in his charge. It was von Steuben's unique combination of perspective, personality, adaptability, dedication, and experience that enabled him to train an entire army in such a short span of time. You might just say he had been sent by "Providence" to rescue the Continental Army.

Absolute proof of the value of von Steuben's training came on May 20, 1778, when a force of 2,000 men under Brig. Gen. Lafayette was out scouting British lines near Philadelphia. About 10,000 British troops came out to corner the Americans, but Lafayette avoided the trap using maneuvers that would have been impossibly beyond the Continentals' capabilities before von Steuben's training. When signal guns alerted the rest of the army at Valley Forge to Lafayette's predicament, it took only 15 minutes for the Continentals to fall out of their huts, prepare for action, and form a line of battle. Not bad, Herr Baron!

On to Victory

Congress formally appointed von Steuben as a major general in May 1778 and his impact continued long after the Continentals left Valley Forge. The Baron worked tirelessly to capture his drill and instructions on paper in a single manual. At the end of March 1779, Congress approved publication of von Steuben's drill in *Regulations for the Order and Discipline of the Troops of the United States, Part I,* the first manual for the United States Army. The "Blue Book," so called because of the color of its cover, contained instructions on every aspect of operating a military organization including tactics, administration, encampments, inspections, maintaining arms and equipment, artillery, treatment of the sick, drum commands, and the proper duties of every rank from regimental commanders to private soldiers. *"A captain cannot be too careful of the company the state has committed to his charge. He must pay the greatest attention to the health of his men, their discipline, arms, accoutrements, ammunition, clothes, and necessaries,"* was just part of the Blue Book's instructions for junior officers, which made it much more than a mere drill manual—it was and still is the foundation of the American professional army.

Continental training continued long after Valley Forge and over the next two years, Washington and von Steuben implemented the Blue Book with new recruits and existing regiments alike. The value of von Steuben's methods was proved time and again. At battles like Monmouth, Stony Point, Cowpens, and Guilford Court House, the now thoroughly trained Continentals consistently maneuvered with skill and often out-maneuvered their "more professional" opponents. Von Steuben obtained a field command in 1780 and his talents in siege warfare helped the Americans win the battle of Yorktown. But by then, the battles listed above had already happened—the Baron's real legacy!

If that's not enough proof of von Steuben's impact, then consider that the Army used the Blue Book until 1812, 18 years after the Baron died and went to the big drill field in the sky. Generations of American military leaders have carried on his principles that officers and sergeants should act as public servants and take genuine interest in their soldiers' welfare. And since the techniques he applied at Valley Forge, dedication, adaptability, enthusiasm, and humor have been handed down from generation to generation of military trainers, it's safe to say there's a little von Steuben in anybody who has ever worn the uniform of the United States of America.

Polish genius American patriot!

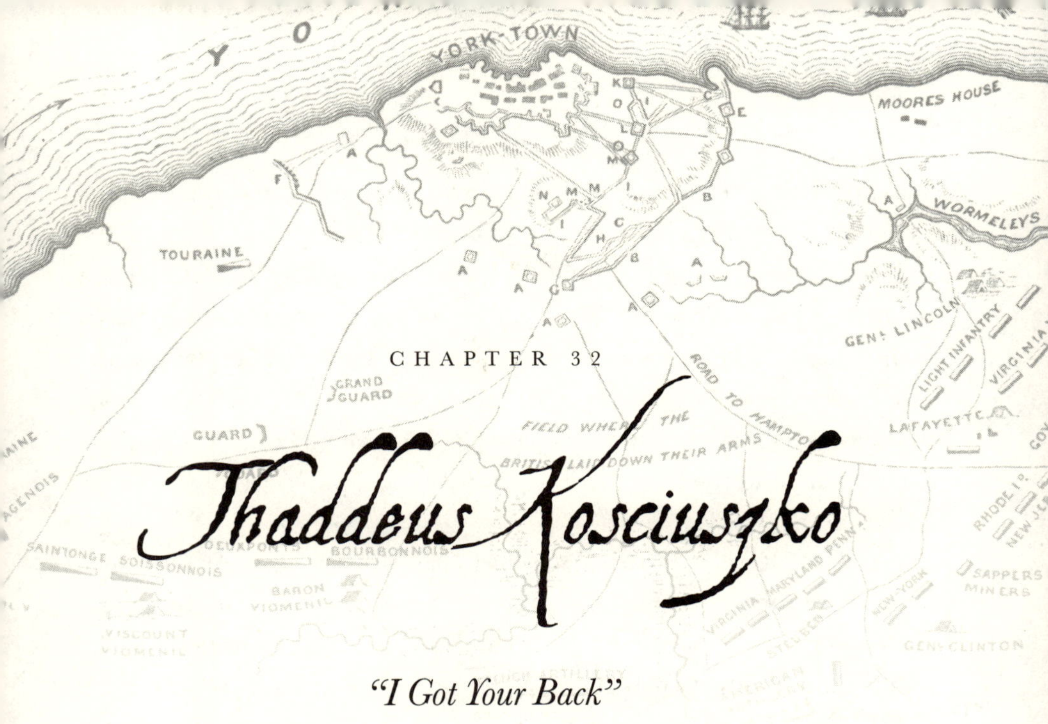

CHAPTER 32

Thaddeus Kosciuszko

"I Got Your Back"

Thaddeus Kosciuszko was born in Poland on February 4, 1746, son of Ludwik and Tekla Kosciuszko. He attended school in Lubieszow at the then Cadet Academy in Warsaw before continuing his engineering studies in Paris. By the time Kosciuszko arrived in America from Poland in 1776, he was a highly skilled engineer who came to offer his sword and his services to the American colonies in their struggle for independence. On October 18, 1776, Kosciuszko was commissioned as Colonel of Engineers by the Continental Congress and began his outstanding service of fortifying battle sites, many of which became turning points in America's war for independence against the British.

Not long after arriving in Philadelphia in 1776, Kosciuszko read the Declaration of Independence and was moved to tears because he discovered in this single, concise document everything in which he truly believed. When he discovered that Thomas Jefferson was responsible for drafting the Declaration, he felt compelled to meet him. A few months later, while moving south with the Continental Army, Kosciuszko stopped in Virginia to meet with Jefferson. After a very warm reception, the two men spent the day comparing philosophies and became fast friends.

In the early days of the war, Kosciuszko helped fortify the Philadelphia waterfront at Fort Mercer. Shortly after, he was transferred to New York where he helped with fortifications along the Hudson and planned the defenses for the Continental positions at Saratoga. The Battle of Saratoga became one of military history's most famous examples of effective militia involvement in the fight for independence and proved to be a turning point in the war.

In 1778, Kosciuszko was made chief engineer of West Point, New York. This fortification became known as the "American Gibraltar" because it was impenetrable to the British Army. In time, West Point became the United States Military Academy.

In 1783, Kosciuszko was appointed Brigadier General and was awarded the Order of the Cincinnati Medal by General George Washington, Commander-in-Chief of the Continental Army himself. Washington also presented Kosciuszko with two pistols and a sword as gifts for his outstanding service to America.

After the American victory in the war for independence, Kosciuszko returned to Poland in 1784 to help his own country gain independence from the surrounding European powers. Kosciuszko was the national hero of the 1794 insurrection. After the successful battle of Raclawice on April 4, 1794, first Warsaw and then Wilno were liberated from Russian occupation. Kosciuszko was wounded in the failed revolt and taken prisoner by the Russians. Upon his release from prison, he returned to America on August 18, 1797, which he considered his "second home." He received a hero's welcome when he reached the Philadelphia waterfront along the Delaware River. Afterward, he secured a residence at 3rd and Pine Streets, which is now the Kosciuszko House, a national memorial to this hero of the American Revolution.

Kosciuszko was admired by officers and soldiers alike, both for his technical knowledge and for his sympathetic understanding and generosity. Jefferson wrote of Kosciuszko, *"He is as pure a son of liberty as I have ever known."*

Tragically, Kosciuszko, a devoted champion of the poor and oppressed, never witnessed the arrival of freedom in his homeland of Poland. He was a firm believer of equality and requested, before leaving the United States for the second time, that the money from his estate be used to buy freedom for slaves, help to educate them, and provide them with enough land to support themselves.

Kosciuszko spent the last years of his life in Switzerland, where on October 15, 1817, he died at the age of 72. He is buried at Wawel Castle in Krakow, Poland, among the tombs of the Polish Kings.

In 1828, a Corps of Cadets erected a monument to Kosciuszko at West Point, where his work was of vital importance to America in the Revolution.

Freedom is the light for which many have died in darkness.

CHAPTER 33

POW / MIA Tribute

A Dream is More Powerful than a Thousand Realities

During the Revolutionary War, almost 25,000 American soldiers, sailors, and marines gave their lives for liberty. Of these, 8,000 were battlefield deaths. Of the over 18,150 American prisoners of war held by the British, more than 15,000 died of disease and exposure while in English custody. The British military saw the American nation as being "in rebellion" and America's soldiers as traitors. These men were treated with inhuman harshness and cruelty during their captivity; many were held in overcrowded prisons in cities under English occupation, most were incarcerated in derelict hulks of ships in Wallabout Bay, New York, and Charleston Harbor, South Carolina. Some were forced to labor in coal mines in Nova Scotia, while others were sent as "slave labor" to British plantations in the West Indies or Senegal. A fortunate few were transported to England and exchanged through the tireless efforts of Dr. Benjamin Franklin and the military prowess of John Paul Jones, whose capture of more than 800 British sailors allowed Franklin to negotiate the release of many American soldiers.

Of the more than 18,000 taken prisoner during the war, fewer than 2,000 returned home. 1,426 are still listed as "missing in action." For most of these men, the promise of "freedom" in exchange for "service to the crown" was unthinkable. They chose suffering, starvation, and death for the dream of Liberty, Independence, and Government of the People. They never betrayed cause, country, or their sacred honor.

Independence National Park in Philadelphia, Pennsylvania, is one of the most visited and active national parks. Here the justly famous and celebrated Founding Fathers debated and adopted both The Declaration of Independence and the U.S. Constitution. Here was where they pledged to one another *"our lives, our fortunes, and our sacred honor,"* placing all on the altar of Liberty and Independence. Just across Sixth Street and a little to the south, The Tomb of the Unknown Revolutionary War Soldier rests quietly on the west side of Washington Square. Upon the stone cover of the tomb are written these words:

> *Beneath this stone rests a soldier of Washington's army who died to give you liberty.*

The busy people of Philadelphia rush by without much notice. Many of Philly's 9 to 5 crowd gather in Washington Square to share a quick lunch and some friendly conversation. If not for the flags of the original states and of the Continental Army and the statue of General Washington *"keeping eternal vigil over the graves of his fallen sons,"* the tomb would be all but obscured by the hustle, bustle, and hurry of everyday business. There is no honor guard, no pageantry as a reminder, but those who gave all that our nation might live and who now sleep in Washington Square must never be forgotten.

The winter of 1777-78, when the English occupied the nation's current capital city of Philadelphia, were dark days indeed. While the British controlled the city, Independence Hall had been gutted (the contents and furniture and such, burned) and was now used as a stable for officers' horses. All churches that were not Anglican were used as hospitals for sick or wounded Redcoats and Hessians. The basements of these buildings were turned into prisons for American soldiers after the Walnut Street prison had been filled to almost three times capacity. Over the course of the bitter months, the prisoners were physically abused, denied food and medical attention, and deprived of any human comforts. They were starved and frozen to death. Common diseases due to overcrowding were rampant in the prisons and these also took a heavy toll on America's first POWs. Several thousand perished from wounds, illness, and privation while in English custody. They were buried in unmarked mass graves in ground thought to be dishonorable and vile—the burial ground of criminals and slaves. Today that ground is known as Washington Square.

All they had to do was take an oath of loyalty to the crown and serve in the British Army and they would have been released from bondage and "restored to the love of king and countrymen." Few, if any, chose to betray the cause, and chose instead a hero's death, keeping faith with brothers in arms and staying true to Liberty and Independence. Can such devotion, service, and love of country ever be forgotten?

Washington returned in December of 1778 to celebrate Philadelphia's liberation from English tyranny. Along with the fanfare and thanks of Congress and the city fathers, the General took the time to inquire concerning "his soldiers" held there during the winter campaign. When he learned of their fate, General Washington wept and was heard to say, *"My sons, my sons!"*

When we walk on Washington Square, we stand on sacred ground.

The Prison Ship Martyrs

During the long campaign for New York and the retreat across New Jersey, the new nation lost more men as prisoners of the English than at any other time of the war. Frankly, the British were not prepared for such a massive influx of POWs. Their response to the problem was horrific: the prison ships. These ships became pest holes where prisoners died at rates of five to ten a day, their bodies tossed overboard and their bones and remains washing upon the shores to be collected by a small band of Patriots in the dark hours before dawn. When the war ended, it was clear that more Americans had died aboard these diabolical hell holes than on the battlefield. These men became the "Prison Ship Martyrs."

The Prison Ship Martyrs Monument is located in Fort Greene Park in Brooklyn, New York. Below the monument rest the remains of over 11,500 American prisoners of war, the largest single Revolutionary War grave in the country. These men were held on British prison ships in Wallabout Bay, now known as New York Harbor, near the Brooklyn Navy Yard.

These are America's first martyrs. Our POWs suffered outrageous and indefensible cruelty resulting in lingering, torturous deaths made more painful by starvation, regular beatings, and diseases. Fatal diseases included yellow fever and smallpox, which spread throughout the overcrowded, filthy prison ships.

One notorious ship, *The Jersey*, was built to hold 400, but when used as a British prison ship, held 1,400 Americans with the portholes sealed to prevent escape. These men spent years suffering from intolerable circumstances, the blistering heat of summer, and the bitter cold of winter. At any time, prisoners could have walked off these ships with their lives had they agreed to defect and enlist in the British Armed Services. With very few exceptions, they all said no and chose a horrid death rather than forsaking their brothers in arms, their new beloved country, and their leader General Washington.

> *"It is foolish and wrong to mourn the men who died. Rather we should thank God that such men lived."*
> —General George S. Patton, Jr.

POW / MIA

You are not forgotten.

Honor their service, keep their trust.

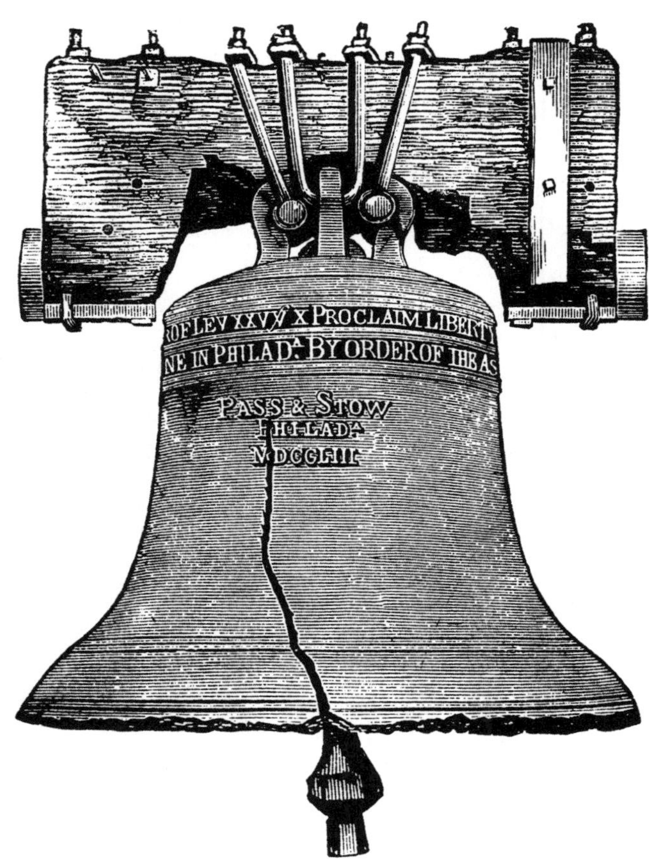
OF LEV XXV X PROCLAIM LIBERT
NE IN PHILADA BY ORDER OF THE AS
PASS & STOW
PHILADA
MDCCLIII

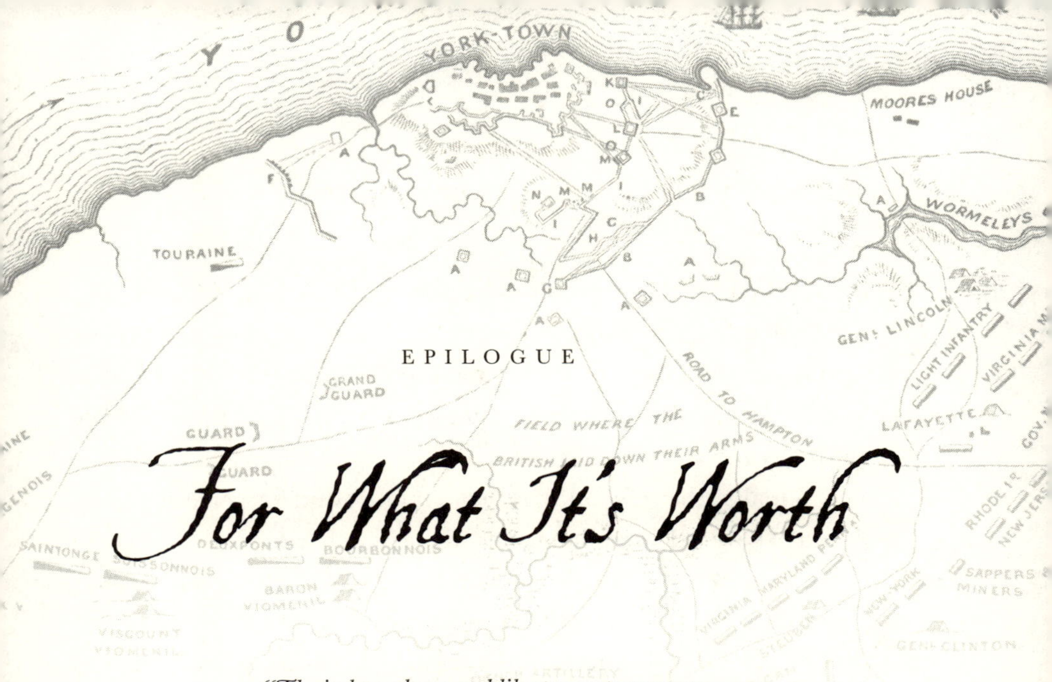

EPILOGUE

For What It's Worth

"The independence and liberty you possess are the work of joint councils and joint efforts of common dangers, suffering, and success."
—General George Washington

After all that has been written about the men (and women) of the Revolution, here's the last thing I will say: They Lived! They saw the need of their day, they stood together, made the necessary sacrifices, and were victorious in the good cause. They were just men and women; not gods or immortals, but men, same faults and failings, same troubles and heartaches, same challenges and trials. But they were driven by something far greater—Faith. A common faith in Liberty, in Independence and Freedom, and in their undeniable faith that theirs was the cause of Heaven!

> *"We hold these truths to be self-evident: that all men are created equal; that they are endowed by their Creator with certain unalienable rights; that among these are life, liberty, and the pursuit of happiness…And for the support of this Declaration, with a firm reliance on the protection of Divine Providence, we*

> *mutually pledge to each other our Lives, our Fortunes and our sacred Honor."*
> —Thomas Jefferson

For this belief, many gave up their lives and fortunes, suffered inhuman cruelties, but never flinched from "the faith." They weren't made of marble or stone; they were flesh and blood. Most were young and in the middle of building their lives—they had families and futures, some had fortunes and security. They were willing to risk all, to lose all, for the chance to make a better world for their children and for generations yet unborn. We have a debt to these souls who gave all and risked all—a debt that we may never be able to repay. Theirs was the sacrifice that gave us our Liberty, our Freedom, and our Independence. Across the globe, we can find the cemeteries that mark the resting places of the honored dead that "kept the faith" to keep our dream alive. From Normandy and across the fields of France, to Pearl Harbor and the *USS Arizona*, to the islands of the Pacific, and in the ocean's sunless depths, their honor and valor sleep stainless and irreproachable.

And now it is our turn. What shall we do to return the blessing? To honor the sacrifice of so many? Abraham Lincoln said:

> *It is rather for us to be here dedicated to the great task remaining before us—that from these honored dead we take increased devotion to that cause for which they gave the last full measure of devotion—that we here highly resolve that these dead shall not have died in vain—that this nation, under God, shall have a new birth of freedom—and that government of the people, by the people, for the people, shall not perish from the earth.*

Freedom: it is the hope of every human heart and the birthright of every American. All who enjoy this great gift share a common culture and sacred obligation to remember. Our endowment of liberty requires that we treasure our history. The legacy of the pilgrims, patriots, pioneers, and the heroes who stood against darkness and tyranny here at home and on distant shores are ours to revere and preserve. These stories *"shall the Good man teach his son, that from this day to the ending of the world,"* they shall always be remembered. We are the guardians of a hallowed heritage and keepers of a solemn trust. We must tell these stories to our children again and again and again so that they will never forget where they came from and will always remember who they are. We must give them a clear understanding of the great gift of liberty and the blessing that is theirs.

So, LIVE! Remember who we are, where we came from, and at what price our Freedom was bought.

Kick a leg over! Throttle up! I'll see you on the Highway! Let's get to Livin'!

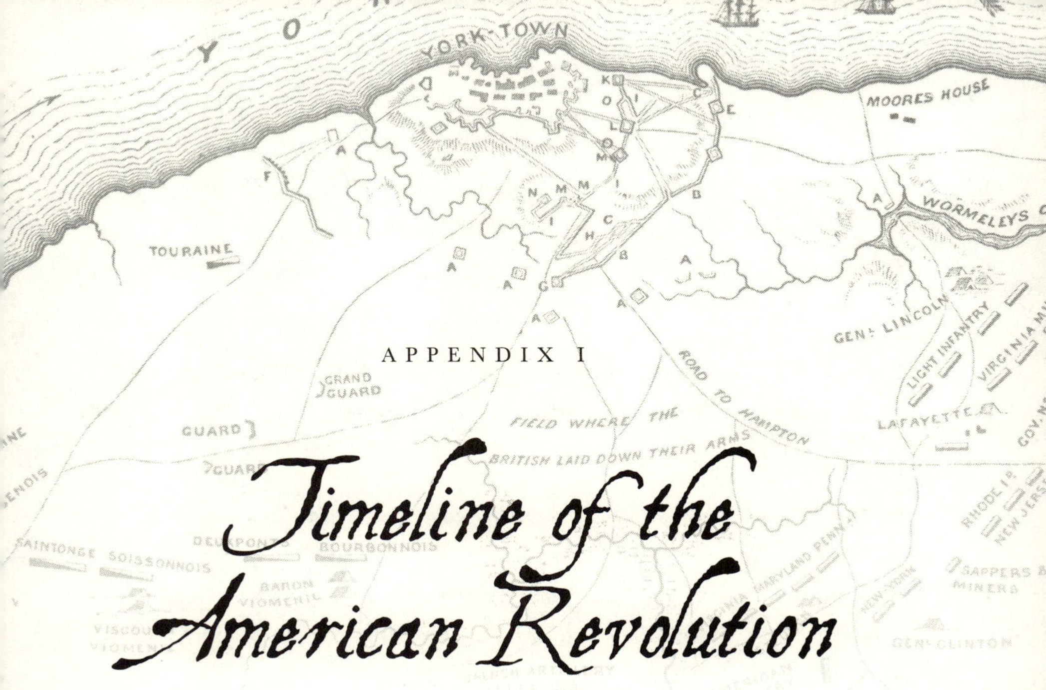

APPENDIX I

Timeline of the American Revolution

1754

May 28 - *The French and Indian War begins*

July 10 - *Albany Plan of Union—Benjamin Franklin proposes a single government for the colonies*

1763

February 10 - *The Treaty of Paris ends the French and Indian War. The English drive the French from North America, and the English national debt soars*

October 7 - *Proclamation of 1763—King George III banned colonists from settling beyond the Appalachian Mountains*

1764

April 5 - *Sugar Act—Smugglers could be tried in Admiralty Courts, without the benefit of a jury*

1765

March 22 - *Stamp Act—Tax on paper goods and legal documents*

March 24 - *Quartering Act—Colonies must provide housing and food for British troops*

March 29 - *Virginia House of Burgesses passes the Virginia Resolves, seven resolutions that challenge the legality of the Stamp Act*

October 7-25 - *Congress meets in Philadelphia to discuss the crisis*

1766

March 18 - *Parliament repeals the Stamp Act and passes the Declaratory Act, which reiterates Parliament's authority over the colonies*

1768

February 11 - *Massachusetts Assembly issues Massachusetts Circular Letter, denouncing Townsend Acts*

August 1 - *Boston Non-Importation Agreement—Boston merchants agree to not import British goods, or sell to Britain*

1770

January 19 - *Golden Hill Riot, NY*

March 5 - *Boston Massacre*

1772

May 10 - *Tea Act—An attempt by Parliament to undercut smugglers by reducing the price of tea to the colonies*

June 9 - *Gaspée Affair—A British ship patrolling for smugglers runs aground in Rhode Island and a local mob burns it; the mob is then accused of treason*

1773

December 16 - *Boston Tea Party*

1774

March 31 - *Boston Port Act—Parliament closes the city's port in response to the Tea Party.*

May 20 - *Administration of Justice Act and Massachusetts Government Act, two of the so-called Intolerable Acts, further anger colonists*

June 2 - *Quartering Act is amended*

September 5–October 26 - *First Continental Congress—Carpenter's Hall, Philadelphia*

1775

March 23 - *Patrick Henry's "Liberty or Death" speech, Richmond, VA*

April 18 - *Revere and Dawes Ride*

April 19 - *Battles of Lexington and Concord, MA*

May 10 - *Ethan Allen and Green Mountain Boys seize Fort Ticonderoga, Second Continental Congress meets*

June 15 - *George Washington appointed commander-in-chief*

June 17 - *Battle of Bunker Hill*

July 3 - *George Washington assumes command of the Army outside Boston*

July 5 - *Congress approves the Olive Branch Petition, a final attempt to avoid war with Britain*

October 13 - *The U.S. Navy is established*

November 10–21 - *Siege of Ninety-Six, SC*

November 13 - *Americans take Montreal*

December 9 - *Battle of Great Bridge, VA*

December 22 - *Battle of Great Canebreak, SC*

December 23-30 - *Snow Campaign, SC*

December 30–Jan 1 - *Battle of Quebec*

1776

January 15 - *Thomas Paine publishes Common Sense*

February 27 - *Battle of Moore's Creek, NC*

March 3 - *Continental Navy captures New Providence Island, Bahamas*

March 17 - *British evacuate Boston*

April 12 - *Halifax Resolves, NC—First colony to authorize its delegates to vote for independence*

June 7 - *Lee Resolution: Richard Henry Lee proposes independence to the Second Continental Congress*

June 28 - *Battle of Sullivan's Island, SC*

July 1 - *Cherokee attack the southern frontier*

July 4 - *Congress adopts the Declaration of Independence*

August 27 - *Battle of Brooklyn, NY*

September 15 - *British occupy Manhattan*

September 16 - *Battle of Harlem Heights, NY*

September 22 - *British execute Nathan Hale, a soldier in the Continental Army*

October 11 - *Battle of Valcour Island, Lake Champlain*

October 28 - *Battle of White Plains, NY*

November 16 - *Battle of Fort Washington, NY*

November 20 - *British capture Fort Lee, NJ*

December 23 - *Thomas Paine publishes The American Crisis*

December 26 - *Battle of Trenton, NJ*

1777

January 3 - *Battle of Princeton, NJ*

January 6–May 28 - *Continental Army winters at Morristown, NJ*

April 27 - *Battle at Ridgefield, CT*

June 14 - *Flag Resolution- Congress declared "That the flag of the thirteen United States be thirteen stripes, alternate red and white; that the union be thirteen stars, white in a blue field"*

July 5 - *British capture Fort Ticonderoga*

August 6 - *Battle of Oriskany, NY*

August 16 - *Battle of Bennington, VT (Walloomsac, NY)*

September 11 - *Battle of Brandywine, PA*

September 19 - *Battle of Saratoga, NY (Freeman's Farm)*

September 21 - *Battle of Paoli, PA*

September 26 - *British take Philadelphia*

October 4 - *Battle of Germantown, PA*

October 7 - *Battle of Saratoga, NY (Bemis Heights)*

October 17 - *British surrender at Saratoga, NY*

October 22 - *Battle of Fort Mercer, NJ*

November 16 - *British capture Fort Mifflin, PA*

December 5–7 - *Battle of White Marsh, PA*

December 19 - *Washington and his army winter in Valley Forge*

1778

February 6 - *The United States and France become allies*

February 7 - *British General William Howe replaced by Henry Clinton*

May 20 - *Battle of Barren Hill, PA*

June 18 - *British abandon Philadelphia, Continental Army marches out of Valley Forge*

June 28 - *Battle of Monmouth, NJ*

July 4 - *George Rogers Clark captures Kaskaskia, in modern Illinois*

July 29–August 31 - *French and American forces besiege Newport, RI*

December 20 - *British capture Savannah, GA*

1779

February 3 - *Battle of Port Royal Island, SC*

February 14 - *Battle of Kettle Creek, GA*

February 23–24 - *George Rogers Clark captures Vincennes, in modern Indiana*

March 3 - *Battle of Briar Creek, GA*

June 20 - *Battle of Stono River, SC*

June 18 - *Sullivan expedition attacks Indian villages in NY*

June 21 - *Spain declares war on Great Britain*

July 8 - *British burn Fairfield, CT*

July 11 - *British burn Norwalk, CT*

July 16 - *Americans capture Stony Point, NY*

July 24–August 14 - *Penobscot Expedition (Castine, ME)*

July 28 - *Battle of Fort Freeland, PA*

August 19 - *Battle of Paulus Hook, NJ*

August 29 - *Battle of Newtown, NY*

September 16–October 19 - *American/French effort to retake Savannah fails*

October 23 - *John Paul Jones and the USS Bonhomme Richard capture HMS Serapis near English coast*

November–June 23 - *Washington's Main Army camps at Morristown, NJ*

1780

January 28 - *Fort Nashborough established (now Nashville, TN)*

March 14 - *Spanish capture Mobile*

May 12 - *British capture Charleston, SC*

May 25 - *Mutiny of Connecticut regiments at Morristown, NJ*

May 26 - *Battle at St. Louis, now in Missouri*

May 29 - *Battle of Waxhaws, SC*

June 20 - *Battle of Ramseur's Mill, NC*

July 11 - *French troops arrive at Newport, RI*

August 6 - *Battle of Hanging Rock, SC*

August 16 - *Battle of Camden, SC*

August 19 - *Battle of Musgrove Mill, SC*

September 23 - *British officer John André arrested for spying*

October 7 - *Battle of King's Mountain, SC*

October 14 - *Gen. Nathanael Greene named commander of the southern Continental Army*

October 18 - *British occupy Wilmington, NC*

1781

January 17 - *Battle of Cowpens, SC*

February 1 - *Battle of Cowan's Ford, NC*

February 12 - *Spanish forces take Fort St. Joseph, now Miles, MO*

March 2 - *Articles of Confederation adopted; Battle of Clapp's Mill, NC*

March 6 - *Battle of Weitzel's Mill, NC*

March 15 - *Battle of Guilford Courthouse, NC*

April 25 - *Battle of Hobkirk's Hill, SC*

May 9 - *Spanish capture Pensacola*

May 15 - *Battle of Fort Granbury, SC*

May 22–June 18 - *Siege of Ninety-Six, SC*

June 6 - *Americans retake Augusta, GA*

July 6 - *Battle at Green Spring, VA*

August 28 - *Battle of Elizabethtown, NC*

September 5 - *Battle of the Capes, Chesapeake Bay*

September 8 - *Battle of Eutaw Springs, SC*

September 28-October 19 - *Siege of Yorktown, VA*

October 19 - *General Cornwallis officially surrenders at Yorktown, VA*

1782

March 7–8 - *Indians attacked by militia at Gnadenhutten, in modern OH*

March 20 - *Lord North resigns as Prime Minister of Great Britain*

April 19 - *Netherlands recognizes American independence*

May 8 - *American and Spanish forces capture Nassau, Bahamas*

July 11 - *British evacuate Savannah, GA*

July 13 - *British/Indian raid on Hannahstown, PA*

August 7 - *Washington establishes the Badge of Military Merit, now known as the Purple Heart*

August 19 - *Battle of Blue Licks, KY*

November 4 - *Encounter at John's Ferry, SC*

November 10 - *George Rogers Clark raids Chillicothe, modern OH*

November 30 - *British and Americans sign preliminary Articles of Peace*

December 14 - *British evacuate Charleston, SC*

1783

March 15 - *Washington addresses the Newburgh Conspiracy and discontent in the Continental Army, Newburgh, NY*

April 19 - *Congress ratifies preliminary peace treaty*

September 3 - *US and Great Britain sign the Treaty of Paris*

November 25 - *British evacuate New York City*

December 4 - *Washington bids farewell to his officers in New York City*

December 23 - *Washington resigns as commander in Annapolis, MD*

MILLMAN

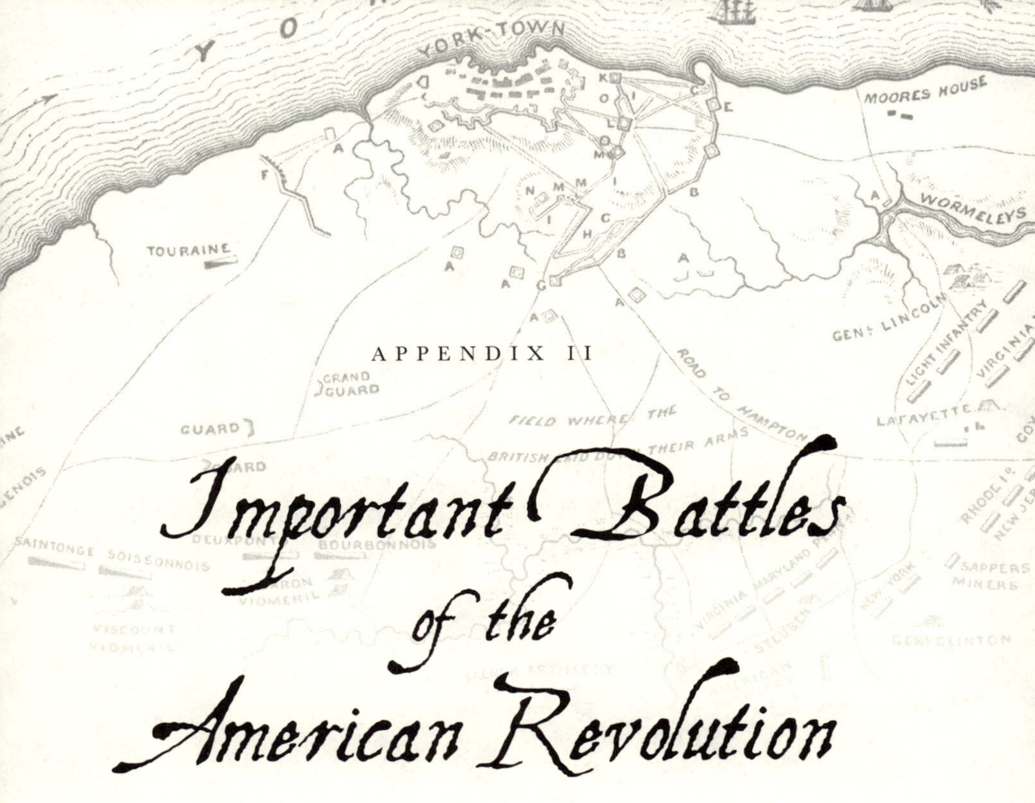

APPENDIX II

Important Battles of the American Revolution

Date of Battle	**Name of Battle**	**Locations and Battlefields**	**Results of Battle**
19th April, 1775	**The Battle of Lexington**	*Lexington Green, Massachusetts*	Colonial Retreat
19th April, 1775	**The Battle of Concord**	*Concord, Massachusetts*	American Victory
April 19, 1775 - March 17, 1776	**The Siege of Boston**	*Boston, Massachusetts. The Siege of Boston included the Battle of Chelsea Creek and the Battle of Bunker Hill*	American Victory
10th May, 1775	**Battle of Fort Ticonderoga**	*Fort Ticonderoga, New York*	American Victory

Date of Battle	*Name of Battle*	*Locations and Battlefields*	*Results of Battle*
27th May, 1775	**The Battle of Chelsea Creek**	*Suffolk County, Massachusetts*	American Victory
16th June, 1775	**The Battle of Bunker Hill**	*Breed's Hill, Charlestown, Massachusetts*	British Victory
31st December, 1775	**The Battle of Quebec**	*Quebec City, Province of Quebec*	British Victory
28th June, 1776	**The Battle of Sullivan's Island**	*Charleston, South Carolina*	American Victory
27th August, 1776	**The Battle of Long Island**	*Brooklyn Heights, Long Island, New York*	British Victory
28th October, 1776	**The Battle of White Plains**	*White Plains, New York*	British Victory
16th November, 1776	**The Battle of Fort Washington**	*Washington Heights, Manhattan, New York*	British Victory
26th December, 1776	**The Battle of Trenton**	*Trenton, New Jersey*	American Victory
3rd January, 1777	**The Battle of Princeton**	*Princeton, New Jersey*	American Victory
6th August, 1777	**The Battle of Oriskany**	*Oriskany, New York*	British Victory
16th August, 1777	**The Battle of Bennington**	*Bennington, New York*	American Victory

Date of Battle	*Name of Battle*	*Locations and Battlefields*	*Results of Battle*
11th September, 1777	**The Battle of Brandywine**	*Near Chadds Ford, Pennsylvania*	British Victory
19th September, 1777 *7th October, 1777*	**The Battles of Saratoga**	*Saratoga County, New York* *First battle: British victory* *Second battle: American victory* *British surrender October 17*	American Victory British Surrender
4th October, 1777	**The Battle of Germantown**	*Germantown, Pennsylvania*	British Victory
28th June, 1778	**The Battle of Monmouth**	*Monmouth, New Jersey*	American Victory
29th December, 1778	**The Siege of Savannah**	*Savannah, Georgia*	British Victory
29th March, 1780	**The Siege of Charleston**	*Charleston, South Carolina*	British Victory
16th August, 1780	**The Battle of Camden**	*North of Camden, South Carolina*	British Victory
7th October, 1780	**The Battle of King's Mountain**	*Near Blackburn, SC and King's Mountain, NC*	American Victory
17th January, 1781	**The Battle of Cowpens**	*Cowpens, South Carolina*	American Victory
15th March, 1781	**Battle of Guilford Courthouse**	*Guilford Courthouse, North Carolina*	British Victory

Date of Battle	***Name of Battle***	***Locations and Battlefields***	***Results of Battle***
8th September, 1781	**The Battle of Eutaw Springs**	*Eutawville, South Carolina*	British Victory
9th October, 1781	**The Battle of Yorktown**	*Yorktown, Virginia*	American Victory British Surrender

Washington at Outposts of Valley Forge

ABOUT THE AUTHOR

Stan Ellsworth is the Harley Davidson-riding host of *American Ride*, the Emmy Award-winning American history program. He was born on the highway and raised in the Carolinas and Virginia. His family lineage includes Revolutionary War patriots Ethan Allen, Henry "Light Horse Harry" Lee, General Daniel Morgan, American folk heroes Daniel Boone and Davy Crockett; the notorious Frank and Jesse James; and . . . General George Washington. Small wonder he went on to earn a bachelor's degree in history.

He also played and coached college football at several universities, including the University of Utah. Among his many adventures, Stan taught high school students where he brought his knowledge and unique personality to the classroom, calling upon his love of liberty to bring American history to life.

As the creator and host of *American Ride*, Stan has brought truth to the retelling of our country's history, especially how Providence has played a big part in the founding and success of the American nation. *American Ride* preserves and preaches that message for all. The show has become a weekly highlight for nearly 11 million Americans, and many viewers in other nations via the Internet.

For *American Ride*, Stan has received recognition from the American Academy of Television Arts with seven Emmys, including numerous Best Host awards. He has also been honored by the following: Sons of the American Revolution, with a Silver Medal of Citizenship; National Coalition of Motorcyclists, with the Silver Spoke Award; Freedoms Foundation at Valley Forge, with the George Washington Gold Medal of Freedom; Boy Scouts of America, for Patriotism; the Honorable Gary Herbert, Governor of the State of Utah, for Service to the State; and several Sergeants Major of the United States Armed Forces, for Distinguished Service to the Nation.

Stan and his wife Stacey are the proud parents of six children and have seven grandchildren. They now make their home in the mountains of Northern Utah.